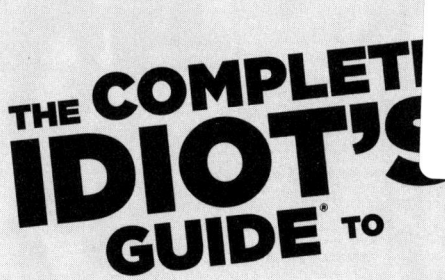

Conducting Music

by Michael Miller

A member of Penguin Group (USA) Inc.

ALPHA BOOKS

Published by Penguin Group (USA) Inc.

Penguin Group (USA) Inc., 375 Hudson Street, New York, New York 10014, USA • Penguin Group (Canada), 90 Eglinton Avenue East, Suite 700, Toronto, Ontario M4P 2Y3, Canada (a division of Pearson Penguin Canada Inc.) • Penguin Books Ltd., 80 Strand, London WC2R 0RL, England • Penguin Ireland, 25 St. Stephen's Green, Dublin 2, Ireland (a division of Penguin Books Ltd.) • Penguin Group (Australia), 250 Camberwell Road, Camberwell, Victoria 3124, Australia (a division of Pearson Australia Group Pty. Ltd.) • Penguin Books India Pvt. Ltd., 11 Community Centre, Panchsheel Park, New Delhi—110 017, India • Penguin Group (NZ), 67 Apollo Drive, Rosedale, North Shore, Auckland 1311, New Zealand (a division of Pearson New Zealand Ltd.) • Penguin Books (South Africa) (Pty.) Ltd., 24 Sturdee Avenue, Rosebank, Johannesburg 2196, South Africa • Penguin Books Ltd., Registered Offices: 80 Strand, London WC2R 0RL, England

Copyright © 2012 by Michael Miller

All rights reserved. No part of this book may be reproduced, scanned, or distributed in any printed or electronic form without permission. Please do not participate in or encourage piracy of copyrighted materials in violation of the author's rights. Purchase only authorized editions. No patent liability is assumed with respect to the use of the information contained herein. Although every precaution has been taken in the preparation of this book, the publisher and author assume no responsibility for errors or omissions. Neither is any liability assumed for damages resulting from the use of information contained herein. For information, address Alpha Books, 800 East 96th Street, Indianapolis, IN 46240.

THE COMPLETE IDIOT'S GUIDE TO and Design are registered trademarks of Penguin Group (USA) Inc.

International Standard Book Number: 978-1-61564-168-0
Library of Congress Catalog Card Number: 2011943391

14 13 12   8 7 6 5 4 3 2 1

Interpretation of the printing code: The rightmost number of the first series of numbers is the year of the book's printing; the rightmost number of the second series of numbers is the number of the book's printing. For example, a printing code of 12-1 shows that the first printing occurred in 2012.

Printed in the United States of America

Note: This publication contains the opinions and ideas of its author. It is intended to provide helpful and informative material on the subject matter covered. It is sold with the understanding that the author and publisher are not engaged in rendering professional services in the book. If the reader requires personal assistance or advice, a competent professional should be consulted.

The author and publisher specifically disclaim any responsibility for any liability, loss, or risk, personal or otherwise, which is incurred as a consequence, directly or indirectly, of the use and application of any of the contents of this book.

Most Alpha books are available at special quantity discounts for bulk purchases for sales promotions, premiums, fund-raising, or educational use. Special books, or book excerpts, can also be created to fit specific needs. For details, write: Special Markets, Alpha Books, 375 Hudson Street, New York, NY 10014.

Publisher: *Marie Butler-Knight*
Associate Publisher: *Mike Sanders*
Executive Managing Editor: *Billy Fields*
Executive Acquisitions Editor: *Lori Cates Hand*
Development Editor: *Lynn Northrup*
Senior Production Editor: *Kayla Dugger*

Copy Editor: *Louise Lund*
Cover Designer: *William Thomas*
Book Designers: *William Thomas, Rebecca Batchelor*
Indexer: *Brad Herriman*
Layout: *Brian Massey*
Senior Proofreader: *Laura Caddell*

ALWAYS LEARNING   PEARSON

To Sherry: Where you lead I will follow.

Contents

Part 1: Behind the Scenes 1

1   What Makes a Great Conductor? 3
    What Exactly Does a Conductor Do? 3
    Who Conducts—and Why? 4
    What Skills Do You Need to Be a Successful Conductor? 5
        Music Theory 5
        Score Reading 6
        Listening Skills 7
        Instrumental and Vocal Knowledge 7
        Performance Skills 8
        Music History 9
        Language Skills 9
        Self-Confidence 10
        Leadership Skills 10
        Positive Communication Skills 10
        Teaching Skills 11
        Rehearsal Skills 11
        Conducting Skills 11
    How to Distinguish Between a Good Conductor and a Great One 12

2   Same Job, Different Roles 15
    The Conductor as Programmer 15
        Why Programming Is Important 15
        Constructing a Program 16
        Should the Conductor Do Programming? 18
    The Conductor as Rehearsal Leader 18
    The Conductor as Teacher 18
    The Conductor as Music Director 19
    The Conductor as Artistic Director 20

3   Preparing the Score 21
    Why You Need to Do Your Homework 21
    Studying the Score 22
        Understanding Musical Scores 22
        Focus on What's Important 28
        Focus on What's Different 29
    Marking Up the Score 30
    Consulting Other Source Material 31
        Recordings and Performances 31
        Books, Articles, and Other Publications 31
        The Composer 32

Preparing to Conduct 32
Planning Your Preparation 33

4 Conducting Rehearsals 35
Why Rehearsals Are Important 35
Planning the Rehearsal 36
Getting Started 37
  Tuning 37
  Warming Up 38
Running the Rehearsal 39
Maintaining Discipline and Creating a Positive Environment 40
Wrapping It Up 41

Part 2: Basic Skills 43

5 Developing Stance and Baton Technique 45
Embracing the Baton—or Not 45
  A Short History of a Short Stick 46
  Should You Use a Baton? 46
  Choosing the Right Baton 47
  Holding the Baton 49
Assuming the Position 50
  The Podium and Music Stand 50
  Why Your Stance Is Important 50
  The Basic Stance 51
Learning the Basics 52
  Conducting the Preparatory Beat 53
  Conducting a Clear Downbeat 54
  Controlling the Rebound 54
  Final Upbeat 55
  … And Repeat 55
  Conducting a Clear Cutoff 56
  Using Your Left Hand 56
Conducting Best Practices 57

6 Conducting Basic Metric Patterns 59
Understanding Beat Patterns 59
  General Principles 59
  Different Approaches to Beat Patterns 60
Conducting in One 60
Conducting in Two 61
  Basic Double Meter Pattern 61
  Alternative Double Meter Pattern 62

Contents   **vii**

       Conducting in Four 63
            Basic Four-Beat Pattern 63
            Alternate Four-Beat Pattern 64
            Conducting Fast and Slow Four 65
       Different Strokes for Different Folks 65

7   **Conducting Triple Meter Patterns 67**
       Conducting in Three 67
            Basic Triple Meter Pattern 67
            Alternative Triple Meter Pattern 68
       Conducting in Compound Triple Meters 69
            Conducting in Six 69
            Conducting in Nine 71
            Conducting in Twelve 72
       Conducting in Fast Triple Meters 73

8   **Conducting Advanced Meters and Subdivided Beats 75**
       Conducting Complex Meters 75
            Conducting in Five 76
            Conducting in Seven 77
       Conducting at Slower Tempos 79
            Subdividing the Beat 79
            Conducting Subdivided Beats 79
            Choosing the Right Beat Pattern 80
       Conducting Through a Change in Time Signature 80
            Changing Beats per Measure 81
            Changing the Underlying Pulse 81
            Changing the Number of Beats and the Rhythmic Value 82
            Practicing Time Changes 82

Part 3:   **Interpretation and Expression 85**

9   **Interpreting and Controlling the Performance 87**
       Interpreting a Musical Work 87
       What Can You Influence? 88
            Timbre 88
            Phrasing 89
            Tempo 89
            Dynamics 90
            Energy 90
            Mood 90
       Controlling the Performance 91

10 Using the Left Hand 93
Things You *Shouldn't* Do with Your Left Hand While Conducting 93
Different Ways to Use Your Nonbaton Hand 94
    Hanging Out 94
    Mirror, Mirror 94
    Expressing Yourself 95
Using Two Hands Together 95

11 Conducting Tempo 97
Setting the Tempo 97
    Choosing the Right Tempo 98
    Understanding Tempo Markings 99
    Setting the Beat 100
    Keeping a Steady Tempo—or Not 101
Conducting at Different Tempos 102
Changing the Tempo 102
    Conducting a Sudden Tempo Change 102
    Conducting a Gradual Tempo Change 103
Conducting Fermati 104

12 Conducting Dynamics and Phrasing 107
Understanding Dynamics 107
Changing Dynamics 109
Conducting Dynamics 109
    Indicating Dynamics with the Baton 109
    Indicating Dynamics with the Left Hand 110
Indicating Phrasing 111

13 Conducting Cues and Accents 113
Cueing Entrances 113
    What Should You Cue? 113
    How Do You Cue? 114
    Making Contact 115
Conducting Accented Notes and Syncopation 116
    Cueing Accents 116
    Cueing Syncopation 116

14 Conducting Recitatives and Other Unmetered Music 119
Understanding Unmetered Music 119
Conducting Recitatives 120
Conducting Plainsong 121
Conducting Cadenzas 122
Conducting Unmeasured Preludes 123

Part 4: Different Types of Conducting 125

15 Conducting Orchestras and Concert Bands 127
Conducting an Orchestra 127
Knowing the Instruments 127
Facing the Orchestra 128
Mixing the Sound 129
Conducting a Concert Band 130
Understanding the Band 130
Achieving the Right Tone 131
Conducting Youth Bands and Orchestras 131
It's a Learning Experience 131
Dealing with Distractions 132
Choosing a Repertoire 132
Conducting in the Real World: An Interview with Manny Laureano 133

16 Conducting Marching Bands 141
Getting to Know the Marching Band 141
Today's Marching Bands 141
Meet the Corps 142
It's All About the Show 143
Understanding the Role of the Drum Major 143
A Short History of Drum Majoring 143
Drum Majors Today 144
Learning Marching Conducting Technique 144
Using Standard Technique 144
Using Military Technique 146
Conducting in the Real World: An Interview with Glenn Northern 147

17 Conducting Jazz Bands 155
What Does the Leader of the Band Do? 155
Conducting the Band 156
Conducting in the Real World: An Interview with Mark Buselli 157

18 Conducting Choirs 165
Conducting Differently—or Not 165
Learning Proper Choral Conducting Technique 166
Conducting Youth Choirs 167
Conducting Elementary School Singers 167
Conducting Middle School Singers 168
Conducting High School Singers 168
Conducting Community Choirs 168
Conducting Church Choirs 169
Conducting Professional Choirs 170
Conducting in the Real World: An Interview with Eric Stark 171

19	**Conducting Musicals and Shows** 179	
	Conducting Musical Theater.. 179	
	Conducting Opera.. 181	
	Conducting Live Shows... 181	
	Conducting in the Real World: An Interview with Dave Hahn....................... 182	
	Conducting in the Real World: An Interview with Larry Yurman............... 185	
	Conducting in the Real World: An Interview with Eric Stern..................... 188	
20	**Conducting in the Recording Studio** 195	
	Conducting Movie Soundtracks... 195	
	Conducting TV Soundtracks... 197	
	Conducting Video Game Soundtracks.. 197	
	Conducting in the Real World: An Interview with Tim Davies 197	
	Conducting in the Real World: An Interview with Pete Anthony 204	

Appendixes

A	Glossary 211	
B	Online Videos 217	
	Index 219	

Introduction

conductor (ken-duk-ter)   A collector of fares in a public conveyance.

No, that's not it. We're not talking about those guys in caps and uniforms who walk from car to car on the train.

conductor (ken-duk-ter)   A material or object that permits an electric current to flow easily.

Nope, that's not right, either. You really don't want to read a whole book about how electricity flows through different materials.

conductor (ken-duk-ter)   The leader of a musical ensemble.

That's it! You want to be a musical conductor, not a piece of metal or a guy on a train. It's music you're interested in, leading and inspiring musicians in performances of great musical works. That's what a conductor does, and it's what you're interested in doing.

Conducting is a unique art. You make music without actually singing or playing an instrument. Just by waving your arms, sounds materialize from thin air, gathering together and taking the shape of chords and melodies and entire passages of music. You move your hand and the music swells, make another gesture and it recedes into a beautiful stillness. You point to a performer and she comes to life, filling the air with a moving melody; point to another performer and a startling counterpoint appears. You speed things up with a wave, then lower your hands to slow them down again. Every musician on stage follows your every gesture; you are in total command of the performance.

That's what a conductor does—lead and inspire. That's what you want to do. That's why you're reading this book.

It may seem daunting, standing up in front of all those musicians and asking them—no, directing them—to do your bidding. It's a big responsibility, and it requires a lot of skill and hard work and no small amount of innate talent.

Well, I can't bestow talent on you; you either have it or you don't. Nor can I demand hard work; you have to provide that, too. But I can help you learn the skills you need to be an effective conductor. It doesn't matter whether you want to conduct a symphonic orchestra or a community choir, the basic information you need is here in this book.

Who This Book Is For

The Complete Idiot's Guide to Conducting Music is written for anyone seeking to conduct any type of musical ensemble. It's written both for students of conducting and those who have conducting thrust upon them. And the skills you'll learn apply to any type of group you might have to conduct—orchestra, concert band, marching band, choir, big band, musical theater, even musicians recording in the studio.

I don't assume that you've ever conducted anything before; we start at square one and go from there. I do assume, however, that you have some musical experience and knowledge—that you know the difference between *fortissimo* and *pianissimo*, for example, and that you know what *ritards* and *crescendos* are. (And if you don't know all this stuff, check out another book I wrote, *The Complete Idiot's Guide to Music Theory, Second Edition* [Alpha Books, 2005]; it will teach you all the basics you want—or need— to learn.)

What You'll Find in This Book

With that basic musical knowledge in hand, I'll show you everything you need to know to conduct most pieces of music. The mechanics aren't that hard, but there are a lot of nuances—all of which you'll learn.

As such, *The Complete Idiot's Guide to Conducting Music* is your step-by-step guide to conducting any type of ensemble, in any genre of music. While you don't have to read the entire book from front to back, it helps if you pick up the initial concepts first before you proceed to the more advanced stuff later in the book.

To that end, I've organized the book into four major parts.

Part 1, Behind the Scenes, is a gentle introduction to the art of conducting. You'll learn what a conductor does, both on and off the podium. You'll also learn how to prepare for conducting—how to read and mark up a score, and how to conduct effective rehearsals. It's all you need to know before you approach a performance.

Part 2, Basic Skills, presents the nuts and bolts of conducting. You'll learn how to wield a baton, assume the proper stance, and conduct that first downbeat. This is where you learn all the basic beat patterns—how to conduct in three and four and other meters, as well as how to tackle advanced time signatures, slow tempos, and changes in meter. This is the real meat of conducting.

Part 3, Interpretation and Expression, moves beyond beat patterns into how you express other types of musical direction and control the performance. I'm talking about conducting tempo, dynamics, phrasing, cues, and accents. You'll even learn how to conduct when there isn't a regular beat, such as recitatives and other solo work. This is the fun part of conducting.

Part 4, Different Types of Conducting, provides a real-world look at different types of conducting. You'll learn the ins and outs of conducting orchestras, concert bands, marching bands, jazz bands, choirs, musicals, and operas. You'll even learn how to conduct TV show and movie soundtracks in the recording studio. It's hands-on advice, augmented by interviews with more than a half-dozen professional conductors in all these fields.

The Complete Idiot's Guide to Conducting Music concludes with a glossary of relevant terms used throughout the book. It's a great place to look up those musical words and phrases that you should know but don't.

There's More Online

But it doesn't stop there. The learning continues after the book is done with a series of online videos that demonstrate basic conducting techniques. The videos are viewable online, from any web browser; just go to www.idiotsguides.com/conducting to view them. (You can find a list of all these videos in Appendix B.)

Also online at www.idiotsguides.com/conducting are the complete transcripts of all the interviews I conducted for Part 4 of this book. We didn't have space to include the complete interviews in the book, so we put them online. I recommend you give them a look; there's a lot of great information there.

And while you're online, take a look around the idiotsguide.com website. There's a lot there about other *Complete Idiot's Guide* books in general, and this book in particular.

How to Get the Most Out of This Book

To get the most out of this book, you should know how it is designed. I've tried to put things together in a way that makes learning about conducting music both fun and easy.

In addition to the main text, you'll find a number of little text boxes (what we in publishing call *sidebars*) that present additional advice and information. These elements enhance your knowledge or point out important pitfalls to avoid, and they look like this:

WHOLE NOTE

These sidebars contain additional information about the topic at hand, as well as useful tips and advice.

THE CONDUCTOR SEZ

These sidebars contain personal comments and advice from our consulting conductor, Dr. Mark A. Boyle. (More about him in a moment.)

FERMATA

These sidebars contain important cautions about things to avoid when conducting—things that might "hold" you up. (Get it?)

DEFINITION

These sidebars contain explanations of key terms relevant to conducting music.

MUSIC VIDEO

These sidebars tell you when there's an online video available that demonstrates a technique discussed in the text.

Let Me Know What You Think

I always love to hear from my readers. Feel free to email me at conducting@molehillgroup.com. I can't promise that I'll answer every email, but I will promise that I'll read each one!

And just in case a few mistakes happen to creep into the printed book, you can find a list of any corrections or clarifications on my website (www.molehillgroup.com). That's also where you can find a list of my other books, so feel free to look around—and maybe do a little online shopping!

Acknowledgments

I extend very special thanks to all the great conductors who agreed to be interviewed for this book, including Pete Anthony, Mark Buselli, Tim Davies, David Hahn, Manny Laureano, Glenn Northern, Dr. Eric Stark, and Lawrence Yurman. I also thank Karyn Gerhard and my neighbor, Linda Tutas Haugen, for recommending several of these conductors.

Thanks also to the usual suspects at Alpha, including Marie Butler-Knight, Lori Cates Hand, Lynn Northrup, Kayla Dugger, and Louise Lund for helping to turn my manuscript into a printed book. Additional thanks go to Amy Elliot, Joseph Laskey, and my wife, Sherry Miller, for transcribing the conductor interviews.

Special Thanks to the Consulting Conductor

All books in the *Complete Idiot's Guide* series are reviewed by experts who double-check the accuracy of the content presented. In this book we went beyond that and partnered with what I'll call a consulting conductor, who not only provided the technical edit of this book, but also contributed his own comments and advice on the art of conducting.

Dr. Mark A. Boyle is Director of Choral Activities and Assistant Professor of Music at Millersville University in Millersville, Pennsylvania. Originally from Wethersfield, Connecticut, Dr. Boyle attended Susquehanna University where he studied music education, tuba, trombone, and voice. He completed his Bachelor of Music in Vocal Performance and Master of Music in choral conducting at Ball State University. He holds the Doctorate of Musical Arts in Choral Conducting from the Mason Gross School of the Arts, the arts conservatory at Rutgers, The State University of New Jersey.

Dr. Boyle has served on the faculties of Rutgers University and Ball State, conducting the Rutgers University Choir and teaching conducting. He has served as a clinician and adjudicator throughout the country and was a semi-finalist in the 2009 ACDA Graduate Conducting Competition, one of eight selected nationally. He is also past editor of the award winning Indiana Choral Directors Association publication, *Notations*. At Millersville University, Dr. Boyle conducts all four of the school's choral ensembles, and teaches private voice lessons, conducting, and vocal methods. More information is available on his website, www.markaboyle.com.

Mark brings this wealth of experience to this project, and I appreciate all of his contributions. You can read his comments in The Conductor Sez sidebars found throughout the book.

Trademarks

All terms mentioned in this book that are known to be or are suspected of being trademarks or service marks have been appropriately capitalized. Alpha Books and Penguin Group (USA) Inc. cannot attest to the accuracy of this information. Use of a term in this book should not be regarded as affecting the validity of any trademark or service mark.

Behind the Scenes

Part 1

So what's this conducting thing all about anyway?

Conducting a group of performers looks easy—just stand up and start waving that little stick. But there's a lot more to it than that, as you'll discover in this first part of the book.

Want to know what separates great conductors from good ones? The answers are here. Want to find out about all the nonconducting stuff a conductor is expected to do? We'll cover that, too. What kind of preparation does a conductor have to do before the first rehearsal? I'll clue you in on that. And what about those rehearsals, anyway—what's important about them? Yeah, you'll find out.

In other words, read the chapters in this part to find out what's involved in conducting a group of musicians—and how you should prepare for the job.

What Makes a Great Conductor?

Chapter 1

In This Chapter

- Learn what conductors do
- Discover who conducts—and why
- Find out what skills you need to be a successful conductor
- Learn how to distinguish between good and great conductors

Conducting isn't that difficult, is it? I mean, you just stand up in front of a group of musicians, count off four, and then start waving your arms to the beat. Anybody can do that.

Well, not really anybody. That's because conducting is a lot more than just counting down and keeping the beat. A good conductor leads the ensemble to discover new dimensions in the music they play; he's a teacher, an interpreter, and yes, a human metronome.

Do you have what it takes to become a great conductor? Read on to find out.

What Exactly Does a Conductor Do?

If you think all a *conductor* does is stand in front of a group of musicians and keep time, you're sorely mistaken. Yes, establishing the tempo and keeping the beat is part of a conductor's job, but only part. There's a lot more to it.

At its most basic, *conducting* involves using gestures to direct a musical performance. That means using your hands (and perhaps a baton) to make sure everyone starts and stops on time, keeps the same tempo, and comes in at the appropriate places. It's the conductor as group leader, the person in charge of getting things going and making sure that they keep going.

Beyond that, the conductor is responsible for getting the most out of a piece of music and group of musicians. Playing music is more than just hitting the notes; it's about going beyond the notes to create a unique and uniquely enjoyable performance. That's the conductor's job, to help musicians go beyond what's written on paper.

Even more, the conductor is responsible for interpreting the music. Keeping the beat is a mechanical thing; interpreting the music is more mental, or even emotional. It's all about emphasizing this part or deemphasizing that one; going just a tad faster here or slower there; playing a little louder than what's written, or maybe a little softer. These subtle changes in interpretation are what make the same piece of music sound different under different conductors. It's how a conductor puts his own personal stamp on the music—and ensures that the composer's vision is carried out as precisely as possible.

THE CONDUCTOR SEZ

I have always held fast to the concept that the conductor must be a source of inspiration for an ensemble. The conductor *empowers* a group. A conductor's power lies in inspiring others to be musically powerful.

A lot of a conductor's work takes place not in public, but in the relative privacy of the rehearsal room. It's during rehearsals that a conductor shapes the ultimate performance by determining tempo and dynamics, deciding which parts to bring out or fade back, and helping musicians tackle difficult passages.

Beyond the obvious conducting duties, many conductors also serve as music directors, in that they audition and choose musicians, as well as select the music they play. Some conductors, especially in community orchestras and big bands, also double as performers.

What you see when a conductor steps up to the *podium*, then, is just a small part of what the conductor does. What goes on behind the scenes defines the conductor as leader, interpreter, and teacher—and informs the quality of the performance you hear.

DEFINITION

A **conductor** is the person who leads a musical ensemble. The art of **conducting** involves directing a musical performance via a large vocabulary of standard hand gestures.

The **podium** is a small platform, situated in front of an ensemble, on which a conductor stands.

Who Conducts—and Why?

Just about every type of larger musical ensemble uses a conductor. Smaller ensembles, such as string quartets and rock bands, typically don't need a conductor; they're small enough to start and stop and keep together all by themselves. But larger ensembles—orchestras, concert bands, choirs, and the like—need a conductor to take charge of and shape the nature of the performance.

THE CONDUCTOR SEZ

The conductor acts as a point of focus to help create sound that is "together"—a sense of ensemble.

Who are these folks who stand up and take charge of these groups of musicians? There's no single answer to this question. You see, some people strive to conduct; others have conducting thrust upon them.

Some people become conductors because they like to work with people. These conductors feel fulfilled when they coax a group of musicians to do something they haven't done before, whether that's tackling a challenging new piece or just stepping up a level, performance-wise. This type of conductor is a people person, a natural leader, a teacher at heart.

Other people become conductors because they like being in charge. Yeah, that's probably not the best reason to become a conductor, but there's no denying that there's a bit of a power thing involved in conducting; it's the will of one person against many, and there's a real sense of accomplishment in that. Not that there's any sort of competition between the conductor and the musicians, of course, it's just that some people do find fulfillment in leading the charge, so to speak.

Other people become conductors because of the music. These conductors are students of great music, and endeavor to share that music with as broad an audience as possible. They strive to create great and unique performances, to stamp the music with their own personal interpretations, to transcend what has come before. These conductors have a unique artistic vision; they hear the music in their heads and just need to get a group to perform that musical vision.

Then there are those folks who are forced into the conducting thing. Maybe it's a member of the congregation with professional performing experience who's cajoled into leading the church choir, or perhaps a lead instrumentalist who has to step in when the normal conductor is ill, or even a school music teacher drafted to conduct the school musical. Not every conductor is formally trained or even self-directed, but every conductor has to conduct—and get the most out of the musicians he or she works with.

> **WHOLE NOTE**
>
> A conductor of an opera is sometimes called a chorus master. A choir conductor is sometimes called a choral director. A conductor of a marching band may be called a drum major or bandmaster. Respected senior conductors are sometimes referred to as maestro—no matter what their gender.

What Skills Do You Need to Be a Successful Conductor?

How, then, does one train to be a conductor? What skills do you need?

There are actually quite a few, some obviously musical and many surprisingly interpersonal. Some of these necessary skills are innate; others can be acquired over time—which means some training is essential.

Music Theory

To be able to lead musicians, you have to know a little bit about music. That's not precisely true; you need to know a *lot* about music. This means you need to know all aspects of *music theory* inside and out. You need to understand time signatures and key signatures, tempo and dynamics, phrasing and construction. You have to know not just what the composer wrote on paper, but what he meant; you have to know enough music theory to get inside the head of the composer, and translate that to your performers.

This means, of course, that you need to be able to read music, and well; I can't imagine being able to conduct without being able to read what you're conducting. And I'm not talking about reading one line at a time; you need to be able to see the whole *score* at one time, all the parts, top to bottom, as you read across the measures, and then hear in your head what it all sounds like. It's a certain talent, to be sure, but one that all successful conductors possess.

In addition, there are functional aspects of music theory that play into a conductor's day-to-day activities. For example, you may find that you want to shift a passage from one instrument to another; this requires you to know each instrument's relationship to concert key, and then be able to transpose the part from one key to another. (This very situation occurs more frequently than you'd expect.)

> **WHOLE NOTE**
>
> Whether you need to obtain basic skills or just do a bit of refreshing, check out my companion book, *The Complete Idiot's Guide to Music Theory, Second Edition* (Alpha Books, 2005). You can also learn more about composition and orchestration from my other books, *The Complete Idiot's Guide to Music Composition* (Alpha Books, 2005) and *The Complete Idiot's Guide to Arranging and Orchestration* (Alpha Books, 2007).

With this in mind, most professional conductors have some sort of formal music education, with music theory being a big part of that. Yes, many music schools today offer a degree in conducting, but you'll also take a fair number of music theory classes. Like it or not, it's a necessity.

How much music training do you need to have? Basic music theory is important, of course, but it also doesn't hurt if you know a thing or two about *composition* and *orchestration*.

> **DEFINITION**
>
> **Music theory** is the study of how music works. The **score** is the written representation of a musical composition; the conductor's score typically contains all the parts of the ensemble, arranged one below another, grouped by section.
>
> **Composition** is the art of writing chords and melodies. **Orchestration** takes a composition and arranges it for multiple instruments and/or voices.

In many ways, composition and orchestration are natural extensions of basic music theory. You take all those notes and rhythms and chords you learned about and put them together into new compositions, then arrange them for groups of instruments or voices to play or sing.

Now, you don't have to be a composer or orchestrator to conduct a piece of music. But knowing a little bit about those two skills can help you better understand the compositions and arrangements you conduct. You'll also be better able to make changes to a piece (which you sometimes have to do, on the spot) if you know how that music was constructed and how it flows from beginning to end. The more you understand the creative process, the better you'll be able to participate in it.

Score Reading

Part and parcel of learning music theory is being able to *sight read* music. Just as any individual musician needs to sight read the music for his or her instrument, a conductor needs to sight read the score for an entire choir or orchestra. You need to be able to read individual parts and to see the big picture.

DEFINITION

Sight reading is the ability to sing or play a piece of music at first sight, without prior preparation.

You also need to be able to delve into a score and dissect it, piece by piece. You need to get inside the score to be able to reproduce the music as the composer intended—and then go beyond the score to interpret the music in your own way.

To do this requires a thorough understanding of music theory, of course, as well as serious sight-reading chops. If you don't have 'em, learn 'em.

Listening Skills

A successful conductor also needs to possess a good ear. You need to be able to hear the difference between pitches, to tell when a single voice or instrument is sharp or flat, and to experience the overall tone of a group of musicians. Yes, you have to be able to pick out wrong notes (this is known as "error detection"), but you also need to hear and then shape the harmonic balance of an ensemble.

It's all a matter of what you hear and how you hear it. Not that you need perfect pitch—the innate (and relatively rare) ability to recognize the exact pitch of any note played—but you do need to be able to hear what's wrong and know why it's wrong—and how to fix it. We're talking issues of intonation, balance, color, and the like.

In addition, developing your listening skills means exposing yourself to all different types of music and performances. You can't learn to conduct in a vacuum; you need to hear the music you'll be conducting, and hear how different conductors approach different pieces. The more you listen to, the more prepared you'll be when you're faced with new musical challenges in the future.

THE CONDUCTOR SEZ

Unlike singers or instrumentalists, conductors can't always have their instruments with them. Time in front of a group is the best way to become a better conductor.

Instrumental and Vocal Knowledge

If you're conducting an orchestra comprised of dozens of different types of instruments, you need to know a bit about those instruments in order to coax the best performances out of your musicians. Not that you need to know how to play each instrument; that would be several lifetimes of work. No, what you need to know is how each instrument works.

Let's say that you're conducting a high school band. In this scenario, you're as much a teacher as a conductor. That means students will come to you if they have trouble playing a passage, to figure out fingerings or positions or whatever it takes to play the music you set in front of them. You need to know enough about each instrument to help your young musicians play what you want them to play. You don't have to play it yourself, but you have to know how it should be played.

The need to know the instruments doesn't lessen if you're conducting more experienced players. For example, if you're conducting an orchestra you shouldn't be surprised if the string section asks how you want a particular section of a piece bowed. You better have an answer, and it better be the right one; if not, you might not get the results you seek—and you might lose the respect of the entire string section.

Again, this doesn't mean you have to be able to bow that section yourself. In fact, you may not even need to know the exact answer—as long as you know where to seek the answer. In our string section example, an appropriate response to the bowing question might be to turn to the *concertmaster* (the leader of the first violin section) and ask, "How do you suggest we approach this?"

DEFINITION

The leader of an orchestra's first violin section is called the **concertmaster** or **concertmistress**. The concertmaster typically makes decisions regarding bowing and other technical issues for the entire string section, and plays most violin solos.

By the way, I don't mean to be instrumental-centric about this. If you're conducting a choir, you also need to know how singing works—that is, the various skills and techniques required to sing a piece. Not that you have to be a virtuoso singer yourself, but you need to know about pitch and breathing and whatnot, enough to communicate with your performers.

Performance Skills

So you need to know how all the instruments or voices of an ensemble work. Do you also need to be a top-notch player or singer yourself?

The answer to this one is, "maybe." That's because conductors in the past have traditionally been virtuoso instrumentalists as well. The thinking here is that you need to master at least one instrument to understand the challenges faced by your players, especially during solo passages. In addition, some believe that a conductor who isn't a master performer won't earn the respect of the musicians he conducts.

THE CONDUCTOR SEZ

Most mainstream conductors are, in fact, soloists in their own right. This certainly adds to a conductor's sense of musicality and overall artistry.

That said, I don't think it's a necessity anymore. That is, conductors today are recognized primarily for their conducting skills, not whether or not they can also pick up a violin and knock out a mean solo. Unless a composer writes a piece specifically for your instrumental skills, it's unlikely that you'll be called to do double-duty as performer and conductor.

Aside from being an instrumental virtuoso, some traditionalists say that to be a successful conductor, you need to learn how to play every instrument. That is, even if you're not proficient with each instrument, you still should be conversant about how the instruments work. While I agree that you need to know the mechanics of each instrument, I think that can come without actually studying trumpet or flute or viola. (Heck, you can learn a lot about a given instrument or voice by having a cup of coffee with a soprano or tuba player and picking her brain about essential technique.)

WHOLE NOTE

If you have to choose a single instrument to play, I recommend piano, if only because it's a better instrument for learning music theory, composition, and orchestration.

This is why many music schools today offer distinct conducting programs and degrees. In years past, however, you may have had to graduate with a performance degree on a specific instrument, thus reinforcing the perceived need to be an instrumental master. Thankfully, today we focus on conducting as a unique skill, not an extension of instrumental prowess.

That said, there's nothing stopping you from playing an instrument or perfecting your instrumental skills. In fact, there's real value in keeping in touch with your performing side; it's always good to view conducting from the other side of the podium. Some of the best conductors of our time are also terrific performers in their own right.

 THE CONDUCTOR SEZ

Almost all conducting programs are graduate degrees. Formal conducting training takes place at the Masters and Doctoral levels. Most of these graduate programs expect you to already be proficient on an instrument or be a solid vocalist.

Music History

When you conduct a piece, it's nice to know a little about its history—where it fits in the canon (an informal list of respected and influential works), what was happening contemporaneously, the general style and period involved. The more you know about what you're conducting, the more accurate you can be in reproducing what the composer intended.

This speaks to gathering a thorough knowledge of music history. You need to know the basic repertoire, the major composers, the important works of all major periods. You need to know your Bach and your Beethoven, and maybe even your Beatles and Bacharach. This will help you not only better understand the music you conduct, but also better select the pieces you perform.

 WHOLE NOTE

Want to learn more about music history? Then pick up a copy of my companion book, *The Complete Idiot's Guide to Music History* (Alpha Books, 2008).

Language Skills

All conductors—choir conductors, especially—deal with words as well as music. Most written musical instructions, after all, are written in Italian, German, or French. And many of the choral pieces you'll conduct will be sung in another language. This means you need to learn some basic language skills.

This is important when it comes to coaching singers on how to sing a particular part, and the words are in French, or German, Italian, or whatever. You need to know what the words mean and how to pronounce them. Not that you have to be at the level of a United Nations interpreter, but some basic mastery of common foreign languages would be helpful.

Self-Confidence

This one probably should go without saying, but if you're going to stand up in front of a dozen or so musicians and try to take charge, you can't really be a wallflower about it. You need to possess and exude the confidence necessary to be the leader.

THE CONDUCTOR SEZ

A group will see right through you if you don't have an idea of how you want things to go already in your head.

If you're too shy to stand up in front of a group, or if you're nervous or apologetic or unsure of yourself, conducting will be very, very challenging for you. You need to have the confidence to stand up, take charge, and not be intimidated by a group of very talented individuals.

Which leads right into …

Leadership Skills

Whatever the musical setting, the conductor is the leader, pure and simple. You need to possess those skills that encourage others to follow you unquestioningly.

As a leader, you need to be able to command attention, motivate allegiance from the troops, and inspire great performances. That requires self-confidence, yes, but also a notable mastery of conducting and other music-related skills. The better you are, and the more sure of yourself you are, the more likely it will be that others will want to follow you.

In spite of what some of the more tyrannical conductors might think, you can't demand respect and loyalty; you have to earn it. Only then can you persuade your fellow musicians to follow you in your quest of musical expression.

Positive Communication Skills

Remember that word "persuasion"; it's important in many different ways. As I said, you really can't demand that talented musicians do things your way. Instead, you have to persuade them. That requires exhibiting solid leadership skills, as well as taking a positive, rather than a negative, approach. Praise is important, as is a focus on what the musicians are doing right—instead of harping on what they're doing wrong. Provide a clear musical goal for the ensemble, and encourage them to strive to reach that goal.

In short, to be an effective conductor, you need strong communication skills. Communicate positively, not negatively; build up your musicians, don't tear them down. Speak to them as equals, not as serfs or peons. Treat them professionally and as adults, even if they're students. If you can't communicate well, they won't know what you want them to do.

Teaching Skills

Positive communication is part and parcel of being a teacher. Obviously, teaching is part of the gig if you're conducting a student ensemble. But conductors are always teachers, even when your "students" are experienced professionals. There's always something new you can bring to the table, and serious musicians will appreciate that.

THE CONDUCTOR SEZ

It's important to have 10 ways to teach each single concept. Everyone learns differently, and if you can relate it to common experience, all the better.

Rehearsal Skills

A large part of your time will be spent in rehearsals—and the time you have will never be enough. That means you need to know how to conduct an effective rehearsal, and get the most out of the limited rehearsal time you have.

As such, developing strong rehearsal skills is essential to your success—and the success of the musicians you're leading. You need to be able to work through the music at hand, of course, but also recognize and correct all manner of technical and interpretive issues—from basic intonation to more sophisticated phrasing. The rehearsal is where you impart your musical interpretation, so you need to know how to work both effectively and efficiently to that end.

THE CONDUCTOR SEZ

Rehearsal management is also key—that is, in what order you rehearse material so that you use your musicians' time effectively.

Conducting Skills

Finally, we come to what you thought this book was about—conducting skills. Yes, you need to know the basic mechanics of the thing, the beat patterns and interpretive gestures. You need to be able to start and stop the group, to set and keep the tempo, to indicate dynamics and phrasings and everything else.

Along this line, you also need to possess some basic physical skills. You need a good right arm, if nothing else; waving around for an hour or so performance (and three to four hours of rehearsal) will tax muscles you weren't aware you had. And you need to exhibit exceptionally proper posture as well. Conducting might be 90 percent mental, but that 10 percent physical part can be a real pain—literally.

THE CONDUCTOR SEZ

I prefer the term "stance" to "posture." Conducting is an athletic event. It really involves the whole body. Posture has always seemed to me a very static term—for skinny models on runways. Stance, like a batting stance or tennis stance, evokes a certain dynamic sense of the thing.

Do you really need *all* these skills to be an effective conductor? Maybe not; it depends a lot on the kind of conducting you're doing. If you're leading a small church choir, you can probably skip the music theory and orchestration stuff; likewise, if you're the drum major for a high school marching band, a thorough knowledge of music history and the ability to speak French and Italian likely aren't that important. Still, the more you know about what you're doing, the better you'll be at it. And a little music theory and history never hurt anyone.

How to Distinguish Between a Good Conductor and a Great One

Why is it that a given conductor can possess all the skills just discussed, have years of practical experience, know the standard repertoire inside and out, but still give relatively unmemorable performances? Put two conductors side by side, both with similar skills and experience, and one is likely to get more out of the orchestra or choir than the other. What makes one conductor more successful than another?

It's about more than basic skills, of course. Experience might be part of the equation, but it's more than that. When it comes to sorting the great conductors from the merely good ones, you have to look beyond what a conductor physically does to the musical and emotional impact he or she can impart.

First, know that there's no one "right" way to conduct a given piece or ensemble. Tempos can edge up or down, passages can be louder or softer, and there's no one to say that a given approach is the only correct one. That makes it difficult to evaluate conductors; it becomes more about creative interpretation and excitement than about strict adherence to the notes on the page.

THE CONDUCTOR SEZ

I think the criteria is this: did the ensemble in question execute the composer's vision? If so, you have a conductor who can lead the ensemble—interpretive issues aside.

It's also important to note that the conductor doesn't actually create the music you hear; that's done by the musicians and their instruments or voices. The conductor only influences what the musicians play or sing. And even a great conductor can't overcome poorly trained or prepared musicians.

That said, conducting is more than just leading a piece straight through from start to finish. It's also about interpreting a piece, bringing out its nuances and subtleties, making the piece your own; it's about shaping a mental vision into audible beauty.

This comes down to how the conductor influences the performance. To be successful, you need to know how to inspire and make others musically powerful.

A great conductor, then, possesses considerable yet delicate interpretive instincts. Some people are natural interpreters; others have to learn it by listening to a lot of different performances and thus forming their own musical viewpoint and vision.

This musical vision and personal interpretation, and the ability to impart such on a musical organization, is a defining quality of great conductors. A great conductor can work with an ensemble to make a piece something more than just the notes on a page. He or she goes beyond basic performance and extracts something new and unique in performance.

In short, great conductors inspire great performances. Their passion and vision are contagious, and translate into unique works of musical art. You can tell a great conductor by listening to the works he or she conducts; there's something special there, something beyond the ordinary, that a more average conductor seldom achieves.

How can you become a great conductor? That's the million-dollar question. You have to master the basic skills, of course, but also possess your own unique artistic vision. You have to be able not just to reproduce musical works in performance, but also to interpret those works in unique fashions. And you have to be able to communicate your vision to your fellow musicians, and inspire them to help achieve that vision in performance.

That's a tall order, involving both trainable techniques and innate skills. Passion and persuasion are key, as is a fair amount of hard work and study—but the results are well worth the effort.

The Least You Need to Know

- At its most basic, a conductor uses visible gestures to direct a musical performance.
- Conducting is more than just starting and stopping a group of musicians—it also involves interpreting the music and creating a unique performance. Much of this work takes place in rehearsal, in preparation for the final performance.
- A successful conductor must possess a variety of musical and nonmusical skills, as well as listening, performance, language, communication, teaching, rehearsal, leadership, and basic conducting skills—plus a heaping helping of self-confidence.
- A good conductor works with musicians to reproduce musically accurate performances. A great conductor interprets musical works and inspires musicians to create unique and exciting performances.

Same Job, Different Roles

Chapter 2

In This Chapter

- Program the music
- Lead rehearsals
- Teach the musicians
- Function as musical director or artistic director

Conducting is a full-time job—which means there's a lot that goes on when you're not on the podium. What other tasks besides conducting is a conductor responsible for? It depends a lot on the conductor, his employer, and the situation—but can include teaching, rehearsing, and even fundraising.

The Conductor as Programmer

Probably the first thing a conductor does—and one of the most important—is pick the music to be played. In the music business this is called programming. Programming is the act of choosing music to play on a given program. The person who chooses the music, in this case the conductor, is the programmer.

When a conductor serves as programmer, he chooses the music to play for a given performance, as well as assembles programs for all the performances in a season. The music you choose not only reflects the playing level and personality of your musicians, but also the perception and culture of your musical organization.

Why Programming Is Important

What music you choose to play has major impact on the success of a musical organization. This is true both in terms of the musicians who play the music and the audience who listens to it.

Let's start with the musicians. It may appear somewhat obvious, but you need to choose music that your musicians can actually play, while still challenging their musical abilities. This itself can be a major challenge. Choose too easy a piece and talented musicians will be bored. Choose too difficult a piece and lesser musicians may not be able to master it. You have to strike a delicate balance in selecting something that can be mastered within the requisite rehearsal time, while still forcing your musicians to stretch a little.

THE CONDUCTOR SEZ

This is particularly important with student and volunteer groups. You need to choose with which the ensemble can enjoy immediate success. Ending a rehearsal with a piece like this sends your musicians out in the world feeling great about the experience. This is an important feature of rehearsal planning.

In fact, when you're dealing with a volunteer organization, the music you program is likely to impact the quantity and quality of musicians you attract. Program a lot of easy, lightweight pieces, and you probably won't get a lot of heavy hitters auditioning; program too many obscure and challenging works, and the typical hobbyist musician may be turned off.

The music you program also impacts the audience you attract, both in terms of size and character. You'll get a much different audience for a concert of little-known modern pieces than you will for one of well-known warhorses. In fact, the public personality of your organization is defined by the music you program. You are what you play. (And not to be too crass about it, a more tightly programmed concert—and, in turn, concert season—allows for a more tightly focused marketing strategy.)

 WHOLE NOTE

One of the quickest ways to change the perception of a musical organization is to change the programming.

Constructing a Program

Whether you're programming a jazz ensemble, symphonic orchestra, or community choir, the music you choose to play will help determine the success or failure of your organization—and of your conducting. Programming is serious business—and, for major musical organizations, big business.

When putting together both a single program and a series of programs, you need to address the following points:

- **Variety.** You don't want all the pieces in a program to be of a kind. Listeners will get bored if you play a half-dozen pieces from the same period, composer, or style. You need to mix it up a bit, so that each piece both contrasts with and enhances the others. Two pieces back to back shouldn't be too similar, yet also shouldn't clash unduly. You need to construct a program so that it has an overall arc, with its own set of climaxes and releases.

  Ensuring musical variety can involve lots of details. Some programmers go to the extreme of not programming back-to-back two pieces in the same key, or of the same tempo. An effective program includes a mix of keys, tempos, styles, and lengths. (Audiences won't sit still for a program of a half-dozen pieces all precisely 10 minutes long.)

  When programming an entire season, you need to include a mix of modern pieces and established repertoire. You could probably program an entire orchestral season of Bach and Beethoven—there's certainly enough quality material there—but you wouldn't be expanding your group's musical horizons, and you'd be giving short shrift to newer composers. Likewise, an entire season of 12-tone pieces might need to be balanced with at least a sprinkling from the old masters. Diversity over the course of a season is desired.

- **Unity.** While some variety is necessary, you don't want the pieces in a program to be too dissimilar. Yes, the individual pieces have to provide some contrast to each other, but they also have to fit together as a whole. There are many ways to do this; some programmers, for example, like themed concerts, performing works of a single composer or period or topic. However you approach it, make sure that the works in a program are of a whole, even as they exhibit some degree of variety.

THE CONDUCTOR SEZ

Think of concert programming like you're planning a meal. You have, for example, appetizers, a main course, and a wonderfully scrumptious dessert. Successful programs are balanced in structure but with contrast—loud/soft, fast/slow, short/long. It's that contrast that makes music exciting to listen to. In addition, your programming should be influenced by the mission and vision of the group at hand. Figure out why your ensemble exists and let that guide your programming.

- **Musical difficulty.** As discussed previously, you need to program music that can be effectively played by the musicians you employ. You want to stretch them, but not so far that the resulting performances are subpar. The difficulty of the music has to match the performance level of your musicians.

- **Audience acceptance.** When you depend on ticket sales to support your organization, you have to pay attention to the audience's likes and dislikes. Public musical organizations are, to some extent, in the business of making their subscribers happy—which means engaging in a bit of a popularity contest. The more popular the pieces you program, the more financially stable your organization will be.

THE CONDUCTOR SEZ

Audience education is important. In this regard, consider the use of program notes and preconcert talks that explain features of the works performed. This goes a long way to increase audience acceptance of unfamiliar works.

- **Cultural appropriateness.** Successful programming involves more than just simple audience popularity. The repertoire you program needs to make sense to the audience, in terms of how it regards your organization. You need to choose works that fit the culture and character of the ensemble.

What you want to avoid are pieces that induce obvious cognitive dissonance. For example, you probably don't want a children's church choir singing an adaptation of a hip hop song, nor do you want a seasoned big-city orchestra playing arrangements of old-timey country western tunes. It's all a matter of situational appropriateness; you have to match the music to the performers and the perception of the organization, in all ways.

That said, you don't want to always play it safe. (Which is the tendency with American performing groups, unfortunately.) It pays to take a few chances, to push the boundaries a little, both to challenge your musicians and your audience. Too much of a good thing can get boring; mainstream is often mundane. Innovation is important.

In short, programming for any type of musical organization is hard but important work. It defines the character of the organization, as well as benchmarks your ability to achieve success.

Should the Conductor Do Programming?

Now, not every organization gives the conductor sole responsibility for programming. In many professional orchestras, for example, programming is a function of a larger committee, of which the conductor is just one (albeit very important) voice. Even in smaller organizations, the conductor may not have final say.

This speaks again to the importance of choosing the right music for the situation. In the case of a professional orchestra, a series' programming affects the organization's revenues, as more popular music will result in larger ticket sales; whether a conductor likes a piece or not is less important than putting posteriors in the seats.

When more is at stake than just your own personal musical enjoyment, be prepared to accept input on your programming choices—or cede programming control to a larger group. When it's that important, more than one voice may be necessary.

THE CONDUCTOR SEZ

Successful conductors realize that they are part of a team. Yes, they artistically lead that team, but they are also a part of it nonetheless.

The Conductor as Rehearsal Leader

Once you've chosen the music for a given performance, you now have to rehearse the musicians for that performance. This is a key function of the conducting job; most conductors spend much more time in rehearsal than in performance.

In fact, many conductors view the rehearsal as the place where they put their personal stamp on a performance. The tempos you set, the dynamics you choose, the way you attack specific passages—all this is taught to the ensemble during rehearsals. The live performance, then, is just a validation of the interpretation you created during rehearsals. I'll talk more about planning and running rehearsals in Chapter 4.

The Conductor as Teacher

With student ensembles, the conductor is a teacher, and vice versa. You teach the individual musicians as they learn the music; you may be conducting, but you're functioning as a teacher as well.

It's the teaching component that many conductors find so rewarding. Realizing the musical progress of a group or individual throughout the course of a semester or performance cycle brings real fulfillment. You've done your job well when the musicians under your charge learn something new while preparing for performance.

With younger students, you may be teaching them specific vocal or instrumental techniques—literally, how to sing or play their instruments. With older students, it's more likely that you're teaching them larger lessons, such as how to play together as a group and develop a sense of ensemble, how to listen to one another, how to work through issues, or how to deal with adversity.

Even conductors in professional situations function as teachers. There's always something new to learn about a piece of music or a performance situation; there's always something new you bring to the table that others can learn from. (For that matter, you can often learn from the musicians you conduct; it's not solely a one-way street.)

THE CONDUCTOR SEZ

This is validation of the notion that the conductor's knowledge of the music must go beyond the score. Would you play a piece differently if you knew it was written in a concentration camp, or if you knew it was written to celebrate the life of Martin Luther King Jr.? A conductor can bring that added knowledge to any ensemble.

Never lose sight of your role as a teacher, especially with student musicians. Your players and singers will look to you not just for leadership but also for answers; how you respond to their questions and needs will determine your long-term success in your role.

The Conductor as Music Director

In certain types of musical situations, the conductor is asked to also function as a *music director*. In very broad terms, a music director is the leader of a musical group, in more ways than just waving the baton.

DEFINITION

A **music director** performs multiple creative and managerial tasks for a musical organization, including conducting, auditioning, and managing musicians.

You typically find conductors as music directors in musical theater productions. Conductors also sometimes function as music directors in live stage shows and jazz ensembles.

A music director is typically responsible for auditioning, hiring, and managing the musicians under his care. Some music directors interface with other creative personnel to ensure the quality of the final performance. For example, the music director of a Broadway musical collaborates with the play's director to guide the stage performance.

Some music directors are responsible for programming a group's music. Occasionally, music directors also function as composers or arrangers. You might see this functionality in a music director for a church choir, for example.

The point is that a music director does more than just conduct. He's involved in multiple creative functions, and also holds some management duties. Not that conducting itself isn't a full-time job, but serving as a music director definitely fills the hours of a day.

The Conductor as Artistic Director

Then we come to the position of *artistic director*. This position is typically found in larger musical organizations—orchestras, choirs, and so forth.

DEFINITION

The **artistic director** is the lead executive of a musical organization, responsible for all music-related tasks.

An artistic director is like a music director, but with more top-level control. In most organizations, an artistic director is an executive-level position; artistic directors not only hire and manage musicians and conduct performances, but also have programming, financial, and even fundraising responsibilities—often with the assistance of an executive director for more business-oriented functions.

As such, an artistic director is very much the public face of a large musical organization. You not only have to deal with music and musicians, you also have to pound the streets and meet with sponsors, donors, and important subscribers. You'll also spend some time working with the media, drumming up favorable press for your organization.

THE CONDUCTOR SEZ

Fundraising starts with what some call "friendraising." There's a saying in the arts—"friendraise first, fundraise second."

If you land a gig as an artistic director, you'll have significant artistic control of the organization. It might not be sole control (many organizations also have active boards of directors), but you'll be able to greatly influence not only the music you play but also the musical direction of the organization. It's a big responsibility, but one that's extremely rewarding—and that perfectly complements your duties as conductor.

The Least You Need to Know

- Many conductors also function as programmers, selecting the music a group plays for a given performance or throughout a performance season.
- Conductors also function as rehearsal leaders, helping their musicians learn new pieces and adding their interpretation of those works.
- In student ensembles, the conductor also functions as a teacher.
- Some conductors serve as music directors, with more responsibility over managerial functions, such as auditioning and hiring musicians.
- In some large organizations, the conductor is also the artistic director, with responsibility for artistic direction and fundraising.

Preparing the Score

Chapter 3

In This Chapter

- Why score prep is important
- Study the score
- Mark up the score
- Review other source material
- Prepare to conduct

You wouldn't get up in front of a big meeting to speak without prepping first. You wouldn't stand on the sidelines to coach a football game without reviewing your plays ahead of time. And you shouldn't conduct a musical piece without first studying it.

Before you stand up in front of a group of musicians, then, you need to do a little homework. You need to learn the score, know where the important bits are and what you need to pay attention to, and gather some sort of idea about how you want to approach the piece. It's basic preparation, but very important.

Why You Need to Do Your Homework

There are many reasons why you need to do your musical homework. First and most obvious is that you need to know what you're in for before you hit that first downbeat. Even seemingly simple musical works involve some degree of complexity—tempo changes, key changes, changes in dynamics, accents, and the like. You need to be ready for the difficult bits as they come up; you don't want to be surprised by anything while you're conducting. Even a student or avocational ensemble will see right through a conductor who is not prepared and doesn't have a vision for the work at hand.

Similarly, you need to prepare your musicians for the difficult bits in a piece. That might mean practicing challenging passages ahead of time, or just knowing when to signal a changeup from the podium. You won't be properly prepared if you're sight reading the score on first pass.

Beyond simply knowing the score, you also need to interpret it in your own unique fashion. That means figuring out how to put your own personal stamp on the upcoming performance, while honoring the composer's intent. How fast should you take the tempo, how soft should pianissimo be, how big a ritard do you want at the end, how long should you hold the final note? These are all decisions you at least need to start thinking about before your musicians gather to practice.

And that brings us to the final reason you need to work through the score ahead of time—you need to consider the best approach to learning this piece as a group. How should you set up your rehearsals? Should you work through the piece from front to back, or focus on the most difficult passages? Do you need to work with certain sections of the orchestra separately? Your advance study of the score will help you determine your best approach to rehearsals.

Studying the score in advance, then, is something every conductor needs to do. It's more than just staying one step ahead of the people you'll be conducting; it's the first step toward putting your personal stamp on the piece.

> **WHOLE NOTE**
>
> Not every conductor has the luxury of studying the score in advance. Studio conductors, for example, might only receive the score the night before a recording session, which doesn't afford much time for study. And if you're subbing for another conductor, you may be sight reading the score as you conduct. (Although you should always try to ask for the music beforehand, if possible!) Still, you should take advantage of any time you have to prepare for a performance—even if it's just a few hours.

Studying the Score

You can't bluff a roomful of talented musicians. You need to know the music inside and out before you start that first rehearsal.

This means studying the score, in detail, much the same way you'd study a book for a book report. Not that you have to memorize every single note of every part played; that's both impractical and unnecessary. However, you do have to know how the music flows, recognize the important melodic lines, know the underlying chord structures and harmonies. You need to know which parts are important, and focus your attention appropriately.

> **WHOLE NOTE**
>
> The formal structure of a piece of music is important. Think of a tree. Every tree is different, and there is some wonderful variance between species, but most have roots, a trunk, big limbs, branches, and leaves. Every piece of music (with very few exceptions) has a beginning, a middle, and an end—and the form is often more detailed than that. A conductor must understand how the music unfolds.

You also need to be comfortable with the time signature and tempo, and be prepared for all time and tempo changes. From there you can work through the beat patterns you'll use to conduct the piece, with proper focus on navigating difficult rhythms and time/tempo changes.

Remember, though, that the score itself is not the music—it's just a blueprint of the music you and your musicians will ultimately create. You need to study that blueprint in advance so you know what to build, and how.

Understanding Musical Scores

What does a typical score look like? It can vary.

A full instrumental score includes staves for each instrument or section. The score can be in either concert pitch (all parts as they sound) or with individual parts already transposed to the instrument's native key. For example, Figure 3.1 shows a typical orchestral score; Figure 3.2 shows a typical big band score. Same idea, different ensembles.

Chapter 3: Preparing the Score   23

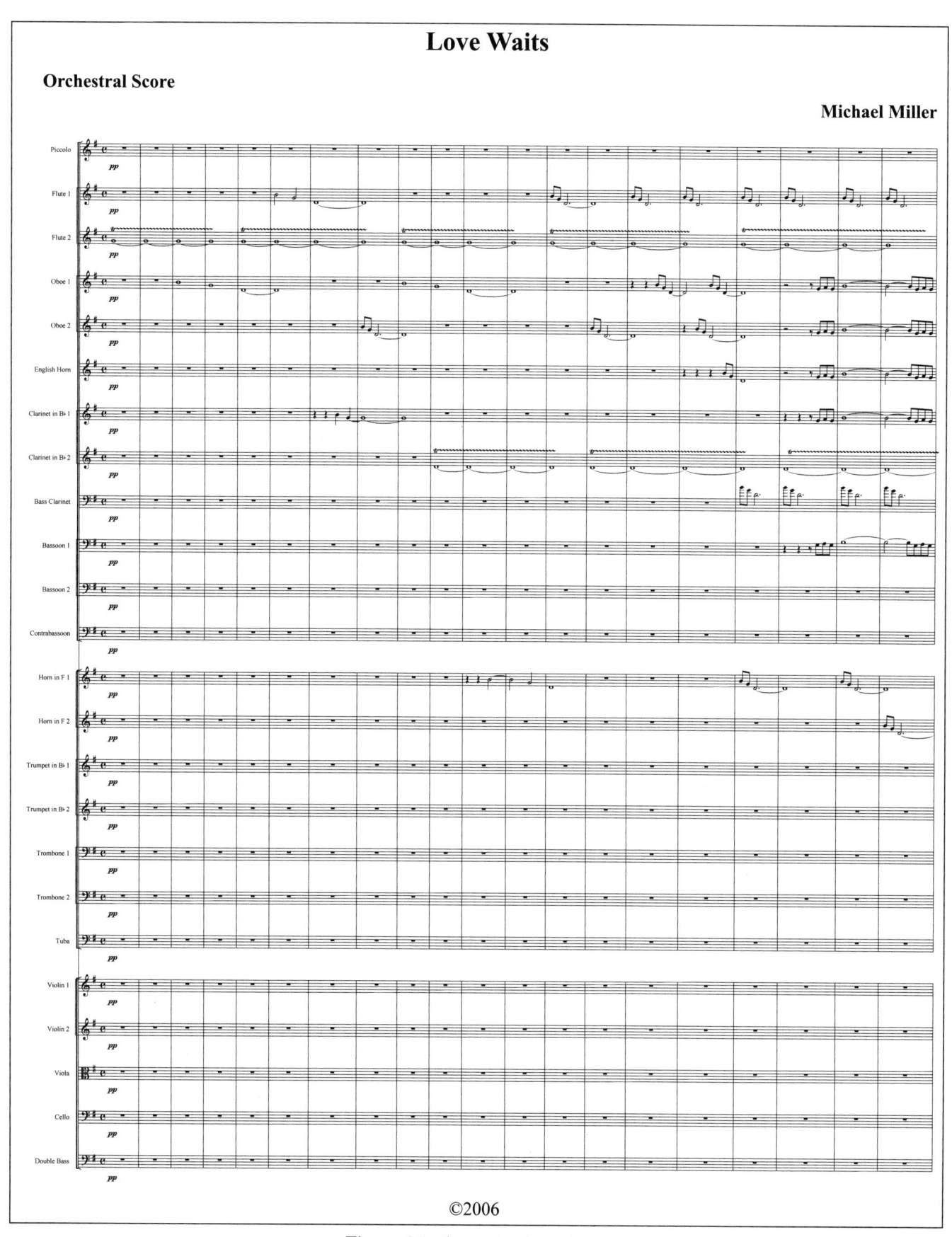

Figure 3.1: *A typical orchestral score.*

24 Part 1: Behind the Scenes

Figure 3.2: *A typical big band score.*

Some scores place an entire instrumental or vocal section on a single staff; others use individual staves for each instrument. Some conductors find the single-staff approach easier to read, as you can more quickly see the entire section at a glance, while the individual-staff approach makes it easier to isolate individual parts. Be prepared to see both in the course of your conducting career.

When reading an instrumental score, you need to familiarize yourself with the instrument's *score order*. Table 3.1 shows the score order for symphonic orchestras; Table 3.2 shows the score order for concert bands; Table 3.3 shows the score order for jazz ensembles. Variations of these basic ensembles, such as pit orchestras and marching bands, have similar score orders.

DEFINITION

Score order is the accepted order of instruments, top to bottom, on the written score.

Table 3.1 Symphonic Orchestra Score Order

Major Section	Individual Instruments
Woodwinds	Piccolo
	Flute (first and second)
	Oboe (first and second)
	English horn
	B♭ clarinet (first and second)
	Bass clarinet
	Bassoon (first and second)
	Contrabassoon
Brass	French horn (first, second, third, and fourth)
	Trumpet (first, second, and third)
	Trombone (first, second, and third)
	Tuba
Percussion	Timpani
	Bells (glockenspiel)
	Xylophone
	Vibraphone
	Marimba
	Chimes
	Snare drum
	Bass drum
	Cymbal
	Other percussion
Keyboards	Harp
	Piano
Vocal parts (if any)	Soloists in voice order (high to low)
	Chorus in voice order (high to low)
Strings	Violin (first and second)
	Viola
	Cello
	Double bass

Table 3.2 Concert Band Score Order

Major Section	Individual Instruments
Woodwinds	Piccolo Flute (first and second) Oboe (first and second) English horn Bassoon (first and second) B♭ clarinet (first, second, and third) Alto clarinet Bass clarinet Alto saxophone (first and second) Tenor saxophone Baritone saxophone
Brass	Cornet (first, second, and third) Trumpet (first and second) French horn (first, second, third, and fourth) Trombone (first and second) Bass trombone Baritone horn Tuba
Percussion	Timpani Bells (glockenspiel) Xylophone Vibraphone Marimba Chimes Snare drum Bass drum Cymbal Other percussion

Chapter 3: Preparing the Score 27

Table 3.3 Jazz Ensemble Score Order

Major Section	Individual Instruments
Woodwinds	Flute (sometimes played by a sax player)
	Soprano saxophone (sometimes played by an alto or tenor sax player)
	Alto saxophones (1 to 3)
	Tenor saxophones (1 to 3)
	Baritone saxophones (1 or 2)
Brass	Trumpets (3 to 5)
	Trombones (3 to 5)
Rhythm section	Guitar (optional)
	Piano
	Bass (electric or acoustic)
	Drums
	Other percussion (congas, tambourine, etc.)

○ WHOLE NOTE

It's not unusual to find scores for some types of ensembles or events in a lead sheet format. This places the melody and perhaps key subsidiary lines on a single staff, accompanied by the underlying chords; individual parts are not detailed. You sometimes see this with jazz band charts, or for charts for various types of popular live shows.

When it comes to vocal pieces, there are two main approaches. Some choral scores put the soprano and alto parts on a single treble clef staff, and the tenor and bass parts on a single bass clef staff, as shown in Figure 3.3. (This is in spite of the fact that the individual tenor part is typically written in treble clef.) The alternate approach, shown in Figure 3.4, uses four separate staves, one for each part. The piano accompaniment is typically placed beneath the vocal staves.

Figure 3.3: *A two-staff vocal score.*

Figure 3.4: *A full vocal score.*

Whether you're looking at an instrumental or vocal score, major sections within a piece should be notated with section numbers (1, 2, 3) or letters (A, B, C). Individual measures may be numbered, or measure numbers may appear only at the start of lines or sections.

> **𝕆 WHOLE NOTE**
>
> Performers also need to number the measures in their parts—at least every other measure. This makes for faster and more efficient rehearsals.

Focus on What's Important

When prep time is limited, as it always is, you need a shorthand approach to score study. Traditional European conservatories recommend a formal method, dubbed Seven Steps Through the Score. This method walks you through the score seven separate times, each step focusing on a particular element. This way you can concentrate on the most important items, one pass at a time.

The seven steps are as follows:

1. **Form analysis.** In the first pass, work through the score with the goal of examining the overall shape of the piece, determining the structure (ABA, verse-chorus, etc.), and noting any special or unusual elements.

2. **Harmonic structure.** In the next pass, pay attention to keys, modulations, points of dissonance, and the like.

3. **Melodic line.** The third pass is all about finding the melody—who has it, and when. Note repeated motifs, counter subjects, and particularly awkward leaps.

4. **Phrasal analysis.** In this pass, look for patterns large and small, cutoffs, breath marks, and the like.

5. **Dynamics, tempo, and rhythm.** The fifth pass is where you note loud and soft passages, tempo markings, rhythmic motifs, and the like.

6. **Instrumentation and transpositions.** Use the penultimate pass to familiarize yourself with the instruments used and their roles in the piece.

7. **Special effects.** In the final pass, focus on any special effects in individual parts—muted brass, pizzicato strings, weird sounds in the percussion section, and the like. Look for extended techniques, such as playing the piano with paperclips on the strings, or vocalists singing into a paper bag.

> **WHOLE NOTE**
>
> For choral pieces, start with an analysis of the text (lyrics); that's where the composer probably started. You should then substitute the instrumentation pass with vocal line analysis—phrasing, entrances, effects, and the like.

Now, there's nothing magical about the number seven. What is valuable, however, is the multiple-pass approach to working through a score. You work on different things on different passes, instead of trying to absorb everything there is about the score in a single pass. It's kind of like overlaying information, one pass at a time.

This traditional approach may or may not work for you, and the focus of each pass may differ, but it's a good place to start. Focus on one thing at a time, then work it all back together when you're ready.

Focus on What's Different

Another equally valid approach starts with the assumption that not all the information in a score is equally important. Yes, you need to familiarize yourself with structure and tempo, but you also need to find and focus on those unusual elements within the score.

The key to this approach is locating those important and distinct elements and marking them for further attention. Be on the lookout for things such as the following:

- Tempo changes, with or without accompanying accelerandos or ritardandos
- Key changes
- Changes in dynamics, with or without accompanying crescendos or decrescendos
- Changes in texture, instrumentation, register, articulation, phrase structure, or harmonic style
- Unexpected accents or syncopated rhythmic patterns
- Individual notes that stretch the boundaries of an instrument's or a voice's range

In other words, be on the lookout for anything that changes the playing field in a major way, or that might be difficult to play. These are the elements, in addition to the overall structure, that will command your attention.

Marking Up the Score

What do you do with the information you glean from studying the score? Well, you use it to inform your personal interpretation, of course, but you also use it to help you conduct the piece—by helping you remember the things to which you need to pay particular attention.

> **WHOLE NOTE**
>
> You may find it more effective to mark each type of item—or the items focused on in each pass through the score—in different colors. This way you'll know that phrase marks are in blue, for example, and those red marks are accents.

The key here is marking up the score to help you focus on the important bits. There are several ways to attack this, but here's a general approach:

- Mark the beginnings and ends of key phrases. If the score does not have measure numbers or section markings, add them.
- Mark tempos and tempo changes.
- Mark dynamics and changes in dynamics.
- Mark fermatas and other key markings.
- Mark important cues—where key instruments or voices enter.
- Mark melodic lines and other key harmonic and subsidiary lines.
- Mark key accents and rhythmic patterns.
- Mark any unusual articulations or effects in individual parts.
- Mark anything else different or unusual from the general flow of the piece.
- Mark any section where you anticipate problems in execution.

> **THE CONDUCTOR SEZ**
>
> Invest in a good set of colored pencils. Use a different color for each big idea—red for cues, green for dynamic changes, and so forth. Be consistent in your use of color throughout and your brain will always know what you're dealing with.

Marking the score in this fashion focuses your attention while you're both rehearsing and conducting. Trying to read all the parts in a score at this speed can be overwhelming; it's better to note those places where you need to place particular focus. When marked properly, your eye will go right to those items that require your attention.

Beyond marking up the master score, you may also want to create your own mini version of the score. That is, you write up a brief "sketch" of the piece, delineating major sections and what happens in each. For example, your sketch might indicate that at rehearsal mark B the brass and woodwinds play the main theme, while from measures 48 through 52 the strings play a countermelody. It's a rough guide, but one that could help you get a better feel for the piece.

> **THE CONDUCTOR SEZ**
>
> Don't be afraid to mark the score! Anything that will help you be more successful is fair game. I know conductors who have scores that look like coloring books—and these people are pros. Use sticky notes, highlighters, you name it. The time you invest in prepping the score outside of rehearsal is inversely proportionate to how quickly you will relate to it in rehearsal. I've found that professionals mark their scores; amateurs say "I'll remember that" and then promptly forget.

Consulting Other Source Material

When prepping a piece for performance, you may find other materials useful, beyond the score itself. While you should always consider the score your primary source, these secondary materials can help add background and nuance to a piece.

What materials might be available? There are a few common items.

Recordings and Performances

Some conductors frown on listening to other versions of a given work, fearing that they may color one's own interpretation. Others welcome the opportunity to see how other conductors approach a piece. Either approach is equally valid.

Here's the thing. Not every conductor has the same inner ear or ability to sight read. If you have trouble "hearing" a score in your head, listening to that piece on CD (or even live, if you have the opportunity) may help you sound out what you see written on paper.

To avoid being unduly influenced by a single conductor, listen to multiple performances of a piece. Instead of listening to a single recording five times, listen to five recordings one time each. This approach also helps you get a feel for the various interpretations possible.

> **THE CONDUCTOR SEZ**
>
> When listening to recordings, try to ferret out why a given conductor made the changes you are hearing. Remember, the performance space has a great deal of influence on tempo and dynamic choices.

Books, Articles, and Other Publications

Reading is a good way to learn more about a given piece, its composer, and the times in which it was composed. It's always good to place a given piece within a cultural and historical context, and referencing the appropriate literature can help you do this.

To that end, seek out books, scholarly articles, magazine articles, music journals, and the like. Look for items that deal directly with the piece you're studying, the composer of the piece, related pieces from other conductors, similar pieces from the same conductor, and the general musical period.

For that matter, some conductors like to read about other artistic endeavors from that period—literature, theater, art, and the like—to provide a thorough grounding of the artistic thinking at that point in time. You don't need to become an expert on Baroque architecture to play a Bach chorale, but a little background on the period certainly can't hurt.

The Composer

If you're preparing a contemporary piece, pick up the phone (or fire up your email program) and talk to the piece's composer. You can gain valuable insight by getting inside the head of the person who wrote it. Of course, if you're premiering a piece, you may get the opportunity to directly interact with the composer, as many composers attend their premieres—and sometimes help in rehearsal. Inside information direct from the horse's mouth, so to speak, can help inform your interpretation of a piece—and create an incredible experience for the musicians in the ensemble as well.

Preparing to Conduct

After working through the score, you need to practice your conducting. And I mean that literally.

Start by setting your tempos. Get out a metronome and set it to the desired beats per minute, then get comfortable conducting to that tempo. If you don't like the way it feels, select a slightly different tempo. Feel free to experiment.

Next, you need to determine your beat patterns, especially in complex time signatures and tricky passages. You also need to work through your expressive gestures, as well as important accents and cues.

You may even want to practice to a recording of the piece. Again, some experts debate the advisability of this, as it could nudge you toward another conductor's interpretation instead of your own, but I think there's value in it, at least in terms of nailing your beat patterns. Still, it's important to hear the piece in your head as you practice conducting; ultimately it's going to be you driving a new performance, not following an existing performance.

> **WHOLE NOTE**
> Consider investing in a full-length mirror or video recorder. You need to somehow watch yourself conduct.

You also need to prepare your interpretation of the piece. That means choosing your desired tempos and dynamics, of course, but also how you handle tempo and dynamic changes. Your personal vision also determines the energy level of a piece, where you want to pump things up and where you want to pull them back. The prep period is where you begin to put your individual stamp on the work; you can't ignore this part of the process.

Equally important, you need to plan how you intend to rehearse the piece. I'll discuss rehearsal tactics in Chapter 4.

> **THE CONDUCTOR SEZ**
>
> Here's the challenge: a trombone player just takes out his instrument to practice. We conductors can't do that! Our instruments are the ensembles with which we work. That makes practicing our skills quite challenging.

Planning Your Preparation

How long should this prep work take? Well, how long have you got? That might sound a bit flippant, but there's some truth there. If you're conducting a major symphony orchestra, you might have a year to prepare for a big performance. If you're conducting a community orchestra, your prep time might be measured in weeks. If you're readying a church choir for a performance this Sunday, you might have a week to prepare, at most. And if you're conducting a movie soundtrack, you'll be lucky to get a glimpse of the score the night before the recording session.

> **THE CONDUCTOR SEZ**
>
> The legendary conductor Robert Shaw was once asked how much time he spent with score prep and study. His answer was, "Every waking moment."

So take all the time you need, but only as long as you have. And teach yourself how to prep quickly, because sometimes you'll have to.

The Least You Need to Know

- You must be familiar with a piece before you can lead an ensemble to play that piece.
- You should work through the score in several passes, focusing on a different element on each pass.
- Feel free to mark up the score, to highlight important or problem passages.
- If other source material is available, such as recordings or books, use them to enhance your knowledge of the piece.
- When all the other prep work is done, get out your metronome and practice conducting the piece—develop the proper beat patterns, prepare for phrasing and accents, and the like.
- With the proper preparation, you should be able to start developing your own personal interpretation of the piece.

Conducting Rehearsals

Chapter 4

In This Chapter

- Discover why rehearsals are important
- Plan your rehearsal
- Get in tune and warm up
- Run the rehearsal
- Maintain discipline
- Wrap up the rehearsal

The rehearsal is where the music takes shape. As conductor, you're responsible for leading rehearsals and teaching your interpretation of a piece to the other musicians.

For these reasons, rehearsals are probably more important than the actual live performance—at the very least, rehearsals enable and shape the performance. It's certainly the case that most conductors spend much more time in rehearsal than they do in performance. It's that important.

Why Rehearsals Are Important

Every musician needs to rehearse, as does every musical group. It's a simple fact that the more you play, the better you get. Rehearsing is a way of life.

Rehearsing a musical ensemble, however, is a bit different from a single musician practicing by himself. Not only does each individual musician need to learn his or her part, but the group needs to learn how to play together. This musical bonding can only happen in rehearsals and performances; a group can't cohere via individual practice. And, since most groups have a lot more time scheduled in the rehearsal room than on stage, it's during rehearsals when things tend to come together.

Rehearsals are also important for the conductor's personal interpretation of a piece. You get a better feel for how you want things played by hearing them played in rehearsal. Plus, you use the rehearsal to teach the group to play a piece your way. That is, you tell the musicians what tempos and dynamics you want, as well as instruct them on how you want the instruments or voices to blend throughout a piece. If you want to emphasize the cellos while getting a little less from the brass, this is the place to do it. There's only so much interpretation you can do on the fly in concert; you have to prepare the musicians for how you want a piece played.

So you use rehearsals to help your musicians learn to play together, as well as how to play a particular piece—your way. It's where they get to know you and your musical vision, and where you get to know them and their own musical strengths and weaknesses.

In this regard, the rehearsal is a unique teaching and learning environment, for both you and your musicians. It is during rehearsal when we perform our most important role—we inspire others to be musically powerful.

> **THE CONDUCTOR SEZ**
>
> I have always maintained that an ensemble's goal should be to "practice perfect." For all intents and purposes, the ensemble is the conductor's instrument. As important as it is for a conductor to know the score and practice on his or her own, the time when a conductor really gets to practice the art of conducting is in rehearsal; it is the only time we get to practice with our instrument. That instrument is made up of people with their own lives and schedules, so we need to be organized and focused and not waste this precious time. A conductor who knows how to "practice perfect" is that much closer to a solid performance.

Planning the Rehearsal

A good rehearsal is one that is well planned in advance. Time is always limited, and you don't want to leave much to chance.

The first step of your rehearsal planning is your personal reading through and preparation of the score. You need to be familiar with the music you're rehearsing in order to teach that music (and your interpretation of it) to your musicians. You should not be learning the score at the same time the other musicians are learning their parts; you need to be a few steps ahead of everyone else. (I cover score prep in much detail in Chapter 3, so be sure to review that chapter.)

> **THE CONDUCTOR SEZ**
>
> You must have a clear idea of what you want before the rehearsal starts, but be flexible and responsive to the moment. Be willing to adjust, based on the musical feedback you receive during rehearsal.

When working through a score, note the most difficult passages and figure on spending extra time on them in rehearsal. Also pull out the most challenging instrumental parts, and plan on focusing rehearsal time on that section individually. Plan out your rehearsal time, allowing for some natural variance, and make sure you have everything you need to get started working.

To that end, you need to create a detailed schedule of what you want to achieve during the practice sessions. If you're rehearsing more than one piece, you'll need to apportion your schedule so that each piece has its own time slot. Also factor in warmup and tuning periods, time to work through difficult passages, and any required breaks.

> **THE CONDUCTOR SEZ**
>
> Plan your rehearsal to effectively use your musicians' available time. Are you doing a piece that only uses the brass of your band? Then plan that at the beginning or end of the rehearsal, and dismiss all but the brass section. Are you doing several pieces that use different combinations of vocalists? Then try and plan the rehearsal so that you move from the largest group to the smallest, to let more people leave earlier. Are you doing the Christmas portions of Handel's *Messiah*? Don't wait until the end to rehearse the "Hallelujah" chorus—your trumpets will be angry. Your musicians will thank you for careful logistical planning.

Here's a common approach to allocating rehearsal time:

1. Start with a warmup period, where everyone settles in and gets in tune. Use this period to not just warm up your vocalists or instrumentalists, but to also build a sense of ensemble, develop intonation, and solidify other basic skills.

2. You can then start playing something easy that everyone can handle. This could be a simple exercise, or maybe something you played (and hopefully mastered) in your last rehearsal.

3. Preliminaries out of the way, the group should now be ready to roll up their collective sleeves and start working. This is where you tackle more taxing material, those pieces and passages that need detailed attention.

4. Finally, wrap things up with another easy piece, so that everyone leaves the rehearsal with a feeling of success.

I like to think of a rehearsal schedule as a template. That is, it's a rough guideline to what you want to achieve and something to measure your progress against, but it's not wholly inflexible. You need to be able to go off-schedule if you encounter problems with specific instruments or passages and need the time to work on those problems; you also need to be able to speed through sections that go more smoothly than you anticipated. But the schedule is a good starting point, and necessary to create.

Getting Started

You can't (or at least shouldn't) just step into the rehearsal room, tap the music stand, and dive right into the deep end. Musicians need to tread gently into rehearsal; they need time to warm up a bit.

> **THE CONDUCTOR SEZ**
>
> I always put the rehearsal order on the board; that way the musicians know where we are headed. It also helps keep me on target, even if we all know we may veer from the schedule from time to time. It's also important to begin and end on time. You have to respect your musicians' valuable time. If you respect their time, they will respect you because of it.

Tuning

Every instrumental ensemble needs to take time to tune up. (Vocalists do their "tuning" during warmup exercises.) You need your players to be not only in tune with themselves, but with each other as a group.

As far as the tuning process, every group has its own rituals. For example, orchestras typically start with the concertmaster getting the strings in tune, followed by the woodwinds and then the brass. It's common to tune to a concert A, as played by the lead oboe. Encourage section leaders to assume responsibility for tuning within their section.

> **WHOLE NOTE**
>
> If you are doing Baroque music and your performers are seasoned pros, they will want to know what your pitch level is for A. Modern players use A440, while early music devotees often use A415—about a half-step lower!

Warming Up

All musicians need time to warm up at the start of a rehearsal. This is true of student and amateur ensembles, naturally, but also for more professional organizations.

You see, many players, even in big-city orchestras, do not live and breathe their music 24/7. Chances are that before they came to rehearsal they were doing their day job, sitting in front of their computers, walking the dog, riding the subway, doing anything but playing their instruments or singing. You need to get their heads back in the game, which you do with group warmups.

So how do you effectively warm up a group of musicians? There are several approaches you can embrace:

- **Breathing exercises.** Start by having your group breathe—literally. Set the metronome to 60 bpm, have everyone inhale for 8 beats, hold their breath for another 8 beats, then exhale over another 8 beats.

> **THE CONDUCTOR SEZ**
>
> For vocalists, it's beneficial to let air out with varying levels of resistance—through a hiss, through a shhhh, through the nose, or through an "ooo" shape. This helps the singers feel the muscles involved in breath management. In addition, choirs need to start in a good midrange key for their warmups; D major is a good key for this. Have them sing descending five-note patterns from A down to D, stepwise to start on a hum, then "ooo," then "aah." Stepwise motion is like easy stretching for the voice. You can then move on to exercise with larger leaps.

- **Unison notes.** After some basic breathing exercises, have the ensemble play long notes, in unison. Try playing a concert F, for example, starting with the lowest instruments and then adding upward. This helps in both breath control and tuning.

- **Scales.** Have the group play through some basic scales, working on intonation, dynamics, phrasing, and the like. Play whole notes then quarter notes, staccato then legato, and so forth. If you're warming up an orchestra, start with open-string (all sharp) keys.

- **Chords.** Here's another good one for intonation. Have the players build a simple triad—F major (F-A-C), for example. Assign the root note to the lowest instruments, the middle note to woodwinds and brass, and the fifth to violins and high woodwinds. Have them hold the chord over an extended period, and listen to the intervals.

- **Rehearsal-specific exercises.** Devise exercises related to the pieces you're focusing on in this rehearsal. For example, if you're rehearsing a 6/8 piece, work up some sort of 6/8 rhythmic exercise. You may also want to focus on scales and chords in the keys of the pieces you're working on.

The point of these warmup exercises is to loosen everyone up, get them listening to one another, and prepare them for the more strenuous part of the rehearsal to come. You also want to build a sense of ensemble; listening to each other is a big part of that.

Running the Rehearsal

What happens during the rest of the rehearsal depends on your own particular needs. If you're just learning a new piece, you may try playing it through all the way to get a feel for it, or you may want to tackle individual passages first before you put it all together. If you're further into the learning process for a piece, there's benefit to focusing on the more problematic passages, either as a complete group or with specific sections of the ensemble.

When working through a difficult passage, it's better to stop at the point a mistake is made than to continue to the end and then start over. Find the exact spot where problems occur and work through that passage until everyone gets it right—even if it's just a single measure. In this instance, repetition is your friend.

> **THE CONDUCTOR SEZ**
>
> I find that a mixture of both these techniques is desirable. If you spend 20 minutes on one measure, your musicians may want to strangle you. If there is a tough section, work on it for a bit, then move on and come back to it later. This is especially true for amateur groups, and can help reduce the frustration level.

Just remember, your rehearsal time is limited. You have to learn the piece, as a group, and impart your own personal stamp on the performance. In essence, you have to teach the musicians your interpretation of a piece, which isn't always easy, especially if they've played the piece numerous times before with other conductors. You have to inspire them to relearn the piece, your way.

Throughout the rehearsal, you want to develop a team spirit. That sometimes means stepping back and letting the group go it on their own. Encouraging the musicians to play without you helps bond them together; you can later step back in to offer your own interpretation of the piece.

> **THE CONDUCTOR SEZ**
>
> I always tell my musicians that you rehearse better when you know the person next to you respects your efforts. You are building a community where it's okay to make mistakes and learn from them. Respect for effort is important.

It helps if you make your rehearsals as interesting as possible. It's hard enough to hold the attention of a large group of creative types without also boring them half to death. Arrange your rehearsal program so that you don't work overly long on any one section or piece; change it up to keep things interesting.

You also need to make your rehearsals challenging, or as challenging as you can. This is particularly difficult in student and community groups, where the talent level may vary wildly. If you pitch your rehearsals toward the least talented players in the room, you'll bore the more talented ones to death. Conversely, if you aim to stretch the more talented players, you'll leave the average and below-average players in the dust. This may argue toward splitting the players at some point, teaching basics to the lower-level musicians and working on advanced techniques with the others.

Naturally, you want to encourage—if not insist on—players taking notes and marking up their parts, as necessary. Make sure all the musicians have a pencil and eraser, so they can mark important passages, articulations, and the like.

> **THE CONDUCTOR SEZ**
>
> A pencil is just as important as bringing your instrument. No musician is complete without a pencil. Just make sure that when he or she is making marks in rented parts to mark lightly!

Finally, remember to be positive, even when things aren't going quite as planned. Let the group know that you enjoy their playing, and offer profuse (but honest) compliments throughout. Don't focus on the negatives, but instead try to turn them around; instead of saying "that really stunk, do it again," try "that was pretty good, but now let's try it a little faster." And if you do find yourself reacting too harshly to an error, try tempering that harsh comment with humor; a little laughter goes a long way.

> **WHOLE NOTE**
>
> For student ensembles, the rehearsal is a good place to wean the group from the tyranny of the beat. Resist counting the group in—instead, get them comfortable with picking up the tempo from the conductor's initial downbeat. If you consistently count in the group, you're training them to listen to you instead of watch you. (Besides, you don't normally count them in during a live performance.) You want your musicians to develop a sense of their own group pulse, and be sensitive to your desired phrasing.

Maintaining Discipline and Creating a Positive Environment

Aside from covering the specifics of the rehearsal schedule, you need to use this time to assert your musical leadership—while fostering a positive environment for the musicians. It's a delicate balance. First, know that leadership is born of mutual respect. And, equally important, recognize that you can't demand the respect of your fellow musicians, you have to earn it.

While there are many ways to lead a group of musicians, some things flat out don't work. Most notably, it's inappropriate and largely ineffective to take charge by yelling at your musicians, or by trying to intimidate them. You have to assert your leadership in more subtle ways; you can command their attention, but you can't demand allegiance. This is particularly difficult when dealing with younger performers, who by their very nature may tend to be a tad unruly. While it may be tempting to play the overtly authoritarian role, there are better approaches. I've found that when the room is unfocused, it's best to stand still at the podium and wait for silence. It will come.

On the flip side, more aggressive methods of gaining attention—tapping the baton on the music stand, clapping your hands, yelling at the miscreants—typically don't work, and actually set a bad example. You want your musicians to *want* to get in line, not to be dragged into it. Treat them like mature adults, and by golly, that's how they'll act. (In theory, anyway.)

> **THE CONDUCTOR SEZ**
>
> I tell my musicians that if they lack focus in rehearsal, they are basically saying with their actions that they are not as important as the conductor when it comes to the ensemble's success. This is obviously not the case—they are incredibly important! So they must have the same level of focus as I do, and I do my best to model what I expect from them.

Wrapping It Up

The learning process doesn't end when the rehearsal is over. It's entirely appropriate, especially with student ensembles, to assign some sort of "homework" for your musicians to work on during the break between rehearsals. Giving the group an assignment of sorts keeps them focused until the next rehearsal or performance.

To this end, you can assign a few difficult passages, and ask your musicians to come back with those passages mastered. You may even want to present some "extra credit" material for your more advanced players, something outside the programmed works, just to keep their interest levels high.

You should definitely be clear with your musicians about what you want them to achieve in the postrehearsal period. That is, tell the group you want a certain piece in concert-ready condition by the start of the next rehearsal. Or that you want all the pieces totally polished before an upcoming performance. Leave them with something to work on and look forward to.

After all, the rehearsal, as important as it is, is just a means to the actual performance. You want your ensemble to master the pieces for performance, of course, but you also want them to grow as musicians. Treat the rehearsal as just one part of the overall learning experience, and expect your musicians to continue learning between rehearsals.

The Least You Need to Know

- Rehearsals are where musicians learn to play specific pieces of music, and to play together as a group.
- Rehearsals are also where a conductor communicates his personal interpretation of a piece.
- Most rehearsals start with a period of tuning and warmup exercises, progress to some easy pieces, move on to learning new pieces and working on difficult passages, and end with a piece that can leave the musicians with a sense of accomplishment.
- A conductor must maintain discipline throughout the rehearsal, while fostering a positive environment for the musicians.
- Always end a rehearsal with some sort of to-do list or assignment, to keep the musicians focused until the next rehearsal or performance.

Basic Skills

Part 2

There's a lot of mechanical stuff involved with being a conductor. I'm not talking about working on engines or lubricating your blender, but rather about the mechanical actions you need to know to conduct a musical ensemble.

In conducting parlance, you need to learn how to work the baton. How to hold it, of course, but also how to wield it to control the performers. That means learning all about what we call beat patterns—those little "one two three four" patterns you draw in the air with that short stick. There's a pattern for every time signature, sometimes more than one, and you need to learn how to conduct your way through all those patterns.

So pick up that baton and get ready to count 'em off—a one and a two and a three …

Developing Stance and Baton Technique

Chapter 5

In This Chapter

- Decide whether or not to use a baton
- Learn how to choose and hold the baton
- Discover the proper conducting stance
- Learn how to conduct preparatory beats, downbeats, rebounds, upbeats, and cutoffs
- Discover best practices for effective conducting

Whether you actually read all of the preceding chapters or just skipped them to get to this point, we now have the preliminaries out of the way—which means it's time to start conducting. But before you start learning the various beat patterns, you need to step up to the podium and learn how to wield your baton. It isn't quite as easy as tapping the music stands and waving your arms around.

Embracing the Baton—or Not

Here's the way conducting is supposed to work. You stand on the podium and glance at the score in front of you. Satisfied that everything is in order and the players are ready to play, you tap the music stand in front of you a few times, then raise your arms and get ready to conduct the first downbeat. (By the way, there are few things orchestras hate more than the sound of a baton tapping on a stand. You should probably avoid doing this.)

Most (but not all) instrumental conductors do their conducting with the aid of a baton—a short wooden or composite stick used by conductors to direct a musical performance. The baton gives musicians something to focus on, and helps novice conductors more easily define beat patterns.

But what kind of baton should you use—and how should you use it?

A Short History of a Short Stick

Where did the whole baton thing come from, anyway? Why isn't a bare hand sufficient for conducting a group of musicians?

The baton, or its earliest predecessor, was used not so much to conduct a musical ensemble, but rather to define the role of the conductor. It all dates back to the Middle Ages and a practice called *chironomy*, which involved the use of hand signals to indicate the shape of a melody in the performance of Gregorian chant. The person using these hand gestures typically held a large staff, which signified his role as leader. Over time, the leader began to get more rhythmic with the staff, moving it up and down to the beat. In this fashion, the staff acted as an early—and quite larger—baton. (And a somewhat more dangerous one; seventeenth-century composer/conductor Jean Baptiste Lully died from a self-inflicted wound on his foot caused by his conducting staff.)

> **DEFINITION**
> **Chironomy** is the use of hand gestures to show the rhythmic elements of a musical work, as practiced in the singing of Gregorian chant in the Middle Ages.

By the seventeenth century, music leaders were using other items to indicate the beat, in addition to the large staff—small sticks, rolled up sheets of paper, and the like. Some leaders even used their bare hands.

In instrumental ensembles, it became common for a member of the ensemble to act as the group's conductor. When this position was held by the principal violinist, as was common, the violinist would use his bow as a baton. When the leader was a lute player, he used the neck of his lute in the same fashion.

The use of the baton became common during the early 1800s; in fact, one of the first conductors to use the short wooden baton was Felix Mendelssohn, the noted composer. Also common during this period was the practice of having dedicated conductors, who did not otherwise play an instrument in the ensemble. The evolution from long stick to short stick was easy to understand; the shorter baton was easier to use than a long stick or a rolled up piece of paper.

Should You Use a Baton?

Some people would argue that whether or not you use a baton depends on the type of group you're conducting. In general, most instrumental conductors use a baton, whereas many choral conductors do not. However, that's not a universal distinction, as many choral conductors do use the stick, while there are some famous orchestral conductors who don't. There is certainly no technical reason for doing it one way or another.

Most musicians believe that a baton makes it easier to see the conductor's beat patterns, especially from the rear or side of large ensembles. Some also feel that using a baton makes it easier for the conductor to delineate precise beats, for more precise direction.

The first point is arguable, and probably depends on where the musician is sitting and the background visible behind the baton; in any case, I'll cede this argument and say a white baton is more uniformly visible than a bare hand. (Unless you're wearing a white shirt, of course.) More important, a baton prevents less experienced conductors from conducting with splayed fingers—which could conceivably provide five "batons" for performers to watch.

As to the second argument, however, it's certainly possible to be just as precise in defining a beat with or without a baton. There's nothing magical about the stick that makes one's conducting more precise.

On the flip side, some conductors (especially choral conductors) argue that using a baton adds a rigidity to the beat that works against the flowing quality needed for legato passages. It's also argued that when you have a baton in your hand, you're less able to use that hand to indicate musical mood. The rigidity argument has some merit, but not a lot, because many conductors are capable of conducting smoothly with the baton. The final argument, however, forgets that most conductors have two hands, and you use the nonbaton one for the expression of mood.

> **THE CONDUCTOR SEZ**
>
> As a choral conductor, I flat-out disagree with the argument that a baton is somehow less expressive; that argument has been allowed to fester for too long. One can be incredibly expressive with a baton if you're sensitive and don't treat it like a drum stick. And one can be incredibly precise without a baton. It all comes down to work and how much time you wish to put into developing your technique.

In short, there is no clear-cut argument in favor of or against using a baton. There is, however, precedent and common practice. The reality is that most conductors of large instrumental ensembles use a baton, as do a fair number of choir conductors.

That said, you certainly don't have to use a baton to be a great conductor. Some of the better-known conductors who eschew use of the stick include Pierre Boulez, Kurt Masur, and Leopold Stokowski. However, if you feel more comfortable conducting without a baton, go for it; there's nothing to say you have to wield the stick.

> **WHOLE NOTE**
>
> The noted conductor Leonard Bernstein, in his book *The Joy of Music* (Leonard Bernstein, Simon & Schuster, 1959), had this to say about using a baton: "If (the conductor) uses a baton, the baton itself must be a living thing, charged with a kind of electricity, which makes it an instrument of meaning in its tiniest movement. If the conductor does not use a baton, his hands must do the job with equal clarity. But baton or no baton, his gestures must be first and always meaningful in terms of the music."

Choosing the Right Baton

If you do choose to use a baton (and you probably will), you're faced with the decision of what type of baton to use. It's not a one size fits all scenario; you can find batons in all shapes, sizes, and weights.

The typical baton, like those shown in Figure 5.1, is made of wood, fiberglass, or graphite, and is relatively thin and light (a few ounces, no more). You can find batons from between 12 to 16 inches in length. The bulb end (the large end you hold in your right hand) may be made of cork or different kinds of wood (oak, walnut, and rosewood are popular); there are also some batons with aluminum handles.

Figure 5.1: *Mollard P-series batons, in 12" and 14" lengths.*
(Photograph courtesy Mollard Conducting Batons, www.mollard.com.)

For what it's worth, most conductors prefer lighter models to heavier ones. As to length, there's less consensus—although you should avoid a longish baton if you're working in a constrained space, such as an orchestra pit of a stage musical.

When you have a choice of color, go with a white model. Darker batons may look cool to you, but are much harder for musicians to see, especially if you're wearing a black tuxedo and standing in front of a darkened concert hall. A light-colored baton presents a much better contrast to all this dark background.

Above all, make sure that the baton you select feels natural in your hand. A baton's balance point is normally right at the joint between the shaft and the bulb, but this is not a requirement. Manufacturers will put the balance point wherever you'd like it—a little further out, or somewhere in the bulb.

For this reason, it makes sense to try out a baton before you buy it, just like you might try on a new article of clothing. A baton is a very personal tool, as you might imagine. In fact, the baton should feel like an extension of your hand; if it's too big or unwieldy, choose a smaller model.

You should be able to find a variety of different types of batons at your local music store, from Donato, King David, Mollard, Newland, and similar manufacturers. Expect to pay anywhere from $5 to $40, depending on how fancy you go. And when you're baton shopping, go ahead and buy two; it's always good to have a spare with you in case the one you're using goes flying out of your hand or breaks during a performance.

Holding the Baton

You hold the baton in your right hand—even if you're left handed. There are lots of different ways to grip the baton; to some degree, it's a personal thing.

> **WHOLE NOTE**
>
> If you're a left-handed conductor, you should conduct as if you're right-handed—with the baton in your right hand. That's because musicians expect to see the baton and the beat in the same place at every performance, even if the conductor happens to be a lefty. Note, however, that this right-handed focus is slowly changing. If you're left-handed, it's good to learn the standard approach—but in the end, if using the baton in your left hand feels more comfortable, that's probably the best way to go for you.

Some people like to grip the baton somewhat gingerly between the thumb and first finger; I find this a bit twee, myself, and somewhat lacking in power. Others go with a death grip, the baton held in the fist with the palm facing downward; this one's a little too inflexible for my tastes.

I recommend the somewhat standard grip that places the bulb of the baton slightly in your palm, more toward your fingers than the base of your hand. Address the baton as if you're shaking hands with it, with your palm about 45 degrees off center, midway between horizontal and vertical. The whole point is for the baton to be an extension of the conductor's arm; you want the baton pointing in the same line as your forearm, which you can't do if your hand is completely flat.

You should, by default, grasp the shaft of the baton between your thumb and your first, second, and third fingers—but not by the fingertips. Instead, curl your fingers around the shaft of the baton. Figure 5.2 shows the proper grip.

Figure 5.2: *The proper baton grip.*

All this said, you can vary your grip or use a grip that feels more natural to you. Again, the point is for the baton to be an extension of your body, pointing straight out from your forearm. If a tighter or looser grip does the job for you, so be it.

> **MUSIC VIDEO**
> See how to hold the baton and assume proper posture in the accompanying video, "The Basics of Conducting," located at www.idiotsguides.com/conmus01.

Assuming the Position

With your baton in hand, you can now step up to (or, more precisely, onto) the podium. But how you position yourself once you're there will affect your performance—and the performance of your ensemble.

The Podium and Music Stand

The setup is as follows: You stand on a podium, behind a music stand, in front of and facing the ensemble. The audience is to your back; from their perspective, you're fairly centered on the stage.

Here's the challenge: The musicians on stage must be able to see the top half of your body (in particular, the baton) over the music stand. You, on the other hand, must be able to read the music on the stand, as well as have relatively free arm movement. In other words, you need to make sure that when your right arm is extended straight out that everyone can see it without straining. You also have to make sure you don't whack the top of the music stand with the baton when you conduct a beat.

Now it's time to do a little geometry.

The ideal solution positions the music stand slightly above your waist level, with the top portion (the part that holds the music) fairly horizontal or parallel with the ground. You want the stand low enough for the other musicians to see you, but not so low that you have to interrupt your conducting to look down on it. In short, the music stand should be high enough for you to refer to it with your eyes without nodding your head.

Why Your Stance Is Important

What your parents told you as a kid holds true when you're conducting—good posture is important. This is especially so for conductors, for a number of reasons.

First, let's call it stance instead of posture. That's because posture is static, where stance is more dynamic—and there's nothing more dynamic than conducting a group of musicians.

When you maintain a proper stance, your movements will be more precise and uniform. If you slouch or crouch or bob up and down, your baton will be sloppy and all over the place. In essence, your baton work reflects your physical stance.

In addition, maintaining a proper and consistent stance helps the musicians concentrate on the baton. You need to control your entire body in order to exhibit total control over the stick.

Finally, the stance you assume will be reflected by the musicians you conduct. You set the example; the more proper and controlled your stance, the more proper and controlled your musicians will be. If you look slouchy and lazy, your musicians will tend to slouch, too—which will affect their tone and playing. Set a good example with your stance, and the musicians will follow you.

The Basic Stance

You might think that since the musicians can only see the top half of your body over the music stand, you don't have to worry about anything below the waist. This isn't the case. (Nor does it argue in favor of wearing Bermuda shorts below your tuxedo jacket.)

The proper conducting stance involves your entire body—above and below the waist. It's a holistic physical thing you have to master.

To attain the proper stance, our conducting advisor Mark Boyle recommends the following seven-point approach—from the ground up:

1. Place your feet shoulder-width apart, with one foot slightly in front of the other. This is for balance in both front-to-back and side-to-side directions.
2. Make sure your knees are not locked; this avoids tension and aids circulation.
3. Position your hips right above your feet, not pushed to the side, front, or back. This aids in stability.
4. Expand your ribs. This provides a good model for your vocalists and wind players.
5. Position your sternum high. This is another good model for vocalists, a kind of stance of pride.
6. Roll your shoulders back and down. Again, a good model for vocalists, but it also looks good and it opens you up to your ensemble.
7. Keep your chin parallel to the ground. Yet another good model for vocalists (good airflow for them) but also helps you keep your eyes up and out.

Remember, you need to stand straight. Don't slouch, don't bend, don't sway back and forth. Hold a constant stance throughout the entire piece; don't be tempted by the enthusiasm of the movement to jump around the podium.

> **FERMATA**
>
> Musicians expect to see the downward stroke of the baton in a single position throughout the piece. If you move around too much, they'll be forced to look around to find the baton, which disturbs their performance. Make it easy on them by staying put throughout.

You can now extend your arms straight out from your body, then bring your hands back in to create an angle of just a little over 90 degrees. Your upper arms should be slightly away from your sides, elbows out but not too far. Your elbows should be positioned between 4 and 5 o'clock and 7 and 8 o'clock relative to the horizontal plane. Your forearms should be positioned slightly above your elbows, and your hands and baton should be a continuation of your forearm. Your palms should be facing inward and downward, at about a 45-degree angle.

> **FERMATA**
>
> Even though your elbows are held out, avoid flapping them. Musicians are generally distracted by anything resembling a large bird on the podium.

Once you're set, stay there. Don't move around, don't flap your arms, and don't wiggle your butt. A good conductor keeps his head and body relatively still most of the time. You conduct with your baton, not with your body.

> **THE CONDUCTOR SEZ**
>
> There's a clear-cut reason for not moving around too much on the podium—moving gestures always stand out in relief against a still body. This should be your default. It's not that you will never move your body, but when you do, it should be purposeful.

Learning the Basics

You're on the podium, in position. You have the baton in your right hand, your music open on the stand in front of you, and you're ready to conduct that first downbeat.

What happens next?

As a conductor, there are a handful of basic movements you need to master. You use these movements to construct the *beat patterns* used to conduct different types of meters.

All of these movements are conducted with your right hand, with or without a baton. Your hand traces a shape in the air for every measure in the music; the shape represents the beat pattern for that specific time signature.

The beat pattern itself is "drawn" on an invisible vertical plane a foot or so in front of your body. Think of it as a virtual piece of clear glass, standing vertically. You draw your beat pattern on the glass, thus maintaining the baton at a constant distance from your body.

The most important parts of any beat pattern are the individual beats of the meter, as indicated by a downward motion of your right hand or baton. The first beat of a measure—in conducting parlance, the *downbeat*—is given particular emphasis, so that all musicians know not only where the beat is, but where each full measure starts.

> **THE CONDUCTOR SEZ**
>
> I once had a principal oboist tell me the following when asked what the most important thing a conductor needed to do when conducting an orchestra: "Respect the downbeat."

A typical beat pattern, then, consists of the one large downward movement for that initial downbeat, followed by smaller downward movements for the other beats in the measure. Each of these following beats is referred to as an *ictus*.

> **DEFINITION**
>
> A **beat pattern** is a pattern a conductor draws in the air, via hand movements, to indicate the time signature of a musical piece. Each beat in a measure is an **ictus** (plural: **icti**), with the initial beat of each measure being the **downbeat.**

You indicate the tempo of a piece by the speed of the beats you conduct—that is, the time it takes to get from one ictus to the next. Changes in tempo are indicated by changing the time between icti.

That's it, in a nutshell. But there's a lot more detail you need to learn, starting with the components of the basic beat.

Conducting the Preparatory Beat

The *preparatory beat* is what you conduct before the very first downbeat of a piece, kind of like the backstroke of a golf swing. It's a full beat before the first real beat that sets the tempo and style of a piece, ensures all musicians start at the same time, and also directs the musicians to take a big breath before jumping in.

> **DEFINITION**
> The silent beat before the first real beat of a piece is the **preparatory beat**.

If you're conducting a piece in 4/4 time, think of the preparatory beat as beat four of the (empty) measure before beat one of measure one. You conduct this beat four as the preparatory beat for beat one of the following measure, thus setting tempo and tone for the entire ensemble.

Conducting a preparatory beat is preferable to counting in the ensemble. While some styles of music are more amenable to a count in (big band jazz, for example), it's really not good form to do the "a one and a two and a three" thing for most serious music. Besides, counting in a piece is lazy, for both the conductor and the musicians; it's more professional and more efficient to get things going with a single, silent preparatory beat. (It also trains your musicians to watch you, rather than look down at their music and listen for you.)

Most musicians will take a deep breath on the preparatory beat. As a conductor, so should you. It should be a natural breath, not an obvious gasp for air, just a simple "in" on beat four. This puts you in sync with your musicians, and prepares you for the start of the piece on the following beat.

The preparatory beat conveys more than just tempo, of course. How you conduct the preparatory beat tells the musicians how they should be playing. Ideally, you should use the preparatory beat to convey all of the following:

- The precise beginning of the first note
- Tempo
- Dynamic level
- Articulation style

> **WHOLE NOTE**
> Younger musicians need to be trained to start from a preparatory beat. Most will be used to being counted in, and losing the numerical countdown is like taking the training wheels off their musical bicycle.

You conduct the preparatory beat the same way you conduct any other beat. For example, if you're in 4/4 time, the preparatory beat is beat four of the measure before the first downbeat. You conduct that fourth beat and then lead right into the initial downbeat.

Conducting a Clear Downbeat

After you move your arm up after the preparatory beat, you swing it back down for the following downbeat. The downbeat itself is indicated by the lowest point on your downward stroke.

You conduct the initial downbeat from the preparatory beat position just discussed. From this uppermost position, bring your right hand and baton back down to the starting position, exactly on the downbeat of beat one. When you hit the bottom, quickly flick your fingers to indicate the actual downbeat. The downward motion should be smooth and steady and in tempo.

Figure 5.3 shows the full motion of the preparatory beat, downbeat, and rebound—which we'll discuss next.

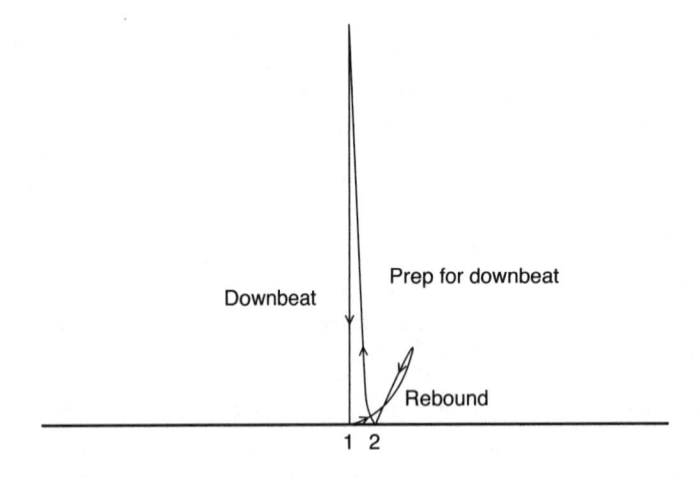

Figure 5.3: *The preparatory beat, downbeat, and rebound.*

> **MUSIC VIDEO**
> See how to conduct a proper downbeat in the accompanying video, "Conducting the Downbeat," located at www.idiotsguides.com/conmus02.

Controlling the Rebound

Each downward stroke of the baton is followed by a rebound—a corresponding upward bounce from the bottommost point of the beat. This rebound emphasizes and helps musicians better see the actual beat.

The rebound should be relatively small, no more than a third the height of the full preparatory beat. In fact, smaller is probably better; a big rebound can be confusing and also wastes energy. You want to use the minimum amount of energy for the desired result; keep it low and in control.

In general, the rebound should move in the opposite direction of the next ictus before changing direction toward the ictus. So if beat two is to the left of beat one, the rebound for beat one should bounce slightly to the right; your stroke then veers left to hit the ictus for beat two. There are exceptions to this rule, especially concerning time signatures with lots of beats, but it's a good place to start.

Interestingly, the type of rebound you employ depends on the articulation desired for a particular phrase. If your rebound is gradual along a U-shaped curve, it implies that the notes end with a tapered dynamic. If your rebound is at a sharp angle and stops suddenly, it implies that notes should end just as suddenly. If your rebound is minimal, so that the baton clearly stops at each beat, it implies a more detached articulation. In other words, the rebound itself is expressive.

Final Upbeat

After the final beat of every measure is a mini-preparatory beat that leads into the downbeat of the next measure. This final upbeat is in the interval between the last beat and the first beat of the next measure (the "and" after four in 4/4 time).

... And Repeat

The combination of downward strokes and rebounds and upbeats leads us into the construction of a beat pattern—that is, the visual metric guide you draw in the air with your baton. Not surprisingly, each time signature has its own beat pattern, and each beat pattern has its own distinct pattern of icti, rebounds, and preliminary beats. I discuss beat patterns in depth in Chapters 6, 7, and 8, so you'll learn more there.

It's important to know, however, that in most instances you want to place all the beats in a beat pattern on the same horizontal plane. This is separate from the vertical plane that defines your forward movement; think of the horizontal plane as a left-to-right line drawn in the air in front of you, or as a table on which each downward stroke hits and rebounds.

The importance of this horizontal plane is that every downward stroke should hit the exact same bottom point. Where the beats hit on the line, from left to right, varies according to the beat pattern.

Musicians will be looking at that invisible horizontal line defined by your downward strokes and expect every single beat to hit on that line. For this reason, you must be precise in where you place your downstrokes; you can't have them bouncing up and down all over the place. (Figure 5.4 shows a typical beat pattern; note that all beats are placed on the same horizontal line.)

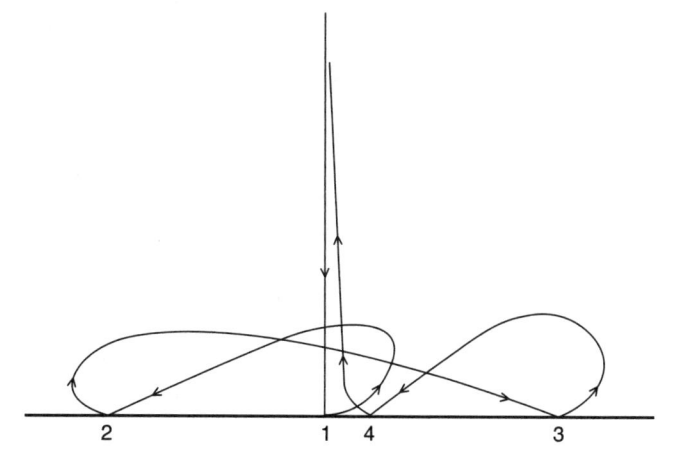

Figure 5.4: *The 4/4 beat pattern, with all beats on the same horizontal line.*

In general, your downward strokes should all hit within your stomach area. For this reason, it's best to draw the horizontal line relatively low—high enough for musicians to see, but low enough so that you have plenty of room to work above the bottom line.

Conducting a Clear Cutoff

Many musical pieces end with a fermata, or held note; it's up to the conductor to define the release or cutoff after the hold.

Even those pieces that have a cutoff on a beat need to have that cutoff clearly defined by the conductor.

For the conductor, the cutoff indicates a sense of finality. It's more than just the last beat in the piece; it's the ending, and that rare opportunity for a bit of theatrical flourish.

As such, a cutoff can be as simple as a standard downstroke, or it can be more dramatic. Some conductors use a rapid sidewise or diagonal stroke, almost like a karate chop, to indicate finality. Others use a slightly higher than normal upward movement before the cutoff, which prepares the musicians (and the audience) for the final release. Still others throw in a little circular flourish on the preparatory beat before the cutoff.

How you approach the cutoff is a personal thing. It just needs to be a little different from all the other gestures in a piece; your musicians need to know that this is the big ending, and there's nothing more after that.

> **THE CONDUCTOR SEZ**
>
> A cutoff or release isn't simply another beat. It's its own unique set of gestures, from a simple pulse with a stop gesture to the big crazy flourish.

Using Your Left Hand

Throughout this chapter we've been talking about conducting with the right hand. That's the hand you use to hold the baton and to conduct your beat patterns. What, then, do you do with your other hand?

It all depends.

You can use your left (nonbaton) hand to indicate dynamics, phrasing, and musical expression. You can use it to cue instruments and singers and to indicate accents and rhythmic patterns. You can even use it to point at musicians for whatever reason you have to point at them.

But if you're not doing any of these things—if the music has no need for expression or reinforcement—your left hand should be kept down at your side. It should not normally be used to mirror your right hand (although a little of that is fine for effect), or just to wave around nonchalantly. Unless it's performing some musical function, or turning pages in the score, your left hand is a distraction. Keep it relaxed at your side until needed. (Learn more about using your left hand in Chapter 10.)

Conducting Best Practices

Proper conducting technique is more than just learning the necessary beat patterns. There's a lot more involved than conducting beats and rebounds. To that end, here are some "best practices" to embrace in your own conducting:

- Remember that all beats should strike on the same horizontal line.
- Every beat should have a rebound, and all rebounds should bounce at approximately the same level—except for the final rebound of each measure, which must rebound to prep the first beat of the next measure. If you don't keep the rebound constant, your performers can't anticipate when you want them to play.
- The height of the rebound is dependent on articulation, dynamics, and, to a lesser degree, the tempo of the music. For example, a loud passage will dictate higher rebounds than a softer passage.
- Conduct the beats, not the rhythms. That is, avoid the temptation to use the baton to draw individual rhythmic patterns, or the notes between the beats. The baton is strictly for beating the metric pulse; doing otherwise will only confuse the musicians.
- As a default, your right hand should always be kept a relatively constant distance from your body. Imagine a plane of glass held vertically a foot or so away from your body; this is your conducting plane, and you should draw your patterns on this plane. You can, however, indicate changes in dynamics by subtly moving the right hand backward and forward through this plane.
- The more complicated the music, the simpler the beat pattern needs to be. You don't want or need to confuse the musicians with an overly complex beat pattern.

> **THE CONDUCTOR SEZ**
> It's an old joke, but it seems that the more you conduct, the less they watch!

- Every gesture you make should be as natural as possible. Your conducting style should be clear and easily understood; don't confuse your players with unnecessary head, arm, or body movements.
- Don't over conduct. Make your movements as economical as possible; use the least amount of energy necessary for the desired result.
- You should always be anticipating the next event in the music. You need to be leading the ensemble, not following the score.
- Don't use your nonbaton hand to brush the hair out of your eyes, scratch your chin, straighten your glasses, or perform similar nonessential functions. Keep it still at your side until you need it; otherwise, it becomes a distraction to the musicians. (You can, however, use your left hand to turn pages in the score—how else are you going to do that?)

- You should strive to maintain as much eye contact with your musicians as possible—and encourage eye contact in return. Keep your head out of the score, and the score in your head.
- You want your musicians to watch not only your hands but your face. Facial expressions are important for conveying musical expression—and for encouraging your musicians.

And here's one last one to remember: There is no one best style of conducting. There are many ways to conduct the same piece of music, and your style defines your own personal approach to the music. So take the instructions and advice in this book and elsewhere as guidelines but not law, and learn to employ these basic techniques in service of your own unique conducting style.

The Least You Need to Know

- Almost all instrumental conductors use a baton; a fair number of choral conductors do, too.
- Most batons run from 12 to 16 inches in length, and are made from wood, fiberglass, or graphite. Choose one that best suits your style and type of music you're conducting; shorter and lighter are generally better.
- A proper stance is essential for effective conducting; stand straight and tall and hold your conducting hand just above waist level.
- Each initial downbeat in a measure is preceded by a preparatory beat that sets the tempo and dynamics.
- When conducting a beat pattern, keep all the beats on the same horizontal plane.

Conducting Basic Metric Patterns

Chapter 6

In This Chapter

- Learn beat patterns
- Conduct single-beat meters
- Conduct two-beat meters
- Conduct four-beat meters
- Conduct fast and slow tempos
- Vary the baton stroke

Basic technique out of the way, let's get down to nuts and bolts—in essence, the mechanics of conducting. I'm talking about beat patterns, folks, the patterns you draw in the air with your baton to indicate the beats of a given time signature.

I'll start in this chapter with the most basic and common beat patterns—those patterns for 2/4 and 4/4 time. (I'll also cover single-beat meters, just because.) In essence, learn the patterns discussed in this chapter and you'll be prepared for the majority of the pieces you'll be called upon to conduct.

Understanding Beat Patterns

Before we get into specific beat patterns, let's take a few moments to look at beat patterns in general. As you recall from Chapter 5, a beat pattern is a pattern you draw in the air with your baton that indicates the individual beats in a given time signature. You typically use the same beat pattern throughout all instances of a time signature in a given piece; given the variables of tempo and style, you'll also use pretty much the same beat patterns for all pieces in a given time signature.

General Principles

All beat patterns are based on a set of common principles. These principles define the movement of the baton within the pattern, as follows:

- The first beat of the measure (the downbeat) is always the strongest, and thus normally has the most emphasis.

- The beat pattern should be constructed so that there is minimal danger of your right (baton) hand colliding with your left.

- In compound meters, the secondary beat is marked by a downstroke almost as strong as that of the primary beat.
- The baton should normally remain in motion, unless special emphasis is required. It should not come to a standstill at the icti that mark the beats, except in special circumstances.
- The baton should not move in a straight line from any one point to another, except in the case of the straight downward movement to the first downbeat of a measure. There should always be a little bounce after each downward stroke, followed by a curved motion to the next ictus.

Simple ideas all, and they combine to create the most effective and efficient beat patterns possible.

> **WHOLE NOTE**
>
> All of the illustrations of beat patterns in this book are drawn from the perspective of the conductor. That is, the left side of the beat pattern represents the conductor's left side, and so forth. If you look at yourself conducting in a mirror, you'll need to deal with the mirror image issue.

Different Approaches to Beat Patterns

You'll note in this chapter and those following that for many time signatures, multiple beat patterns are presented. That's because there isn't one single best way to approach any given meter.

While I've indicated one preferred beat pattern in each instance, not every conductor agrees, and you don't always have to use that pattern. Alternate patterns exist, and are also presented.

Which beat pattern you use depends a lot on your personal style and the style and tempo of the music being played. That said, it's probably a good idea to learn the recommended patterns first (you can't go wrong with them), then branch out to the alternate patterns to vary your repertoire.

Conducting in One

The most basic meter you can conceive is a basic one beat per measure concoction. Now, you seldom find pieces written in 1/4 or similar time signature, although fast triple meters (such as 3/8 or 3/4) are sometimes simplified to a single beat per measure. That said, by focusing on a single beat, you can learn a lot about more complex beat patterns and using the baton.

If you're conducting a single-beat meter, the pattern of the baton looks like the pattern in Figure 6.1.

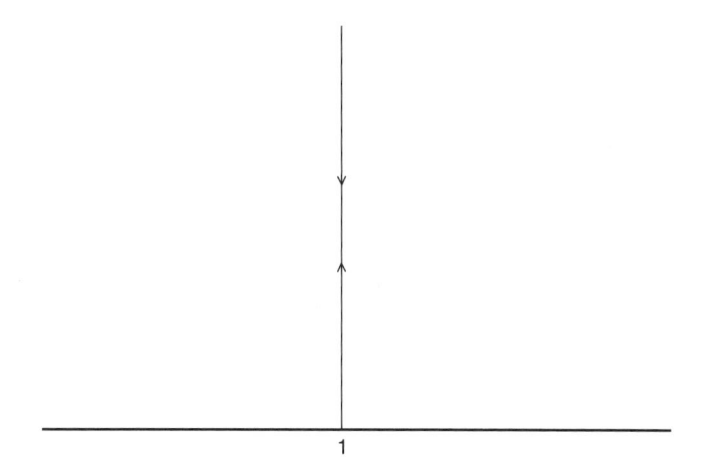

Figure 6.1: *The basic one-beat pattern.*

That is, the downbeat (the repeating "one") is always at the bottom of the stroke. The rebound—that is, the top of the stroke—is always on the "and" after one. It's a simple up and down motion: one-and one-and one-and one-and ad infinitum.

In this single-beat pattern, the stroke hits the bottom (on one) and immediately moves to the top-most position (on the "and" after one). It's regimented, somewhat stiff motion up and down; there are no flourishes or movement outside of the vertical plane.

Conducting in Two

As I mentioned, it's unlikely that you'll find yourself conducting in single meter. (Unless you're doing a fast waltz, that is.) Double meter is much more common, in the form of 2/4 and 2/2 time signatures.

MUSIC VIDEO

See how to conduct double meter patterns in the accompanying video, "Conducting in Two," located at www.idiotsguides.com/conmus03.

Basic Double Meter Pattern

There are several different two-beat patterns. The most common, shown in Figure 6.2, looks a little like a letter "J." The downbeat (beat one) is placed dead center, as with the single-beat pattern. The second beat is placed slightly to the right of beat one. You get from beat one to beat two by sliding the baton upward and to the right, hence the "J" or hook pattern.

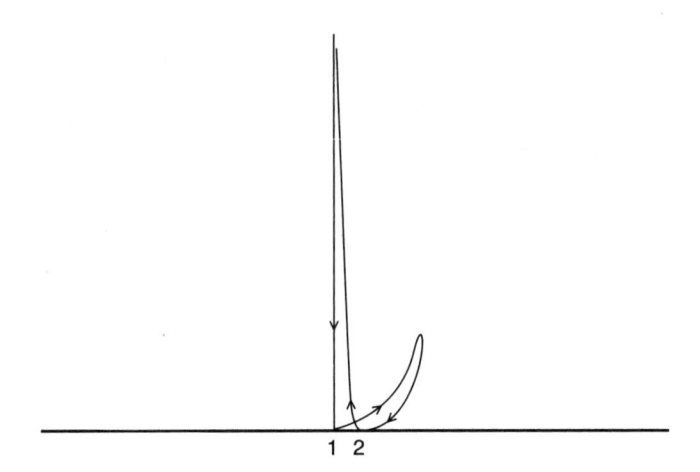

Figure 6.2: *The basic two-beat pattern.*

> ⵔ **WHOLE NOTE**
>
> You use the same double meter pattern whether you're conducting in 2/4, 2/2, or even 2/8; it's the number of beats that's important, not the rhythmic value of each beat. For that matter, you can use these same patterns for fast 6/8 pieces, with the dotted quarter note as the beat.

Alternative Double Meter Pattern

When you're conducting at slower tempos, consider the two-beat pattern shown in Figure 6.3. This pattern is a bit more showy than the basic pattern, with the movement from beat one to beat two drawing a circle in the air. For this reason, this pattern is sometimes called the rounded two or "golf club" pattern. (Look at it; it looks a little like a golf club.)

As noted, the rounded two pattern is more appropriate for slower tempos and more legato styles, where you have the time to more fully define the second beat. It's also commonly used for pieces in fast 6/8 time, where you essentially conduct in two groups (of three eighth notes each) instead of six individual beats.

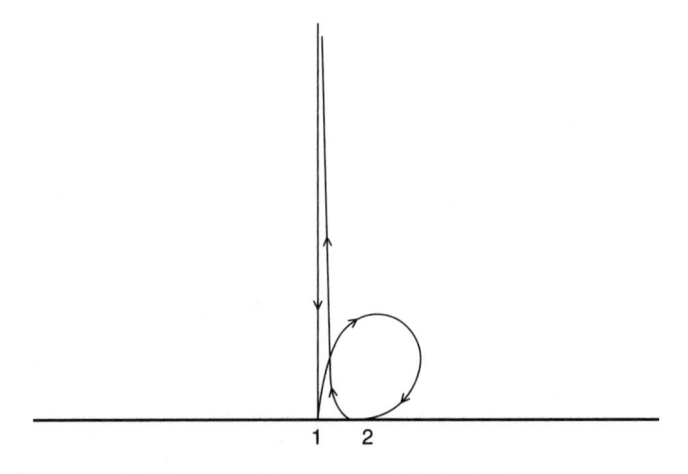

Figure 6.3: *The more elaborate rounded two double meter pattern.*

Conducting in Four

Next we come to the most common time signature, 4/4—or, for that matter, any other meters with four beats to the measure, such as 4/2, 4/8, or even 12/8 (with dotted quarter note beats). These are the beat patterns you'll probably use most often.

> **MUSIC VIDEO**
> See how to conduct quadruple meter patterns in the accompanying video, "Conducting in Four," located at www.idiotsguides.com/conmus05.

Basic Four-Beat Pattern

Figure 6.4 shows the most common four-beat pattern. This pattern uses four distinct beats, like this: down, left, far right, slightly left. (That is, the final beat is to the left of beat three—between beats three and one.)

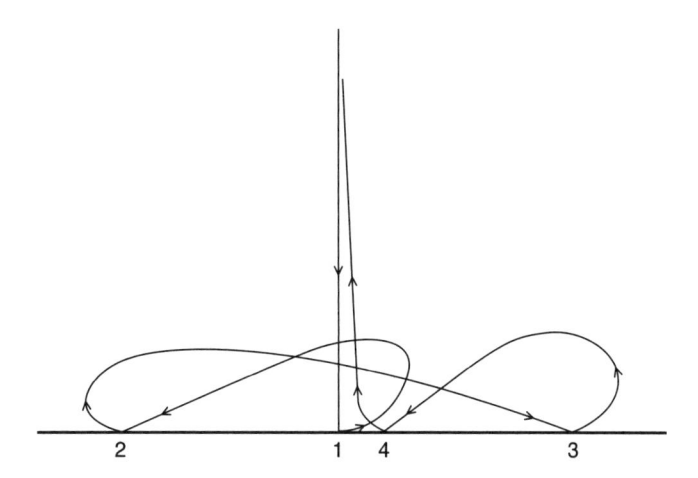

Figure 6.4: *The basic four-beat pattern, with four distinct beats.*

With this pattern, all four beats are placed at separate points on the horizontal plane. Theoretically, at least, the third beat has secondary emphasis, meaning that it's stronger than beats two and four (but not as strong as beat one, of course). As you might imagine, this pattern is better suited for slower and moderate tempos, where you have time to hit all four beats.

> **THE CONDUCTOR SEZ**
> This need to assign beat three secondary emphasis is why it's clear across the body from beat two, to show its emphasis as the next strongest beat after beat one. It is the largest movement other than the downbeat. The distance from beat two to three should be about the same as from the top of the first stroke to the ictus of beat one.

Note the position of the rebounds in this pattern. Each rebound, save the last, is in the opposite direction of the next beat. So the rebound for beat one is to the right, because beat two is to the left. And so forth.

The slower the tempo or the more legato the piece, the more elaborate and decorative your strokes can be—although you want to avoid getting too elaborate. (Remember, the more you conduct, the less the musicians actually watch.) On the flip side, the faster the tempo and the more staccato the piece, the straighter the strokes between beats, and the lower and sharper the rebounds.

Alternate Four-Beat Pattern

There's an alternative four-beat pattern that is actually somewhat common in certain types of music. As you can see in Figure 6.5, this pattern consists of a strong, straight downbeat for beat one; a weaker stroke to the left on beat two; a similar stroke to the far right on beat three; and a broad upbeat on beat four. That's down, left, right, up—repeat as necessary.

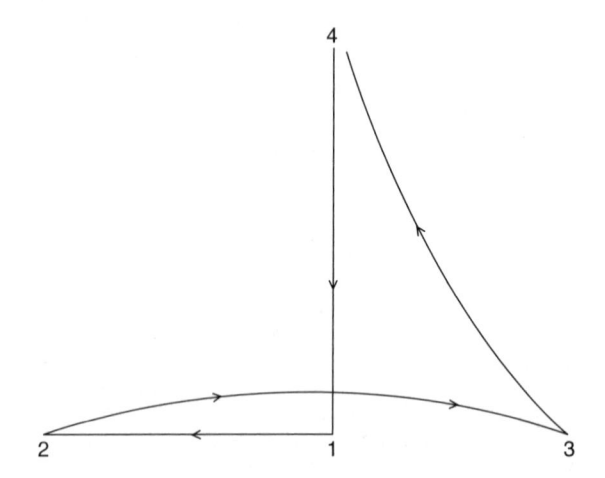

Figure 6.5: *An alternate four-beat pattern.*

In practice, especially at rapid tempos, this pattern is often conducted without distinct rebounds. That is, beats two and four are more like slashes to the left and right (respectively) as opposed to distinct beats on the horizontal plane. It's kind of a lazy pattern in this respect, but it does minimize arm movement—which, at faster tempos, might be practical.

This alternate pattern is often used to conduct marching bands, especially those with a more traditional or military bent. I also see it used by a lot of choral conductors, especially untrained ones. It's certainly a pattern that is easy to learn and do—and thus more appealing to occasional and amateur conductors.

That said, I feel it's best to learn the basic four-beat pattern from the get-go, as it teaches proper conducting technique—especially the need to give each individual beat its own downstroke. It's easy enough to simplify the basic pattern for use at faster tempos; it's much harder to go back and insert that fourth beat if you're used to putting the upbeat on four instead.

> **FERMATA**
> Because of its lack of distinct contact points for each beat, the alternate four-beat pattern is less effective than the recommended four-beat pattern at transmitting a clear tempo for your performers. It's definitely not recommended for slower tempos, and you should use it with the appropriate caveats.

Conducting Fast and Slow Four

What do you do when you're conducting a *very* fast piece in quadruple meter? Well, if the tempo is that fast, you may not be able to delineate all four beats—at least not without going through heroic gyrations. You can employ the alternate beat pattern, of course, but even that might not be achievable at extremely fast tempos.

When the tempo is that fast, it may be better to conduct the piece in half time—that is, using a two-beat pattern with beat one as the downbeat (nothing changes here) and beat three as the second downstroke. Two and four then become part of the rebounds from beats one and three. It's a matter of thinking in gestures exactly half as fast as the piece proceeds.

You face a similar dilemma when conducting a very slow piece. That is, you may have more time and space between beats than you know what to do with. The solution here is to subdivide the beat, effectively conducting in eight instead of four—that is, each eighth note gets a beat. Learn more about subdividing beats in Chapter 8.

Then there's the unique situation that is 12/8 time. At faster tempos, you conduct 12/8 in four, with each dotted quarter note getting a beat and the overall feel being that of a triplet background. But at moderate to slower tempos, you can conduct each and every eighth note. (It's the same thing with 6/8 and 9/8, of course.) Learn more about conducting these and other triple meters in Chapter 7.

Different Strokes for Different Folks

As noted throughout this chapter, the length and curvature of the baton stroke depends to no small degree on the tempo and style of the piece you're conducting. In general, you should alter the strokes within your beat patterns as follows:

- At slower tempos, you can spread out the pattern more from left to right; make it a bit broader.
- At faster tempos, narrow the pattern and use a shorter and more vigorous stroke with lower rebound.
- For more legato pieces, use a more flowing stroke between beats, as well as more curved or "bouncy" rebounds.
- For more staccato pieces, use a sharper stroke between beats.

This all speaks to the point that the way you conduct—that is, your baton strokes and conducting style—helps define the tempo, style, and feel of the music. It's part of how a conductor interprets and expresses his own unique musical vision.

The Least You Need to Know

- Beat patterns are constructed based on several general principles concerning strong and weak beats, as well as the motion of the baton.
- A single-beat meter is conducted with a simple up-and-down stroke.
- A two-beat meter is conducted as two downstrokes with a minor rebound between the two.
- A four-beat meter is conducted with a strong downstroke on one, a leftward stroke on two, a rightward stroke on three, and a slight leftward stroke on four.
- There are variations for each of these beat patterns. In addition, the stroke you use within a pattern defines and is defined by the piece's tempo and style.

Conducting Triple Meter Patterns

Chapter 7

In This Chapter

- Conduct three-beat patterns
- Conduct six-beat patterns
- Conduct nine-beat patterns
- Conduct twelve-beat patterns
- Conduct fast-tempo triple meters

In Chapter 6 we discussed the beat patterns for simple double and quadruple meters—2/4, 4/4, and the like. Now it's time to move into triple meters, and learn the beat patterns for 3/4, 3/8, 6/8, 9/8, 12/8, and similar time signatures.

Conducting in Three

Let's start with the beat patterns for simple triple meters—that is, those time signatures with precisely three beats per measure. I'm talking 3/4 and 3/8, what some might call waltz time.

Basic Triple Meter Pattern

As with our examination of simple double and quadruple meters, there are multiple ways to approach patterns in three. The most common beat pattern, shown in Figure 7.1, goes down, right, then back to the left—that is, the third beat is to the left of the second beat, but still to the right of the first downbeat.

Note that the rebounds for beats one and two go in the opposite directions of the following beats. So the rebound for beat one veers to the left, before the stroke travels to the right for beat two. The rebound for beat two veers to the right before the stroke travels to the left for beat three. (The rebound for beat three, however, travels straight up to prepare for the following downbeat.)

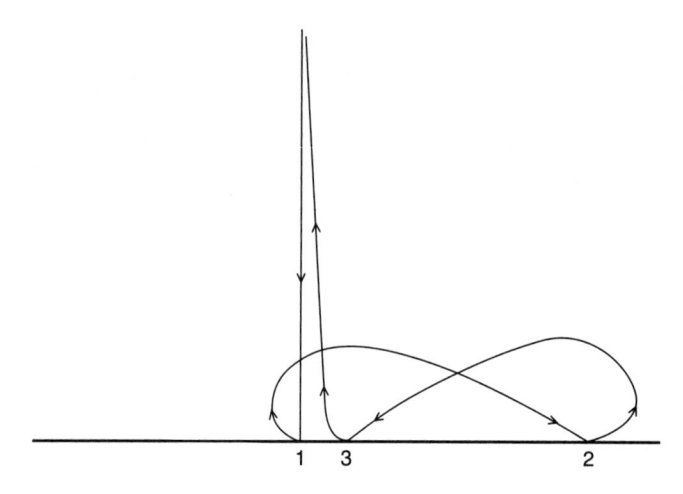

Figure 7.1: *The basic triple meter pattern.*

> **MUSIC VIDEO**
>
> See how to conduct triple meter patterns in the accompanying video, "Conducting in Three," located at www.idiotsguides.com/conmus04.

As you might suspect, this pattern works best when you have time to conduct all three beats—which means slower and moderate tempos. For faster tempos, there's an alternative pattern to consider, which we'll discuss next.

> **WHOLE NOTE**
>
> Why does the three-beat pattern always go to the right of the downbeat and never to the left? I think it has to do with the way the upward motion of the final rebound is typically conducted in almost all beat patterns. Remember back to the one-, two-, and four-beat patterns presented in Chapter 6; all described the final rebound as an upward stroke from the conductor's right to the straight up position. Looking at it another way, the final beat (and subsequent rebound) almost always falls to the right of the downbeat, no matter what the pattern.

Alternative Triple Meter Pattern

There's one primary alternative pattern used for conducting in 3/4 and 3/8, albeit primarily for faster tempos. This pattern is conducted as a simple down, right, up motion, with that final upward stroke leading back to the strong downbeat in the following measure. Figure 7.2 shows what this pattern looks like.

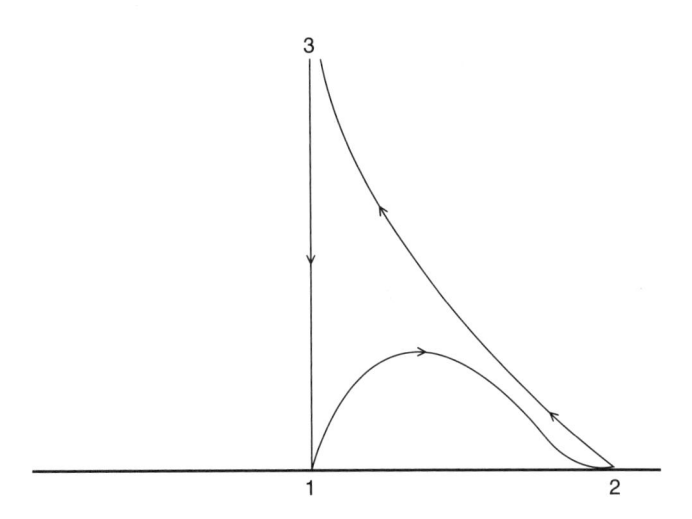

Figure 7.2: *The simplified triple meter pattern.*

Conducting in Compound Triple Meters

Now we come to *compound meters* in three. These are time signatures built on a multiple of three, such as 6/8, 9/8, and 12/8. For example, 6/8 is typically constructed of two pulses of three beats each; 9/8 consists of three pulses of three beats each; and 12/8 is four pulses of three beats each. These meters are slightly more difficult to conduct than simple three-beat patterns.

> **DEFINITION**
>
> A **compound meter** is one in which each beat is divided into three parts instead of two.

Conducting in Six

The most common compound meter is 6/8. This time signature is used a lot in martial music, but also in other types of instrumental and choral works.

When conducting 6/8 at a slow or moderate tempo, you have your choice of several equally functional beat patterns. (At faster tempos you're likely to conduct 6/8 with just two beats per measure, as we'll discuss later in this chapter.)

> **MUSIC VIDEO**
>
> See how to conduct in 6/4 and 6/8 in the accompanying video, "Conducting in Six," located at www.idiotsguides.com/conmus07.

The first 6/8 beat pattern is shown in Figure 7.3. In this pattern all six beats are defined on the horizontal plane, divided into two halves. Beats one, two, and three define the first half of the pattern, falling center and left of center; beats four through six are the second half, all falling right of center.

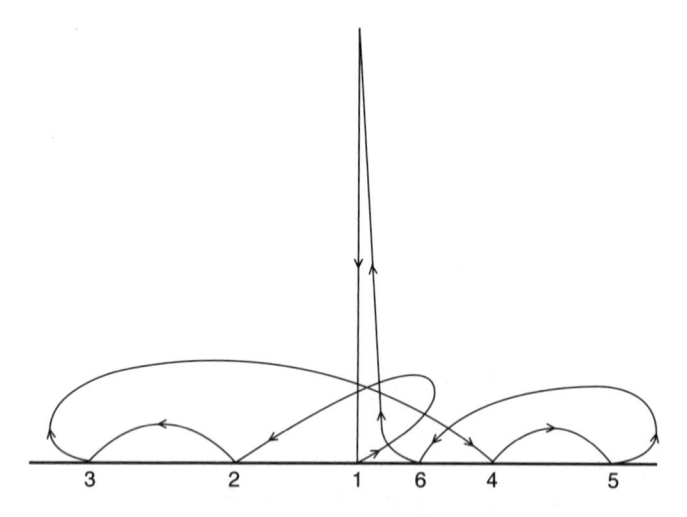

Figure 7.3: *The basic six-beat pattern.*

WHOLE NOTE

By placing the first three beats on one side of center and the second three beats on the other, most six-beat patterns emphasize the two main beats of 6/8 meter. That is, the big across-the-body movement to the right (past the center point) provides for a secondary emphasis on beat four—the secondary pulse in a measure of 6/8 time.

Next, consider the pattern known as the French six, shown in Figure 7.4. This pattern places the second and third beats to the right of the downbeat, but then swipes the final three beats up the horizontal axis. It looks a little like you're drawing a Christmas tree in the air. It's also unusual in that it breaks the rule that says all beats should fall onto the same horizontal plane—the final three beats are placed well above the horizontal. You conduct this pattern as down, right, further right, up and left, further up and right, then up and left again for the final beat.

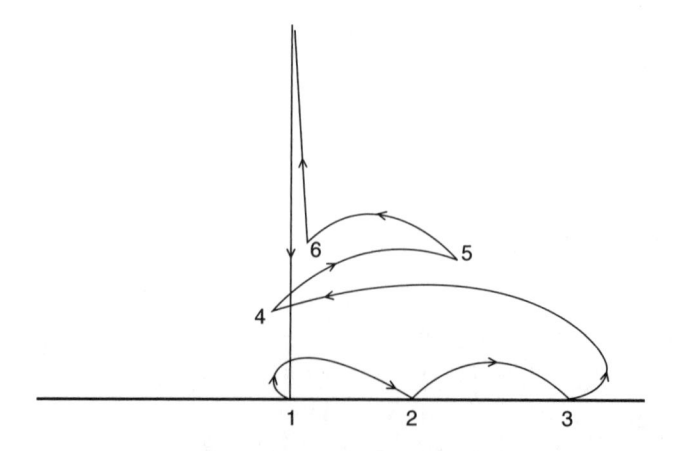

Figure 7.4: *The French six pattern mixes a standard triple pattern (for the first three beats) with an ascending center-based pattern for the final beats.*

> **THE CONDUCTOR SEZ**
>
> Very few trained conductors use the French six pattern. It lacks clarity and it's very easy to get lost in the last three beats. I do not believe it defines all six beats as well as the standard six pattern.

Conducting in Nine

The more beats you add per measure, the more difficult a piece is to conduct, if only because the beat pattern becomes even more complicated. Which, of course, brings us to those nine-beat meters—9/8, 9/4, and 9/2.

> **MUSIC VIDEO**
>
> See how to conduct nine-beat patterns in the accompanying video, "Conducting in Nine," located at www.idiotsguides.com/conmus09.

As you can see in Figure 7.5, what you end up with is a six-beat pattern augmented with three additional beats. The extra beats are not placed on the normal horizontal plane, but instead move up and inward in a stepward motion.

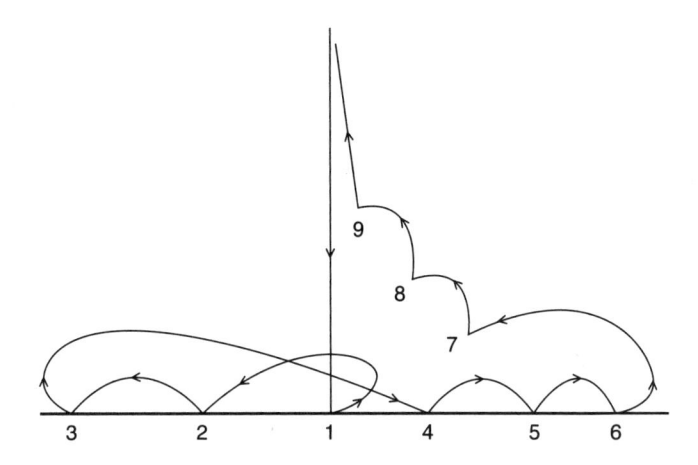

Figure 7.5: *A nine-beat pattern with upward and inward motion for the final three beats.*

The variation of this nine-beat pattern, shown in Figure 7.6, is similar but with a different approach to the final three beats. It's kind of like the last part of the French six pattern (the Christmas tree part) grafted onto a basic six pattern.

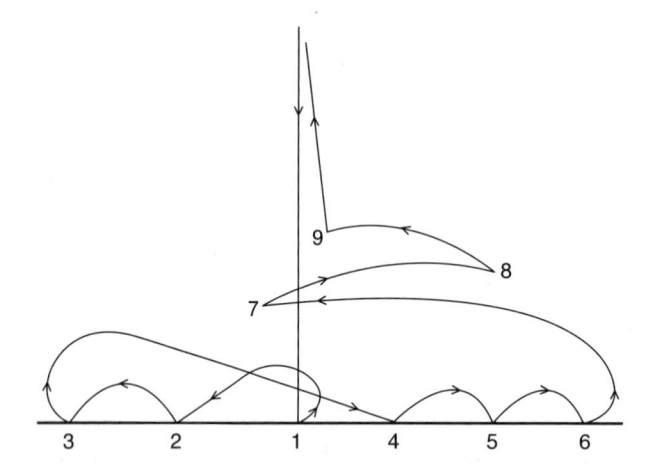

Figure 7.6: *A nine-beat pattern with a French six–like pattern for the final beats.*

> **THE CONDUCTOR SEZ**
>
> The final three beats of the second nine-beat pattern works better than the similar beats in the French six pattern, as it's the only place to put these last beats if you want an actual pattern. Notice that when done correctly, the last beat is always closer to the center axis, with its rebound moving up and inward to the top of one. (This is true for the twelve-beat pattern as well.)

Conducting in Twelve

If you thought nine was complex, wait till you get to twelve-beat meters, such as 12/8, 12/4, and 12/2. You have a lot of beats to account for when conducting in these time signatures.

The thinking behind the basic twelve-beat pattern, shown in Figure 7.7, is to divide the beats into groups of three. Hence the first group that starts with the downbeat and moves to the right; the second group that is conducted to the left of center; the third group that fits to the far right; and the final group that moves up the center axis in a French six type of pattern.

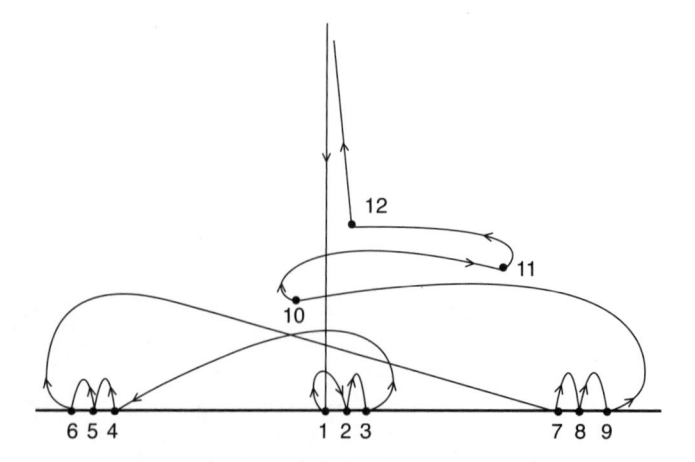

Figure 7.7: *A twelve-beat pattern, divided into four groups of three beats apiece.*

> **WHOLE NOTE**
>
> The advantage of approaching twelve-beat meters as four groups of three is that by starting each group of three beats in a different position, you emphasize the four strongest beats of the meter.

That said, most 12/8 or 12/4 pieces are fast enough that you can and probably should conduct them in four instead of twelve. That is, you conduct beats one, four, seven, and ten; each beat you conduct represents three beats in the measure, as we'll discuss next.

Conducting in Fast Triple Meters

All the beat patterns we've discussed so far in this chapter are ideal for slow and medium tempos. However, as the tempo increases, these stock beat patterns become somewhat unwieldy; when beating a fast nine, for example, you end up wagging your baton hand so fast as to be somewhat incomprehensible to your musicians. (You also wear yourself out!)

The solution for conducting fast-tempo triple meters is to simplify the beats you conduct. That is, assuming that the piece was written this way, you group every three beats together into a single conducted beat.

In this fashion, a measure of 6/8 gets conducted in a two-beat pattern, with each beat representing a dotted quarter note. Put another way, three eighth notes fit into each beat you conduct; this gives you two conducted beats to a measure. (See Chapter 6 for more on two-beat patterns.)

Likewise, a measure of 9/8 gets conducted in a simple triple pattern, with three beats to a measure. And 12/8 gets conducted in a quadruple pattern, four beats to a measure.

The Least You Need to Know

- Simple three-beat meters are conducted down, right, left.
- Patterns for six-beat meters place half the beats to the left of the downbeat and half to the right.
- Patterns for nine-beat meters start with a basic six-beat pattern then move the final three beats up the center axis.
- Twelve-beat patterns are typically divided into four groups of three, with each group positioned individually along the horizontal axis.
- Fast triple meters are often conducted with one downbeat per three normal beats; this results in a measure of 6/8 being conducted in a two-beat pattern, for example.

Conducting Advanced Meters and Subdivided Beats

Chapter 8

In This Chapter

- Conduct in quintuple meters
- Conduct seven-beat patterns
- Subdivide the beat at slower tempos
- Conduct changing time signatures

Conducting in three or four isn't that hard—well, at least the beat patterns aren't that difficult to learn. But what do you do when you get some really unusual time signatures, something like 5/4 or 7/8? That's when things, from a conductor's perspective, get really interesting.

It also gets interesting when you're conducting at a relatively slow tempo—so slow that you tend to lose the basic beat in the pattern. It's also interesting when you have to conduct through a change in time signature, a challenge that can vex the most experienced conductors.

So this chapter is about "interesting" stuff. Read on, if you're interested.

Conducting Complex Meters

As musicians, we're most familiar with a handful of common time signatures. In Western music we live and breathe in 4/4 time, and 3/4 is almost as familiar. Of course, we know the popular variations (2/4, 2/2, 3/8, and so forth), as well as a handful of compound basic meters, such as 6/8 and 9/8.

What all these time signatures have in common is that they're easily divided by either two or three. For example, 4/4 time can be divided into two equal parts of two beats apiece; 6/8 time can be divided into two parts of three beats apiece.

Less familiar to us are those time signatures that do not easily fit the double or triple mold—that don't divide into equal halves or thirds. Call these *complex meters*, because they're not simple to deal with.

> **DEFINITION**
>
> A **complex meter** is a time signature that does not divide into two or three equal parts.

The key to conducting (or even counting) a complex time signature is breaking it down into two or more parts. That is, you really don't count up to five or seven or whatever in a single measure; instead you create two submeasures of more traditional meter.

For example, when playing or counting or conducting a measure of 5/4, you don't really deal with five beats straight in a row. Instead, you subdivide the measure into two unequal parts. It's kind of a math problem, really; you can count 5/4 as either 2+3 or 3+2. That is, you count one two, one two three (or one two three, one two) instead of one two three four five. Dividing a long, complex measure into shorter, less complex parts makes the whole thing easier to deal with.

How you divide a complex meter depends on the pulse of the piece. You'll need to determine this when first prepping the score. Does that 5/4 piece have a 3+2 pulse or a 2+3 pulse? You can generally tell from the underlying accents within the piece.

Back to our 5/4 example, take a listen to the Dave Brubeck Quartet's *Take Five* (composed by saxophonist Paul Desmond). This piece has its strongest pulses on beats one and four, which means you're dealing with a 3+2 pattern.

It's the same thing when dealing with any work in a complex time signature. Figure out the underlying grouping, which defines the subdivided pattern, then conduct using a beat pattern that fits the subdivided measures.

Conducting in Five

We've already used a 5/4 piece as an example, so let's start there with our beat patterns. As noted, you can divide any five-beat meter (5/4, 5/8, 5/2, you name it) into two unequal parts—either 3+2 (like *Take Five*) or 2+3. How you divide the measure determines the beat pattern.

If you're using a 3+2 division, you use the beat pattern shown in Figure 8.1. You conduct down, left, left, then right, and back toward the center; the final rebound moves up and in.

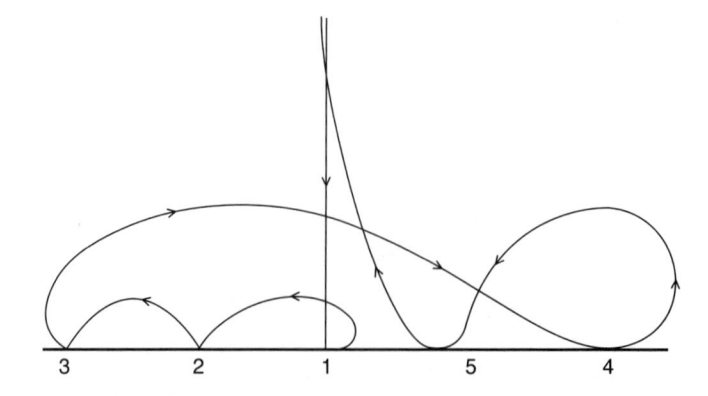

Figure 8.1: *A five-beat pattern with a 3+2 grouping.*

If you're using a 2+3 division, the beat pattern is conducted as in Figure 8.2. That is, you conduct down, left, then right, right, and back to the left, with the final upbeat again after beat five.

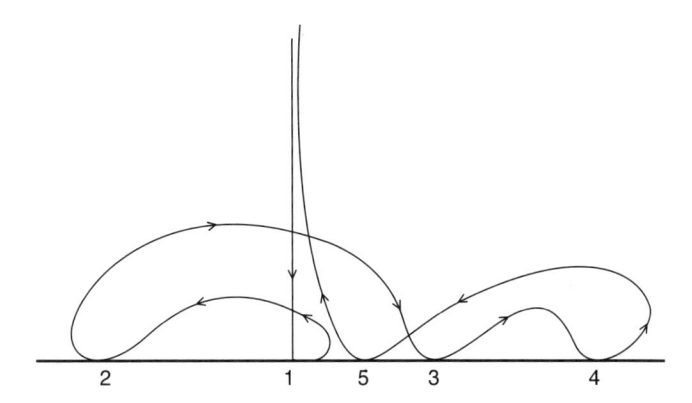

Figure 8.2: *A five-beat pattern with a 2+3 grouping.*

> **MUSIC VIDEO**
>
> See how to conduct five-beat patterns in the accompanying video, "Conducting in Five," located at www.idiotsguides.com/conmus06.

Another option, especially at faster tempos, is not to conduct in five at all, but rather to use an asymmetrical two-beat pattern, focusing on the two dominant beats in the measure. In a fast 3+2 piece, for example, you'd conduct beats one and four, using one of the standard two-beat patterns. It's not an even two-beat, of course, as the downbeat lasts for three beats of the measure while the second downstroke lasts for just two beats, but it works with faster quintuple meters. For 2+3 meters, of course, you conduct beats one and three.

Conducting in Seven

You face the same challenge when conducting a seven-beat measure—that is, you have to organize the beats into two or more groups. The challenge holds whether you're conducting in 7/8, 7/4, or 7/2. In any instance, you normally have two variations: 4+3 and 3+4. (With meters of seven and higher, there are actually a lot more variations possible, but these are the most common.)

> **FERMATA**
>
> Resist the temptation to conduct 7/4 as two separate measures of 4/4 and 3/4, each with their own strong downbeats. This will confuse your musicians; you only want a single downbeat per measure.

> **MUSIC VIDEO**
>
> See how to conduct seven-beat patterns in the accompanying video, "Conducting in Seven," located at www.idiotsguides.com/conmus08.

Figure 8.3 shows one way to conduct the 4+3 grouping. This pattern places the first four beats to the left of center and the last three beats right of center.

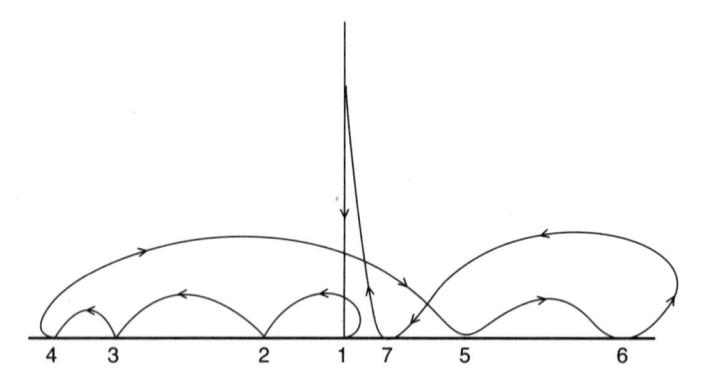

Figure 8.3: *A seven-beat pattern with a 4+3 grouping.*

Figure 8.4 shows one way to conduct the 3+4 grouping. Here the first three beats are placed to the left of center, while the last four beats are right of center.

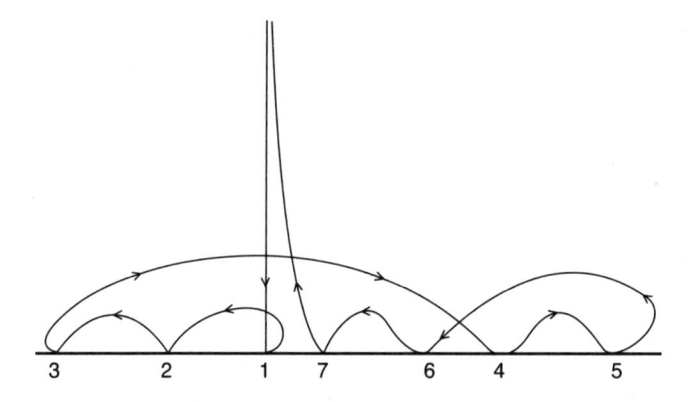

Figure 8.4: *A seven-beat pattern with a 3+4 grouping.*

As with quintuple meters, you can conduct fast seven-count meters with a two-beat pattern. For a fast 4+3 grouping, conduct beats one and five. For a fast 3+4 grouping, conduct beats one and four.

> **WHOLE NOTE**
>
> We won't be discussing even more complex meters (11/8, 13/8, and so forth), since it's unlikely you'll run into them, at least early in your conducting career; these meters represent a more advanced topic for more experienced conductors. If you do meet an overly complex meter, you'll want to divide each measure into smaller beat groups, and base your patterns on these smaller groupings.

Conducting at Slower Tempos

If you're conducting a piece at a very slow tempo, the baton ends up moving so slowly between positions as to be functionally useless to the performers; it just kind of waves around in an endless curve. This makes it difficult for performers to track the underlying subdivided pulse of a piece—for example, the underlying eighth notes in 4/4 time.

The solution is often to double-up on the beats you conduct. When you subdivide the meter in this fashion, you conduct a downstroke for each underlying note division—four downstrokes in a measure of 2/4 time, for example, or eight downstrokes in a measure of 4/4. In other words, the tempo of a piece determines how many beats per measure you conduct.

Subdividing the Beat

Here's how it works. If you're conducting a slow 4/4 piece, for example, you subdivide the beat so that you conduct one beat for each eighth note, for a total of eight beats in a measure. In essence, you turn the 4/4 time into 8/8 time, at least in terms of your conducting.

Now, the beats between the primary beats—in this example, on the "ands" after each beat—should not be as strong as the main beats dictated by the time signature. The subdivided beats you insert are conducted as additional pulses very close to the main beats. They aren't as big as the primary downstrokes, so musicians can tell the difference between the main beats and the subdivisions.

Conducting Subdivided Beats

How do you conduct these subdivided beats? It's really quite simple, and an extension of your regular beat pattern. What you do is add these extra beats/bounces as smaller movements of the baton in the same direction as the movement for the original beat.

Figure 8.5 shows how this works in a measure of 4/4 time. Using the basic 4/4 beat pattern as the template, the "ands" you insert continue in the same direction as the preceding stroke, but bounce a little lower than the main beats.

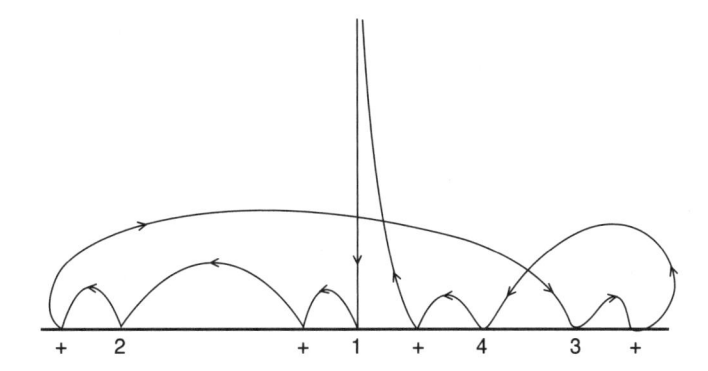

Figure 8.5: *The beat pattern for a measure of subdivided 4/4 time.*

> **THE CONDUCTOR SEZ**
>
> Though they may appear similar, subdivisions are quite different from the normal rebounds you use in your beat patterns. A rebound happens immediately after hitting the ictus, whereas a subdivision happens on the "and" after the ictus.

It's the same thing no matter which time signature you're subdividing. As another example, Figure 8.6 shows a subdivided three-beat pattern—let's call it 3/4. The subdivided beats (eighth notes all) are little bounces along the established path of the baton stroke.

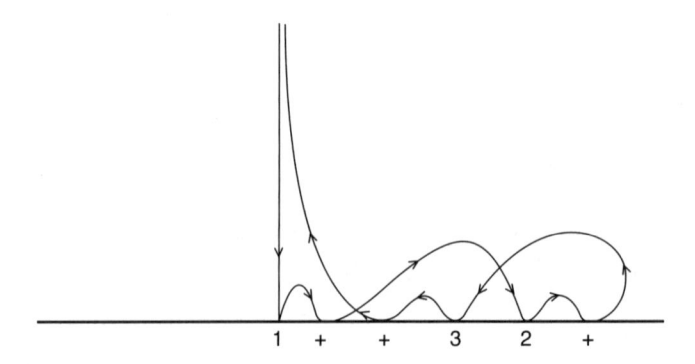

Figure 8.6: *The beat pattern for a measure of subdivided 3/4 time.*

Choosing the Right Beat Pattern

One thing to keep in mind when conducting subdivided beats—or any piece at a slower tempo—is that you should *not* start with the basic patterns that use an upbeat for the final beat of the measure. This leaves you no place to insert the subdivided beat after that last beat. Instead, use a beat pattern that requires you to conduct each and every beat in a measure. You can then convert that final subdivided beat (the last "and" in a measure of quarter-note time) into either a separate bounce or, at fast tempos, a simple rebound.

> **MUSIC VIDEO**
>
> See how to conduct subdivided beats in the accompanying video, "Conducting Subdivisions," located at www.idiotsguides.com/conmus10.

Conducting Through a Change in Time Signature

What do you do when the time signature changes in the middle of a piece? It's simple—you change from one beat pattern to another.

For example, if the meter changes from 4/4 to 3/4, you switch from a four-beat pattern to a three-beat pattern. It's not much harder than that … in theory, anyway.

Changing Beats per Measure

In practice, changing time signatures requires you to shift your thinking midstream. Your body gets into a bit of an unconscious pattern after conducting multiple measures with the same beat pattern; you have to consciously make the effort to change beat patterns when the time signature changes.

> **FERMATA**
>
> Be careful not to change the tempo when you move through a change in time signature, unless the score says to do so. Any time you change beat patterns there is a danger of losing the basic pulse—of unconsciously speeding up or slowing down. Focus on keeping the underlying pulse steady even as the beat pattern changes.

To be honest, it isn't that difficult to change time signatures when the tempo and beat value remain the same. That is, if you move from one quarter-note meter to another (from 4/4 to 3/4, for example, or from 4/4 to 5/4), you need do nothing more than add or subtract one or more beats per measure.

> **THE CONDUCTOR SEZ**
>
> The technical term for the underlying pulse of a piece is *tactus*.

Let's look at changing from 4/4 to 3/4, as an example. The two-measure switch is counted, at an even pulse, like this:

ONE two three four ONE two three

The tempo stays the same; the only thing that changes is the number of beats you count and conduct per measure.

It's the same thing if you move from 3/8 to 4/8, or from 2/2 to 3/2; the underlying pulse and tempo remain the same, you only have to change the number of beats per measure.

Changing the Underlying Pulse

It's more difficult, however, to conduct through changes in the basic pulse—that is, when you move from an eighth-note time signature to one based on a quarter note or half note. For example, moving from 3/8 to 2/4, or from 2/2 to 3/4. In these situations, you have to not only change the number of beats you conduct, but also the speed of the beat pattern and what rhythmic value gets the beat. Fortunately, most such tempo changes move in multiples of a given pulse—which lets you utilize those subdivision skills I just discussed.

> **WHOLE NOTE**
>
> Sometimes changing the beat value doesn't change the tempo at all. Look for score instructions for a time change along the lines that a quarter note equals an eighth note. This is fairly common, actually, and in this instance nothing changes except perhaps the number of beats per measure.

Consider a simple example of a meter change from 4/4 to 4/8. In this instance, the tempo of the second meter is exactly twice that of the original meter—assuming there are no other tempo instructions, of course. You still stroke four beats per measure after the time change, but each beat is exactly half the duration as previous—that is, you beat twice as fast.

Here's another relatively simple example, moving from 4/4 to 2/2. When you move to 2/2, each beat you conduct is twice as long as the ones before; essentially, you're conducting at half speed. In addition, though, you need to change the number of beats per measure. So you change from conducting four fast beats per measure to conducting two slow beats.

The key here is subdividing the meters to focus on the common pulse between the two time signatures. In the case of the shift from 4/4 to 4/8, subdivide the 4/4 meter to focus on the eighth notes, which remain constant between the two time signatures. In your head, start counting eighth notes in the measure preceding the time change; this sets you up for the eighth-note pulse after the change. Here's how you'd count it, keeping a steady tempo/pulse:

> ONE and two and three and four and ONE two three four ONE two three four

For that matter, you can actually conduct a subdivided measure or two leading up to the time change. This will prepare your performers for what's coming up and keep them on track.

It's the same thing when you go in the other direction. When you move from 4/4 to 4/2, for example, just keep counting the common quarter notes in your head for a measure or two after the time change, like this:

> ONE two three four ONE two three four ONE and two and three and four and

Each word has the same duration, which lets you keep the same pulse as you change time signatures.

Changing the Number of Beats and the Rhythmic Value

What's really difficult is when you're faced with both a change in number of beats per measure and the prevailing rhythmic value; for example, if you have to move from 3/8 time to a 2/4 time signature. You have to shift from beating three eighth notes per measure to beating two quarter notes. There's no getting around it; this is challenging. You have to employ all your skill and technique to make the time change work. That means focusing on the underlying common pulse *and* changing beat patterns.

Practicing Time Changes

Negotiating this type of time change—heck, negotiating *any* time change—is something you probably want to practice. When you prep the score before the first rehearsal, mark any time changes you encounter. Then work through, in your mind, the beat patterns you'll be using for each time signature.

> **THE CONDUCTOR SEZ**
>
> The most important thing here is understanding the math involved and knowing all the variables. Does the composer want a change of tempo? Of tactus (prevailing pulse)? Is there a relationship given?

You can then get out your baton and start practicing both beat patterns and the actual meter shift. Practice until you can conduct through the time change without thinking about it—until it's muscle memory. Preparation and practice—that's how you prepare for a complex time change.

The Least You Need to Know

- When you're conducting complex time signatures, divide and count the measure as two or three unequal parts. For example, you can divide a five-beat time signature as 2+3 or 3+2, and then employ beat pattern to match this division.
- When conducting an odd-time piece at a faster tempo, you can use a two-beat pattern, focusing on the two dominant beats in each measure.
- When conducting slower tempos, you may need to subdivide the beat—that is, to conduct every half-beat as a separate downstroke.
- When the time signature changes within a piece, find the common pulse to conduct through the meter change, and then change your beat pattern after the time change.

Interpretation and Expression

Part 3

Beat patterns out of the way, it's time to move beyond the basic stuff and learn how to deal with more expressive direction. That means learning how to interpret a score and control a performance. It also means learning to use your other hand—the one you don't hold a baton in.

You use your left hand for all sorts of things when conducting, and we'll talk about all of them—things like tempo, dynamics, phrasing, cues, and accents. To put your personal stamp on a piece of music, you'll have to use both your hands—and be prepared to work up a little sweat.

Speaking of sweat, just how do you conduct a passage that doesn't have a formal beat, like a recitative in opera? That's a very special case, and it requires a bit of forethought—which you'll get in this part.

Interpreting and Controlling the Performance

Chapter 9

In This Chapter

- Learn how to interpret a musical work
- Discover those elements a conductor can influence
- Understand timbre, phrasing, tempo, dynamics, energy, and mood
- Find out how to control a performance from the podium

I've said it several times already in this book, but conducting is more than just tapping out a beat pattern with your baton. While the mechanics of baton work are important, a good conductor also interprets the music and guides the performance, creating a unique musical experience—even if it's a piece we've all heard hundreds of times before.

Just how does a conductor do this? After all, it's you versus the ensemble, and all you have is the score and your baton. How do you entice the performers to play a piece your way?

Interpreting a Musical Work

A piece of music is a piece of music is a piece of music—or is it? Is every performance of Beethoven's Ninth Symphony exactly the same? Does every choir sing *Amazing Grace* exactly the same way every time? What makes one big band's performance of *Autumn in Paris* sound different from that of another band?

Naturally, the performers involved will color the sound of a given performance. But equally if not more important is the vision of the conductor—the tempos and dynamics he chooses, the expression he coaxes from the performers, the excitement he imparts. It's all about how a conductor interprets a given piece of music, and how he conducts the performers in service of that interpretation.

All performers interpret the music they play or sing. Every performer has his own idiosyncrasies, his own style, that he imparts on even the most innocuous pieces he plays. This is most obvious in jazz and popular music, but also the case in classical music and other serious musical forms.

In this fashion, the conductor is no different from other musicians. Naturally, a conductor approaches each piece of music from his or her own unique perspective. Maybe he hears the piece as a more driving pulse, or maybe he hears it as more lyrical. Perhaps he hears certain parts performed staccato, and others more legato. He may even hear specific tempos and dynamics different from those of other conductors. In this regard, the conductor has much latitude in putting his personal stamp on a piece of music.

> **THE CONDUCTOR SEZ**
>
> I am of the opinion that what the musicians bring to the table is equally important as what the conductor brings. No one is more important—though I would point out that without musicians, a conductor is a crazy person alone in a room waving his or her arms around.

What Can You Influence?

A composition is more than just a cold collection of notes; a great conductor can breathe life into the music, arousing the emotions of the audience. He does this by bringing out the essential character of the music (or at least his view of this character) by emphasizing certain key elements in a piece and deemphasizing the unimportant ones.

Just what elements of a musical work can and should a conductor impact? While the basic notes and rhythms are set by a piece's composer, there are a half dozen or so variables present in just about every piece of music. These include the following:

- Timbre
- Phrasing
- Tempo
- Dynamics
- Energy
- Mood

All of these points need to be aligned with the composer's intent, of course. We'll look at each of these elements individually.

> **FERMATA**
>
> While a conductor can (and should) personally interpret a piece of music, he doesn't actually *change* the original work. The conductor doesn't go in and rewrite the notes, alter rhythms, or turn pianissimo passages to fortissimo. No, the original music remains as written; the conductor merely puts his own personal stamp on how that music is performed.

Timbre

Timbre (or "color") is the character or quality of a musical tone. When working with an ensemble, that tone can be either that of an individual instrument or of the ensemble as a whole. To this end, the conductor can work with individual musicians to achieve a desired timbre, with specific sections of the ensemble, and with the ensemble as a whole.

In addition, the conductor is responsible for the overall mix of the entire ensemble. That means bringing certain parts or sections to the fore and sending others to the background. For example, a composer might want the string section to play softer so that a passage in the woodwinds becomes more prominent. It's the same piece of music either way, but by emphasizing one part over another, the piece takes on a completely different character. You might find it surprising just how much changing this mix can affect the overall sound of a piece.

> **WHOLE NOTE**
>
> The conductor's interpretation and manipulation of timbre is most often achieved during the rehearsal process. Performers must learn how the conductor wants a piece played well before the actual performance.

Phrasing

Phrasing is the expressive shaping of a musical passage. A passage can be phrased in many different ways, in effect changing the passage's musical meaning. It's the musical equivalent of how speaking a sentence different ways can change its meaning. On paper, a sentence is nothing more than a series of words, one after another, just as a musical passage is a series of notes on paper. One orator can speak those words rapidly and make them sound light and inconsequential; another orator can slow them down and give them greater import.

It's the same thing with musical phrases. Whether a given passage sounds light or heavy, thrilling or pensive, depends wholly on how a conductor interprets the phrasing. It's a matter of which notes are stressed and which are subordinated, and how those notes are performed together.

> **WHOLE NOTE**
>
> In vocal music (and with wind instruments, too), phrasing also involves breathing—where the performers take their breaths during a passage. In choral music, phrasing is guided tremendously by the piece's lyrics.

Tempo

Tempo is the speed or pace of a musical passage—how fast the rhythmic pulse is. While the composer indicates general tempos, the conductor is free to interpret these directions and indicate exact tempo for a performance.

The conductor has this type of freedom because there is no general agreement as to what precise tempos are indicated by our general tempo markings. That is, we can't say for sure exactly how fast *adagio* or *allegro* is, just that *allegro* is faster than *adagio*. It's up to the conductor to set the precise speed for a given tempo marking.

The exception to a conductor's interpretation of tempo is when a composer indicates an exact tempo in terms of beats per minute (bpm). You often see this in marching band music, musical theater, and film scoring, but bpm markings can appear in any type of work.

> **THE CONDUCTOR SEZ**
>
> Tempo is often influenced by the acoustics of the concert hall or performing space. A dry acoustic calls for a faster tempo interpretation; a wet acoustic, a slower one.

Dynamics

Dynamics involves the volume level of a musical passage—how loud or how soft it is. Dynamics is similar to tempo in terms of how much latitude a conductor has, and for the same reason. That's right, there are no official decibel levels assigned to *forte* or *pianissimo* or any other dynamic marking. We know that *forte* is louder than *pianissimo*, but we don't know by how much. Just how loud is *forte*, and how soft is *pianissimo*? That's entirely up to the conductor. And, of course, the volume levels chosen greatly affect the performance of a piece.

> **THE CONDUCTOR SEZ**
>
> When working with dynamics, the conductor needs to consider many variables, such as the number of performers (*forte* for a string quartet is very different from the *forte* of a 200-voice choir), the size of the venue, and whether there is any amplification involved.

Energy

Different performances of the same musical work quite often have different energy levels. It's a matter of vigor, or the ability to generate a given level of excitement.

There are many factors that affect energy level, but the conductor has a big say in the whole thing. Yes, lethargic performers can pull down the energy level, but a good conductor can goose the ensemble to pump up the energy. Likewise, the conductor can hold energy in reserve, restraining the performance and lowering the level of excitement.

It's all accomplished by how a conductor conducts the work. Some conductors are very expressive and enthusiastic, and thus drive high-energy performances from their ensembles. Other conductors are more reserved, and this is reflected in lower-key performances. How you feel, and how you employ other key elements, will define the energy level of any given performance.

> **WHOLE NOTE**
>
> Changing the tempo a few beats per minute one way or the other can greatly affect the energy level of a performance.

Mood

Many musical works were created to evoke a particular mood. The conductor can help bring out that mood and lend emotional weight to a piece. It's up to the conductor whether a piece has a somber mood or a joyful one, whether a piece is full of hope or expresses hopelessness, whether a work evokes nostalgia or tranquility or anger or despair. Notes on paper are one thing; the mood invoked by the performance of those notes is something else entirely.

How do you do this? It's all about the motions and gestures you use, and your body language. For example, to evoke a tender mood, use small and delicate movements. To evoke a joyous mode, use more exaggerated arm movements. You can also use facial expressions to set a mood; looking a little wild-eyed will convey a more raucous mood. Let your demeanor help set the musical mood.

> **THE CONDUCTOR SEZ**
>
> Mood and energy are greatly influenced by the conductor's face. You wouldn't want to smile during a funeral march, for example, or look somber during *Deck the Halls*. Physically approach a given piece with the body language (including facial expression) that matches your desired level of energy and mood. Your eyes become incredibly useful tools as you lead an ensemble.

Controlling the Performance

With so many elements under his control, the conductor truly does have a crucial role in the interpretation of a performance. The conductor is more than just the guy who starts and stops the thing; he's the leader of the ensemble, the person who defines the expression of a work in performance.

But how does a conductor imprint his interpretation on a group of performers? For that matter, how does a single person, standing in front of a huge group of people, get that group to do anything at all? How much control over a choir or orchestra does a conductor really have?

The answer to that last question is, a lot. In reality, a group of trained musicians is surprisingly sensitive to the ministrations of the conductor; great performers willingly follow the direction of great conductors. This assumes, of course, that the conductor knows how to conduct—not just how to follow basic beat patterns, but also how to instruct and cajole performers in both direct and subtle ways.

A conductor uses his right hand to define the time signature and tempo, of course. The right hand can also help define phrasing and style, the length of the basic stroke, the type (rounded or angular) and height of the rebound, and so forth. That's a lot of control and expressiveness right there, in one hand.

The conductor has another hand, however, which controls even more musical expression. The left hand is used to indicate dynamics and phrasing, as well as general shape and style. The left hand is also used to indicate accents and rhythmic patterns, and to cue passages and instruments. It handles the bulk of the nontempo work. (Learn more about using your nonbaton hand in Chapter 10.)

The gestures you make are just part of the story. The conductor can also get his point across by employing different facial expressions, body language, eye contact, and the like. It's all a matter of using every element at your disposal to tell the performers what you want them to do.

And, as discussed in Chapter 4, a large part of this communication takes place before the actual performance, during the rehearsal process. During rehearsal you can actually tell the performers what you want, using your voice; you don't have to play conductor charades to get the point across. When you effectively use the rehearsal process to shape the piece's artistic direction, the gestures you make during the actual performance are just subtle reminders.

The Least You Need to Know

- A conductor has wide latitude in interpreting just about any musical work.
- A conductor has influence over several key musical elements, including timbre, phrasing, tempo, dynamics, energy, and mood.
- A conductor controls the ensemble with his hands (both right and left), facial expressions, body movements, and overall demeanor.
- Much of a conductor's musical interpretation is imparted verbally, during the rehearsal process.

Using the Left Hand

Chapter 10

In This Chapter

- Discover what you shouldn't do with your nonbaton hand
- Learn how to mirror your right hand with your left
- Find out how to use your left hand to express musical direction
- Learn how to use your two hands together

So far in this book we've focused almost exclusively on the conductor's use of the right, or baton hand. But most of us have two such fully functioning appendages; what, then, should we do with our left hands?

It all depends on what you want to do, of course, and what kind of music you're conducting. Your left hand can get quite a workout—or just hang around for the ride.

Things You *Shouldn't* Do with Your Left Hand While Conducting

Before we get into the different ways you can use your left (nonbaton) hand while conducting, let's look at some things you really shouldn't do with that hand. Here's a list of things to keep in mind:

- *Don't* put your left hand in your pocket and twiddle your change during a performance.
- *Don't* pick up your cell phone and start texting.
- *Don't* pick up your favorite beverage and take a long refreshing drink.
- *Don't* point toward the rear of the stage to signal where you'll hit your next home run.
- *Don't* light up a smoke. (Most concert halls are smoke-free, in any case.)
- *Don't* wiggle your fingers shyly at that cute little clarinet player in the third row.
- *Don't* do the wave.
- *Don't* make a fist with your left hand, extend your middle finger, and gesture rudely at the trombone section—no matter how much they might deserve it.

And never, never use your left hand to pick your nose in concert. (For that matter, you shouldn't use your baton for this, either.)

Different Ways to Use Your Nonbaton Hand

Okay, that little bit of levity out of the way, how then *should* you use your left hand while conducting? Your right hand does all the heavy lifting, after all; it's responsible for setting and keeping the tempo, and for defining all the beats of a given time signature. What's left for Mr. Left to do?

> **WHOLE NOTE**
>
> Throughout this book I refer to your right hand as your baton hand. This is accepted practice, even if you're left handed. In most instances, you should conduct with the baton in your right hand; that's what performers expect to see. Times change, however, and we're starting to see some real southpaw conductors. If that's what feels natural to you, then go for it—but be prepared for some pushback from more traditional musicians.

Hanging Out

First things first. Your left hand should not be a distraction; you want the musicians you're conducting to focus on your baton hand. To that end, when you're not using your left hand, you should keep it loosely at your side. It should not be up in the air, interfering with the view of the baton; you shouldn't wave it around without purpose. Unless you're using your left hand to perform some musical expression, keep it out of sight.

Mirror, Mirror

Some conductors like to use their left hand to mirror what their right hand is doing. That is, each hand makes the same motions, but in the opposite directions. (Figure 10.1 shows this mirroring with the alternate four-beat pattern.)

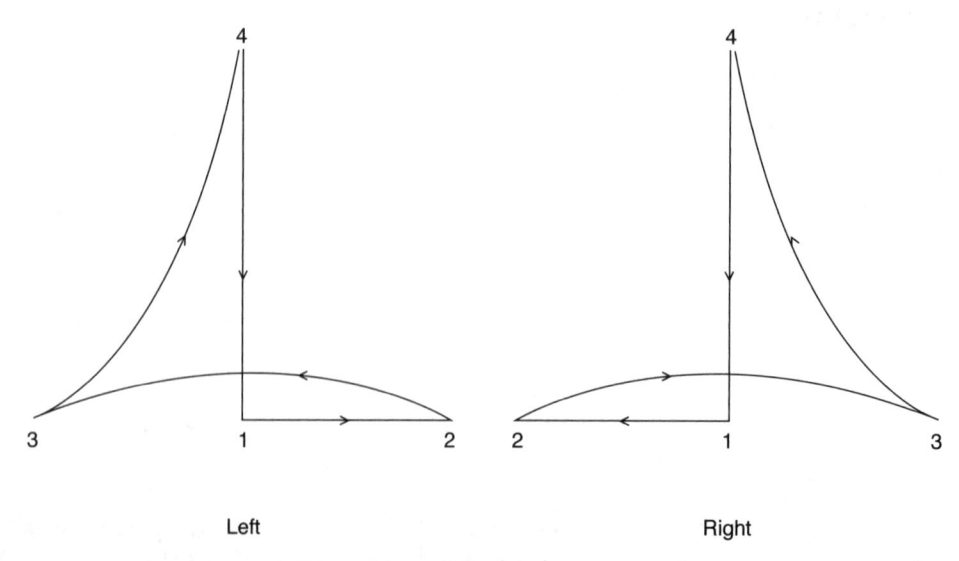

Figure 10.1: *The four-beat pattern mirrored in the left hand.*

The advantage of mirroring your hands is that you get increased visibility. This is why some drum majors employ this approach, especially those in old school military-type bands. You'll also find some choral conductors, especially those without formal training, using this technique.

Mirroring your hand movements throughout a piece isn't accepted practice, however, and I don't recommend it. It's wasted energy, and puts too much motion in front of the performers; quite frankly, it's distracting. The left hand is better used to express specific musical demands, as we'll discuss next, or left out of the picture completely.

> **THE CONDUCTOR SEZ**
>
> Mirroring the right hand should not be the default use of the left hand. Mirroring should be used sparingly, for special emphasis. Remember: the more you conduct, the less they watch.

Expressing Yourself

The proper role of the left hand is to emphasize particular musical elements and instructions—things you can't do with your right hand while keeping the beat.

In particular, you use your left hand to indicate the following:

- Dynamics
- Phrasing
- Mood and expressiveness
- Key accents and rhythmic patterns
- Cues for the entrance of different instruments and voices, including pointing out numeric cues or counting down measures or beats before an entrance

You can also use your left hand to get the attention of distracted or misbehaving individuals. Many conductors also use their left hands to correct any mistakes that may arise during the course of a performance.

Using Two Hands Together

As you can see, the left hand is free to do all the things that your right hand isn't free to do. That means you need to ensure that your two hands work together as a team, the better to express all necessary musical direction. With that in mind, there are some best practices you should keep in mind when working your two hands together.

- Never cross your hands. Keep your right hand planted on the right side of your body (actually, from the center to the right), and your left hand on the left.
- That said, you can move your left hand over the top of your right hand when expressing phrasing. But make sure the hands are relatively far apart if you do this.
- While the right hand should be kept at a relatively constant distance from your body, your left hand can move out further and come in closer, as musical direction dictates. (You can also move your right hand in and out on occasion, as we'll discuss in later chapters—but sparingly.)
- Your left hand can also move higher and lower than your right hand. (But not too much lower, or no one will see it!)
- Don't let movement with your left hand affect the tempo you keep with your right hand. The right-hand beat should remain steady, no matter what your left hand is doing.

When using both your hands together, you need to exhibit something that drummers call *coordinated independence*. That is, each hand (and, if you're a drummer, both feet, too) need to be able to move independently of each other, but in a coordinated fashion. It's kind of like patting your head and rubbing your tummy at the same time. (Just don't try to chew gum, too!)

> **THE CONDUCTOR SEZ**
>
> Here's what I tell my students: your default right-hand gesture should show nothing more than tempo. That's it. This is what you should always return to; this way, when you change the gesture to show a different mood, a dynamic change, a specific articulation, and so on, your musicians will readily be able to appreciate the change and respond to it. When you add the left hand, it must have a reason for being there. If you decide to bring the left hand up, it should be for something the right hand can't show at the time. Overuse of the left hand (for example, simple mirroring or vague waving) will cause musicians to not watch you—and perhaps even cause confusion.

The Least You Need to Know

- Some conductors mirror their right hand with their left, although this isn't accepted practice for most types of music.
- Instead, use your left hand to indicate musical directions—cues, accents, dynamics, and the like.
- When not in use, your left hand should remain loosely at your side.
- Make sure that your left hand doesn't interfere with your right—and that you never cross hands while conducting.

Conducting Tempo

Chapter 11

In This Chapter

- Determine the tempo
- Get to know tempo markings
- Learn to conduct at different tempos
- Discover how to conduct tempo changes
- Find out how to conduct fermati

One of the conductor's primary responsibilities is to set and maintain the tempo of a piece. That also involves guiding performers through any change in tempo, up to and including a full stop.

Tempo is the one form of musical expression that you do mainly with your right, or baton hand. It's all about how you conduct the beat—after setting it in your head.

Setting the Tempo

The pace of a piece—the tempo—helps set the musical mood. The tempo you choose can make a piece sound energetic or lethargic, exciting or pensive, driven or laid back. Tempo is one of the prime factors in explaining how the same musical work can sound so different under different conductors.

No less a light than the famed composer Richard Wagner, himself a talented conductor, had this to say about the importance of conducting tempo in his essay *On Conducting* (1869):

> The whole duty of the conductor is comprised in his ability always to indicate the right tempo. His choice of tempi will show whether he understands the piece or not. With good players, again, the true tempo induces correct phrasing and expression and, conversely, with a conductor, the idea of appropriate phrasing and expression will induce the conception of the true tempo.

In other words, tempo not only has to do with beats per minute, it also influences the phrasing and expression of the performance. It's something you have to get right.

Choosing the Right Tempo

How do you set the tempo of a piece? It all depends. Some composers dictate a very specific tempo, in terms of exact *beats per minute* (*bpm*). When bpm is specified, that's what you should conduct—using a metronome to set the beat, if necessary.

Other types of conducting involve working with a metronome-like *click track*. When you have to synch a performance with a click, you have to match that tempo. There's no leeway for expression; hit the required tempo or else.

> **DEFINITION**
>
> **Beats per minute,** or **bpm,** literally defines the tempo in terms of how many beats are played per 60 second period. (In some older pieces you may see the notation M.M. instead, for "metronome marking.") A **click track** is a sound that plays on each beat of a measure, defining the tempo of a piece, much like an electronic metronome. Click tracks are typically heard in musician's headphones and not on the final recording; musicians play to the click to keep a steady tempo.

Some types of conducting, such as studio and stage conducting, increasingly require performers to play along with prerecorded or digitally generated tracks. This is like conducting to a click (and often includes a click along with the prerecords), in that you have to hit the precise tempo of the pre-existing material; there is no room for interpretation.

> **THE CONDUCTOR SEZ**
>
> Contemporary art compositions often use electronic components or prerecorded material, and thus have their tempo dictated in advance. This was quite common in the 1960s and has found resurgence in the past decade.

Most music, however, does offer room for interpretation of tempo. What you typically find is that the composer used an established musical term to indicate the tempo; you, as the conductor, have some amount of leeway in defining that tempo in terms of beats per minute. For example, the beginning of Gershwin's *An American in Paris* is indicated as *allegretto*, or fairly fast. So what exactly does "fairly fast" mean? Technically, *allegretto* is to be performed somewhat faster than *andante* and a little slower than *allegro*, but that really doesn't pin things down.

In reality, some conductors perform this piece at a kind of brisk walking pace, around 80 to 90 bpm. Other conductors will rev things up and perform it at a much more energetic 110 to 120 bpm. Now that's a big difference, but it's allowed; when setting tempo, there's no right or wrong. It's all about how the conductor hears it in his head.

> **THE CONDUCTOR SEZ**
>
> The venue can have a tremendous effect on tempo choice. The more ringy or "wet" a room's acoustics, the slower the tempo. The drier the space, the faster the tempo. Think about it—if you have fast harmonic rhythms in a wet room, those harmony changes will fall all over each other and sound very muddy. You must slow the work down to get it to sound correctly. In this aspect, the venue is the silent member of every ensemble and is often overlooked.

Understanding Tempo Markings

Before we get too far into the ins and outs of conducting tempo, you need a solid understanding of the standard Italian tempo markings. (There are also German and French tempo markings, but the Italian ones are more common.) You'll run into these terms in just about every piece you conduct. Table 11.1 details the more common of these tempo markings, arranged from slowest to fastest. Make sure you're familiar with the tempos they indicate.

Table 11.1 Tempo Markings

Tempo	Description
Very Slow Tempos (20–40 bpm)	
larghissimo	Very, very slow
grave	Very slow; solemn
Slow Tempos (40–75 bpm)	
lento	Slow
largo	Slow and dignified; broadly
larghetto	A little faster than *largo*
adagio	Moderately slow; stately
adagietto	A little faster than *adagio*
Moderate Tempos (70–115 bpm)	
andante	A "walking" tempo
andantino	A little faster than *andante*
moderato	Moderate pace
Fast Tempos (120 bpm and faster)	
allegretto	Not quite as fast as *allegro*
allegro	Fast, cheerful
vivace	Lively
presto	Very fast
prestissimo	Very, very fast

> **THE CONDUCTOR SEZ**
>
> It's important to understand that these terms have as much to do with character as actual tempo. In fact, in the Baroque era, many terms are actually associated with mood rather than tempo.

Sometimes you'll see these tempo terms accompanied by the word *molto*, which means "very." So if you see *molto vivace*, you know that the music should be played "very lively."

Remember, these tempo markings are approximate, and even their order is not always fully observed. What's important is that composers use these terms to get across the "spirit" of the music. For example, the word *allegro* in Italian really means "cheerful." The precise tempo, then, is always left to the discretion of the conductor—which you should do during your score prep, before you begin the very first rehearsal.

> **THE CONDUCTOR SEZ**
>
> My favorite crazy tempo marking comes from Beethoven's Missa in C, for the first movement (Kyrie): *Andante con moto assai vivace quasi Allegretto ma non troppo*. Translated, this means "At a walking pace with motion, very lively, a bit quick but not too much."

When you're determining the tempo of a piece, you need to consider several factors:

- **Tempo markings.** These give you a general feel of where the tempo should be.
- **Fastest rhythmic value.** Look for the fastest rhythmic value—that is, the smallest note value. If a piece has a lot of thirty-second notes, for example, you'll probably set the tempo slower than a piece that primarily consist of eighth notes.
- **Tradition.** Certain pieces have historically been performed a certain way; you may want to hew to that tradition or break with it.
- **Performer's abilities.** In reality, the fastest and slowest tempos at which a piece can be performed are dictated by its most difficult passages, and your musicians' ability to play or sing those passages. If you're dealing with younger or less experienced performers, for example, you may need to take a difficult piece at a slower tempo than if it were being played by more skilled performers.

> **FERMATA**
>
> While it's good to push your performers, don't turn a piece into a suicide run. Try to avoid tempo-related train wrecks, if you can.

Setting the Beat

Once you determine the tempo of a piece, how do you convey that tempo to the performers? The tempo is completely in your hands—predominantly your right hand.

That's right, you set the tempo with your right hand. It doesn't matter whether or not you use a baton, the hand you use to conduct the beat is the one that also sets the tempo. That's because the speed of the beat pattern you conduct *is* the tempo; each beat you conduct represents a single metrical pulse in a measure. The speed at which you conduct these beats is the tempo of the music.

You set the initial tempo of a piece by the relationship of your preparatory gesture and your first beat. That is, the speed of the preparatory beat defines the tempo of the piece.

That's the mechanics of it. The speed you beat the baton sets the tempo of the music—it's that simple.

But how do you get that tempo when you're standing on the concert stage? You have to remember the tempo in your head, which takes some practice. You can always cheat and carry a portable metronome with you, but it's better if you can actually feel the tempo. Like I said, experience will help you develop this skill.

> **WHOLE NOTE**
>
> Practice setting the tempo in your head, and then check the resulting bpm against a metronome. You can also gauge tempo against your own heartbeat; typical resting pulse is close to 70 bpm.

Keeping a Steady Tempo—or Not

Once you get the group started at a set tempo, it should be a snap to keep them going at the right speed. Well, it *should* be .... In reality, though, large groups of performers sometimes have trouble keeping a steady tempo. They speed up when excited and slow down when bored; the tempo gets slower when the notes get harder, and speeds up during easier passages. It's just natural—and more pronounced with less experienced musicians, of course.

It's your job as the conductor to ensure a steady tempo throughout the course of a piece of music. You have to resist the temptation to speed up here or slow down there. In fact, you may have to physically hold back entire sections of musicians who want to pull or push the beat. It can be difficult.

Holding a steady tempo requires strong leadership. This is one part of the job that's not really nuanced; you have to wield an authoritative baton to keep everybody in check. (And I do mean everybody; oftentimes one section will want to go at one tempo and another section at another.)

> **FERMATA**
>
> Weak or less confident conductors have a tendency to follow a group's tempo rather than lead it. There's nothing more embarrassing than an inexperienced conductor being pulled by a group of rushing musicians right off the virtual cliff.

When the tempo starts to waver, you have to beat more firmly to keep everyone in line. Remember, though, the more you beat, the less they watch; it can be more effective to pull everything back and force them to watch you more closely. Use smaller and cleaner gestures—don't start waving your arms around with larger gestures.

It's important that you conduct a distinct beat, which means no fuzzy patterns; everybody has to be clear about where the beat is and what the tempo should be. When things start getting a little wobbly, focus on the beat—and the exclusion of other expression—until things return to normal.

This assumes, however, that you *want* to maintain a steady beat. That isn't always the case. The character of a piece may benefit from a slight pulsing of meter, slowing down a tad here and speeding up a little there. A slight—and I do mean *slight*—variation in tempo can lend expressiveness and emotion to a performance. Use your own best judgment, but feel free to nudge the tempo up or down a bit as you feel necessary.

Conducting at Different Tempos

How does conducting differ at different tempos? In general, not much. That is, you pretty much do what you'd expect to do—at faster tempos, you beat faster; at slower tempos, you beat slower. But there are some nuances.

The most significant tempo-related issue concerns the speed of your baton stroke. For example, you may need to separate your icti to a greater degree to indicate a slower tempo; if your icti are at the same physical points in space, you end up moving slower from point to point.

At faster tempos, keep your rebounds shorter and quicker, and don't gesture as broadly throughout the beat pattern. Keep your upper arm relatively still, with most of the movement centered on your elbow. In essence, the faster the tempo, the more you conduct with your forearms; eliminate as much extra motion as possible.

As the tempo decreases, let your rebounds take a bit more time; you can also use a bit broader stroke throughout the pattern. The slower the tempo, the more you center your arm movement from your shoulder. Your beat patterns should be bigger as well.

> **WHOLE NOTE**
>
> As the tempo gets even slower, consider subdividing the beats you conduct. Learn more about subdivisions in Chapter 8.

Changing the Tempo

Many compositions change tempo throughout the course of the piece. A tempo change may be immediate or it may be gradual; in either case, you have to lead the performers through the change of tempo.

> **MUSIC VIDEO**
>
> See how to indicate changes in tempo in the accompanying video, "Conducting Tempo Changes," located at www.idiotsguides.com/conmus11.

Conducting a Sudden Tempo Change

Conducting a sudden change of tempo is like changing gears in a car. You just shift up or shift down and keep going, as the case may be. There's typically no time to prep the tempo change; you have to be able to feel the new tempo immediately, and shift your beat pattern on the fly.

Imagine that you're marching along at a nice *allegro* when the composer hits you with an immediate change to *largo*. You have to immediately shift your beat to the slower tempo, which means you have to have the new tempo fixed in your head beforehand. This requires—wait for it—practice, which you do by yourself before the first rehearsal. Obviously, rehearsing the ensemble through the tempo change is also beneficial.

In some instances, you can use beat subdivision to affect a tempo change. If you're lucky enough that the new tempo is an easy division or increment of the original tempo, subdividing the beat will get you through the change with flying colors. For example, if the tempo changes from 60 bpm to 120 bpm, you start subdividing the original beat a few measures before the change, then the subdivision becomes the new beat after the tempo change.

If the new tempo is not an easy multiple of the original tempo, some have advocated a mathematical preparation, where you calculate the new tempo as a percentage of the original tempo. I can't say I recommend this approach; the calculations get way too messy and the result, if you can pull it off, can sound too mechanical. It's better to just hear the new tempo in your head, with a little prep and practice, and proceed by feel.

> **THE CONDUCTOR SEZ**
>
> A new, sudden tempo change is best shown in the rebound immediately before the change. Say your change is on beat three of a 4/4 bar, and you're going from *lento* to *allegro*. The rebound from three will be in the new tempo, moving to four at the *allegro* speed.

Conducting a Gradual Tempo Change

Perhaps more common are gradual tempo changes, where the original tempo slowly speeds up or slows down to a new tempo. This is typically indicated by one of the commonly used Italian markings described in Table 11.2.

Table 11.2   Tempo Change Markings

Marking	Description
ritardando (*rit.*, *ritard.*)	Gradually slow down
rallentando (*rall.*)	Gradually slow down
ritenuto (*riten.*)	Hold back the tempo
accelerando (*accel.*)	Gradually speed up
doppio movimento	Twice as fast
a tempo	Return to the previous tempo
tempo primo	Return to the tempo at the beginning of the piece

Speeding up and slowing down are relatively easy to do. You just start changing the speed of your beat pattern until you gradually hit the desired new tempo—where indicated in the score, of course. Naturally, you need to have the new tempo fixed in your head, but that's no different than it is with any type of tempo change.

When you're conducting an *accelerando*, use smaller beat gestures as you speed things up—or simply move faster in your current pattern. When you're conducting a *rallentando* or *ritarando*, use larger beat gestures to help slow things down.

> **WHOLE NOTE**
>
> Avoid the temptation to use larger motions when speeding up the tempo. Unfortunately, these broader gestures increase the weightiness of the beat and can actually serve to slow down the beat.

Conducting Fermati

Then there's the issue of conducting *fermati*. That's the plural of *fermata*, which is one of those little bird's-eye signs in the music that indicate a "hold" or indefinite prolongation of a note. When it comes to conducting a fermata, the length of the hold is left up to the conductor's discretion.

There are three commonly recognized types of fermati, defined by the nature of the hold and typically referred to as A, B, and C:

- A, a hold with no true break afterward
- B, a hold with a cutoff and followed by a preparatory gesture in tempo—basically, an in-tempo break
- C, a hold with an out-of-time break afterward—anything longer than a metric pulse requiring a full stop

You conduct each type of fermata in a similar fashion; the main difference is the length of the silence between the end of the fermata and the restart of the music afterward. Once you strike the fermata beat, you conduct a slightly slower rebound and then hold the baton raised and steady, at the rebound level, for the duration of the fermata; you may also mirror this motion with your left hand. The musicians continue playing/singing the held note until you choose to end it.

For the type A fermata, you do *not* execute a cutoff at the end of the hold. Instead, simply lift the baton from the held beat and move to the next beat. You do not repeat the held beat at all, nor do you give a preparatory beat for the next beat played. It's a very smooth movement forward.

For the type B fermata, you restrike the held beat as both a cutoff and prep for the next entrance. This cutoff and prep are done in either the previous tempo or in a new tempo, depending on what's indicated in the score.

Finally, for the type C fermata, you need to execute a cutoff at the end of the hold, since there needs to be a space between the fermata and the start of the next passage. You do this as discussed in Chapter 5, by making a sharp diagonal or vertical movement with your baton hand. Then pause for the desired amount of time as dictated by the piece. (And really pause—don't move at all or your musicians will think you're going on!) You resume the piece *a tempo* with a preparatory gesture before the first beat of the following passage. This is typically done by lifting the baton from the point in space where your cutoff gesture ends; this lift becomes the preparatory gesture for the next entrance.

> **FERMATA**
>
> You should *not* beat time during a fermata. Instead, keep your arm raised and steady, as the tempo literally stops during the held note.

The Least You Need to Know

- It's the conductor's job to interpret the composer's tempo markings and set the tempo for a piece.
- The tempo you choose influences the character of the performance.
- You should have the initial tempo set in your head before you launch into the preparatory beat.
- Conducting through a tempo change requires a sense of the target tempo, and a firm hand in getting from tempo A to tempo B—either immediately or gradually, as dictated in the score.
- When conducting a fermata, hold the note with your arm raised and steady at the rebound level. End the fermata with either a clear cutoff or a preparatory beat to resume the piece *a tempo*.

Conducting Dynamics and Phrasing

Chapter **12**

In This Chapter

- Understand musical dynamics
- Discover how to change dynamics
- Learn how to conduct dynamics
- Indicate phrasing in your conducting

Once you get meter and the tempo out of the way, there are lots of other ways to put musical expression into a performance. As the conductor, you can interpret a piece's soft and loud passages, shape its musical phrases, even put a point on specific articulations.

Now all these things are quite subtle in and of themselves, but can have substantial impact on the final performance. A raise of the hand here or the point of a finger there can distinguish your performance of a work from all others.

Understanding Dynamics

Let's start with *dynamics*—the volume level of a piece or passage. We interpret dynamics based on the composer's intent, overall mood of the piece, forces present, and the acoustics of the hall.

As you can imagine, the conductor has substantial say into just how loud or soft an ensemble plays at any given point in time. Unlike tempo, which can be precisely defined in terms of beats per minute, there is no way to strictly define the exact volume level of a piece or passage. You could, I suppose, get all scientific and indicate a specific volume level in decibels, but that isn't very practical and is never done. (Who carries around a sound level meter anyway?) Instead, the conductor must interpret just how loud or soft a piece or passage is to be played, based on the composer's initial markings.

You start by gaining a thorough understanding of the common Italian dynamic markings. These provide a general indication of the volume level, which is a good starting point for the final interpretation. Table 12.1 details the most common dynamic markings.

Table 12.1 Italian Dynamic Markings

Marking	Dynamic	Means …
ppp	*pianississimo*	Very, very soft
pp	*pianissimo*	Very soft
p	*piano*	Soft
mp	*mezzo piano*	Medium soft
mf	*mezzo forte*	Medium loud
f	*forte*	Loud
ff	*fortissimo*	Very loud
fff	*fortississimo*	Very, very loud

> **WHOLE NOTE**
>
> In most works, you find an initial dynamic marking at the very beginning of the score; if there are no additional markings, this same volume level is maintained throughout the piece. If you don't see a dynamic marking, that means the piece should be played at a medium volume.

Naturally, these are relative markings; there is no universal consensus of just how soft *pianissimo* is, for example, or how loud *fortissimo* is. That is where the conductor's interpretation comes in. That is, it's the conductor's job to determine just how loud a group should play *fortissimo* in a given piece. *Fortissimo* doesn't always have to be (and seldom is) the same level from piece to piece, or even in different sections of the same piece. It's all a matter of interpretation—and the volume levels you choose can affect the mood and energy level of a performance.

> **THE CONDUCTOR SEZ**
>
> The size of the ensemble, the type of group, venue, amplification, and even the makeup of the audience have a place in interpreting dynamics.

In addition, the dynamic levels you set during rehearsal may change once you get to the actual performance. That's because sound levels change from setting to setting; you might think you're playing loud within the confines of the rehearsal room, but find out it isn't very loud at all when you get to the larger concert hall. You'll often need to adjust volume levels (as well as the mix of individual sections and instruments) on the fly during the performance itself. Be prepared to gesture to the ensemble to play a little louder than normal here, or to soften it up a bit there. That's the sort of fine-tuning that the conductor is responsible for during a performance.

Changing Dynamics

Dynamics can—and often do—change throughout the course of a piece of music. A change in dynamics can be abrupt or gradual.

A sudden change in dynamics is indicated by a new dynamic marking in the score. A gradual change in dynamics is indicated by *crescendo* (getting louder) and *decrescendo* (getting softer) marks. The *crescendo* mark (which looks like a giant hairpin, closed at the left and widening to the right) indicates that you gradually increase the volume from the current level to the new level indicated at the end of the *crescendo*. The *decrescendo* mark (which looks like a hairpin open at the left and closed at the right) indicates that you gradually decrease the volume from the current level to the new level indicated at the end of the *decrescendo*. (These gradual changes can also be indicated by the words themselves or their common abbreviations—*cresc.*, *decresc.*, or *dim.*)

> **WHOLE NOTE**
>
> While *decrescendo* is a commonly used term, it's actually a made-up one. The proper, though less frequently used, term is *diminuendo* (abbreviated *dim.*).

Crescendos and *decrescendos* can be relatively short (just a beat or two) or extend over multiple measures. Obviously, the longer the *crescendo* or *decrescendo*, the more gradual is the change in volume—and the more difficult it is to effectuate by the ensemble.

Conducting Dynamics

The dynamic level can be indicated by either your right or left hand—or, sometimes, by both.

> **MUSIC VIDEO**
>
> See the different ways to indicate dynamics in the accompanying video, "Conducting Dynamics," located at www.idiotsguides.com/conmus12.

Indicating Dynamics with the Baton

Right hand first. When conducting a beat pattern, the overall size of the pattern will indicate the general dynamic level. That is, you use a wider pattern (more space between icti) with louder dynamics, and a narrower pattern (less space between icti) for softer dynamics. In essence, a big pattern means a loud passage, while a small pattern means a softer passage.

It's not just the size of the pattern, of course; the dynamic level is also indicated by the intensity of the stroke and the height of the rebound. A shorter rebound indicates a softer passage; a higher rebound indicates a louder volume level.

For that matter, any change in the baton stroke and rebound suggests a change in dynamics. To indicate a *crescendo*, make the baton travel a longer distance from one beat to the next, and increase the height of the rebounds. To indicate a *decrescendo*, make the baton travel a shorter distance throughout a series of beat patterns, while lowering the height of the rebounds.

To prepare performers for a sudden change in dynamics, use the final rebound before the volume change. That is, if you're going from a *pianissimo* to *fortissimo* on beat one of the next measure, use a very large rebound to prepare for that louder downbeat. If you're going in the other direction (loud to soft), use a very short rebound from that last beat. The key is to show the ensemble what's coming before they do it—which you do with that preparatory upbeat before the change in dynamics.

> **THE CONDUCTOR SEZ**
>
> You can also indicate dynamic changes with subtle shifts of the pattern toward your musicians. If you move the pattern away from your body, this will indicate a louder dynamic; if you move closer to your body, a softer dynamic. This works better with smaller ensembles, as it can be difficult to appreciate from the greater distances involved with larger groups.

Indicating Dynamics with the Left Hand

All that said, it may be more visually evident to indicate dynamics with your left hand. You do so with simple hand movements—literally raising and lowering your left hand.

Here's what to do:

- To indicate a *decrescendo*, start with your left hand raised, palm down, then lower your hand toward the floor.
- To indicate a *crescendo*, start with your left hand at a lower level, palm up, then raise your hand toward the ceiling.

Got that? To tell performers to decrease the volume, lower your left hand with the palm down. To tell them to increase the volume, raise your left hand with the palm up. Pretty simple, eh?

> **THE CONDUCTOR SEZ**
>
> Here's a good exercise for gaining left hand independence. Conduct a simple four pattern with your right hand, while showing four-beat *crescendo* and then *decrescendo* with your left hand. Try to show a smooth gesture up or down, without the pulse of your right hand evident in the left.

You indicate how fast the volume changes by the speed at which you raise or lower your left hand. For a long *crescendo*, take your time raising your hand. For a relatively rapid *crescendo*, raise that hand quickly.

To conduct a sudden change in dynamics, use sudden movements of your left hand. For example, to indicate a softer volume level, bring your left hand close in to your body. To indicate a louder volume level, give a quick upward sweep of your hand, palm up.

> **WHOLE NOTE**
>
> You can also get creative with your left hand, by doing things like putting your pointing finger in front of your lips in a "shushing" gesture to indicate a softer passage.

Indicating Phrasing

Musical notes are often grouped together in *phrases*. Singers or wind players may sing or play a phrase in a single breath. Even string players will connect the notes in phrase and put a natural break at the end of a phrase.

> **DEFINITION**
>
> A musical **phrase** is a connected group of notes, played one after another without a breath or break.

As a conductor, you have several ways to indicate phrases and breathing points, using both your hands.

One way to indicate a phrase is to make a smooth, sustained side-to-side motion with your left hand. (I like going from the right to the left, but that's not set in stone.) The higher and broader the hand motion, the smoother the phrase. For longer phrases, you can move your hand in a circle or figure-eight pattern.

Another way to indicate a phrase, or even just a single held note, is by holding your left hand flat with the palm up; this indicates that your musicians should carry through. To indicate the end of the phrase or held note, quickly close your left hand into a fist.

You can also indicate smooth flowing phrases with your right hand. Simply use smooth strokes in your beat pattern, with rounded rebounds and movements. (Using more angular movements indicates a more staccato passage.)

> **THE CONDUCTOR SEZ**
>
> Phrasing is normally worked out ahead of time in rehearsal. Your performance gesture becomes a reminder of rehearsed interpretation.

To indicate a breathing point, you briefly pause the baton where the breath should occur. This puts a short break in the beat pattern, letting the performers take a quick breath at that point.

Know, however, that you don't have to conduct every phrase in every piece. It's probably more important for *legato* phrases where you don't want any discernable breaks in the melodic flow—that is, when you have a sweeping, expressive, melodic line. In this instance, your conducting can help emphasize the shape of the line, giving it a smooth, natural curve. Your job here is to help the musicians express the phrase, not necessarily dictate phrasing to them.

> **MUSIC VIDEO**
>
> See how to indicate phrasing in the accompanying video, "Conducting Phrasing," located at www.idiotsguides.com/conmus13.

The Least You Need to Know

- Dynamics indicate how soft or loud a piece or passage is to be played.
- Since dynamic markings are somewhat general, it's up to the conductor to determine the exact volume level.
- The dynamic level can change suddenly or gradually via *crescendo* and *decrescendo*.
- Dynamics are indicated with the right hand, via the size and height of the baton stroke and rebound.
- Dynamics are also indicated by raising and lowering the left hand.
- The left hand also can indicate phrasing and breathing points.

Conducting Cues and Accents

Chapter 13

In This Chapter

- Discover what and when you should cue
- Learn how to cue entrances
- Discover how to cue accents
- Find out how to conduct syncopated rhythms

The conductor is the leader of the ensemble, and as the leader is charged with making sure that all the performers hit their marks and work their way through tricky passages. In practice, that means conducting cues, accents, and syncopated passages—making sure that everyone comes in on time and plays together.

Cueing Entrances

In most musical works, individual instruments and singers, as well as complete sections, amble on and off the performing stage, so to speak. That is, not every instrument plays straight through most pieces; performers must count their rests and come back in at the exact right spot in the score.

The act of directing a performer to begin playing or singing is called *cueing*. A conductor is responsible for issuing cues to the ensemble, to ensure everyone comes in on time in the right place. You give performers a cue, and they know it's time to join the party.

What Should You Cue?

If you're conducting a long piece for a large ensemble (think a typical orchestral work), there are going to be lots of comings and goings for the various sections and individuals in the ensemble. Should you try to conduct every possible cue? The string section, for example, might have dozens of breaks throughout the scope of the work, with the corresponding dozens of reentrances that could be cued. Does every entrance need to be cued, or can you rely on the strings to enter on their own, without your assistance?

Not every entrance is created equal, either. Some entrances might be quite major—when a new melody line starts, for example, or when multiple sections enter together. Other entrances are less important and less noticeable—background padding, harmony lines, and the like. Should you cue all entrances the same way?

Then there's the example of a single instrument with a relatively small but important part—a cymbal player who sits through a hundred or more measures of rest to hit one extremely powerful crash. If this performer misses his cue, the whole piece falls apart; the problem being, however, that it's easy to get lost when you're sitting there doing nothing for so long. Should you devote your attention to a single note from a single performer?

The answer, of course, is that there's no universal rule. Not only is every musical work different, but each group of performers is different; one ensemble might require more cueing than another. For that matter, different conductors approach cueing in different ways; two conductors might cue the same piece performed by the same ensemble two different ways.

Like I said, there aren't any rules.

That said, there are some general guidelines to keep in mind:

- Younger and less experienced performers require more cueing than do more experienced and professional ensembles. That is, you can generally count on the pros to find their own way in; youngsters may need a little more help.

- The more important the entrance, the more you might want to cue it. Not only does it help to be safe, but cueing an entrance emphasizes its importance to the work.

- The more musicians entering at once, the more you might want to cue them in. Let's face it, it's hard to ignore it when half the orchestra enters on the same beat; you might as well welcome them with a hearty cue.

- The longer an instrument or section has sat out, the more they need to be cued. As one of those lonely percussionists playing a single triangle note after resting throughout an entire movement, I can attest to this; a little visual reinforcement from the conductor does wonders.

Remember, though, these are not hard and fast rules. You cannot and should not cue every single entrance in a piece; not only is it not humanly possible, it also suggests a false equality of importance. Some entrances *are* more important than others, and thus deserve your attention.

How Do You Cue?

You can cue performers with either your right or left hand. If an entrance is on the beat, use your baton hand to cue the entrance by exaggerating the rebound from the last beat of the previous measure, and thus the downstroke for that entrance. In this instance, the larger-than-normal rebound serves as the cue that a big entrance is coming.

> **MUSIC VIDEO**
>
> See how to cue in the accompanying video, "Conducting Cues and Entrances," located at www.idiotsguides.com/conmus14.

You can also use your left hand to cue the performers. While any number of gestures might work, one popular approach is to conduct a preparatory upward motion and subsequent downstroke for the cue with your left hand. Use a similar approach when the cue falls between beats. You should never disrupt your beat pattern to conduct a cue; instead, use your left hand to point out the entrance.

Note that any left-hand cue you make should indicate that the cue is coming. That means not holding your gesture for the cue itself. Instead, move your left hand into play before the entrance, then look at the section or individual you want to cue. In this respect, cueing is done as much with the eyes as with the hands.

> **FERMATA**
>
> Inexperienced conductors sometimes have trouble when cues or accents occur between beats, either broadening their normal baton movement or breaking into an unexpected subdivision of the beat with the right hand—both attempts to "hit" the accent with the baton hand. Don't do this. Your baton hand should conduct a steady series of beats, in tempo, even (and especially) when cues and accents occur between beats.

Making Contact

As noted, it's important to direct your cue at the specific section of performers who will be entering at the cue point. Don't aim your cue at the entire ensemble; you need to indicate who you're cueing as much as what you're cueing.

You can do this by using a variety of communication skills. Pivot your body toward the section in question. Look at and make eye contact with the performers you're cueing. Nod at them when ready. Do whatever it takes to direct your cue at the appropriate individuals.

> **THE CONDUCTOR SEZ**
>
> You should avoid pointing while conducting; there are better ways to let a section know they need to be ready. A former teacher of mine called pointing the "finger of death." While you may find use for it, it's best kept for very specific instances. The less you use it, the more effective it will be when you do. That said, pointing works far better for jazz and big bands than it does with concert bands, orchestras, and choirs.

Of course, different individuals respond differently to different cues. Again, there's a big difference between cueing inexperienced and experienced players. Cueing up a student ensemble may require more pronounced hand gestures; cueing up a group of pros may require nothing more than a raised eyebrow. For the most part, professional musicians are looking for little more in a cue than confirmation that they're coming in correctly. Amateurs often need more concrete direction.

You can also cue differently during rehearsals than during the actual performance. You're free to communicate verbally during rehearsals; it's okay to yell "trumpets!" to get their attention when you're practicing. You can then scale back on the cues after everyone has better learned their parts. You can be more overt during rehearsals, and more subtle during performances.

It's also okay to help performers count in their parts—especially when they've been resting for extended periods of time. For that lonely triangle player standing at the back of stage, make eye contact a few measures in advance of the entrance, then hold your left hand close to your body and hold up four fingers (for four measures to go), then three, then two, then one. There's your cue right there.

The point is to connect with the performers being cued and ensure an accurate entrance. You need to be clear with your gestures which instruments or voices you're "talking" to, and where they need to come in.

Conducting Accented Notes and Syncopation

The conductor may also want to cue heavy accents within a passage, as well as difficult rhythmic passages—especially those that incorporate heavy *syncopation*. With accents, you're helping the ensemble hit the notes with major impact; with syncopated passages, you're helping them play a passage with a heightened degree of difficulty.

> **DEFINITION**
>
> **Syncopation** is a rhythm that places notes on unexpected or normally unaccented beats or parts of beats.

Cueing Accents

Conducting accents and syncopation is actually quite similar—and similar to conducting cues. You use your left hand to cue the accents and rhythms, while your right hand continues to conduct a steady beat.

You cue an important accent by using your left hand (or the pointing finger on that hand) in a pointing or whipping movement. You can prepare for the accent with a kind of preparatory backstroke—kind of like how you draw a whip back before whipping it forward.

> **THE CONDUCTOR SEZ**
>
> If you have a syncopation on the "and" of one, a strong downbeat with a crisp rebound can serve as the cue for that syncopation. A cue should occur before the entrance, not at the entrance. If you wait to cue until the entrance itself, you're too late.

Cueing Syncopation

You cue a syncopated passage pretty much the same way. That is, you use your left hand to whip out the rhythm. You must, however, keep a steady beat with your right hand—your beat pattern should not be interrupted. The reality is, the ensemble probably needs that beat reinforcement more than it needs you to cue the syncopated rhythm. In fact, a clear beat reinforcement provides context for the syncopation. It's easy for performers to lose track of the beat while playing a difficult syncopation; it's your job to keep them on the beat.

What you *don't* want to do is interrupt your beat pattern to conduct the syncopated figure. It's a steadfast rule: *Never* conduct the syncopation with the right hand. You should continue to conduct a steady series of beats and let the ensemble syncopate around the beat. During syncopated passages, they need to clearly see where the beat is, no questions asked, so they can play against it.

> **THE CONDUCTOR SEZ**
> What makes syncopation interesting is its relief against the steady strong beat. It may feel good to conduct a syncopation with your right hand, but you aren't helping anyone out by doing so.

The challenge is that it's easy to get pulled away from the underlying beat by a heavily syncopated pattern, and thus stroke the syncopation with your baton instead of the beat. If you do this you will not only confuse the performers, you may find yourself unable to get back on the beat. Focus your attention on providing a steady beat through the syncopated figure; you can add syncopated cues with your left hand only if you're rhythmically capable of doing so.

Here's something else to watch out for. It's not uncommon for an ensemble to rush through a syncopated passage, thus getting ahead of the conductor and basic beat—which is another reason for the conductor to keep a firm and steady beat through syncopated passages.

> **MUSIC VIDEO**
> See how to indicate accents and syncopated rhythms in the accompanying video, "Conducting Accents and Syncopation," located at www.idiotsguides.com/conmus15.

The Least You Need to Know

- Not every entrance needs to be cued, only the most important ones.
- If an entrance falls on the first beat of a measure, use your right hand to show a clear rebound from the previous beat as a cue, or use your left hand instead.
- For other entrances, use various body movement—including left-hand gestures—to cue the performers.
- Use your left hand to cue major accents.
- During syncopated passages, keep a steady beat with your baton hand—then direct the syncopation with your left, if you can.

Conducting Recitatives and Other Unmetered Music

Chapter 14

In This Chapter

- Understand unmetered music
- Learn how to conduct recitatives
- Find out how to conduct plainsong
- Discover how to conduct cadenzas
- Learn how to conduct unmeasured preludes

Now we come to the most difficult type of passage to conduct—one that doesn't have a clear beat or bar line. We're talking things like operatic recitatives, solo cadenzas, unmeasured harpsichord preludes, and even chants in various sacred music traditions. How do you beat the beat when there's no beat to beat?

Understanding Unmetered Music

What we're talking about here is something called *unmetered music*—literally, music without a steady meter or pulse. This is a passage in a larger work where the normal beat comes to a halt and a soloist does his or her own thing, without the normal confines of a steady beat or distinct measures. It's just a series of notes, as played or sung by the soloist, sometimes with the backing of other musicians. The duration of each note—in some instances, the notes themselves—are left up to the whim of the performer, typically with some input from the conductor.

> **DEFINITION**
>
> **Unmetered music** is a passage without a steady, pulsed meter, where the duration of each note is essentially left to the performer(s).

There are many types of passages that fall under the heading of unmetered music:

- In opera, the *recitative* is a passage where a soloist sings in a free-form fashion, utilizing the rhythms of ordinary speech. Recitatives often have instrumental backing, following the rhythms of the soloist.

- In sacred music, *plainsong* (also known as *chant*) exists as a way to sing unmetered biblical texts, such as psalms and canticles. Plainsong is typically performed to the natural speech rhythms of the text.

- In many types of music, a soloist is often required to perform a *cadenza*, a free-form, unmetered, often virtuosic passage. In classical or art music and most jazz, cadenzas are typically improvised; in more recent classical music, the cadenza may be written out beforehand. Cadenzas are solo passages, with the ensemble often required to enter at the conclusion.

- In the Baroque music of the seventeenth century, an *unmeasured prelude* is a free-form introductory passage, typically played by the harpsichord or organ.

How does one conduct an unmetered work or passage? Obviously, it's not about downbeats and beat patterns; it's much more complex than that.

Conducting Recitatives

A recitative is an odd beast, but a common one in operatic music. During a recitative, the vocal soloist almost "speaks" through the text, matching the rhythm of the music to the natural speaking rhythm of the words. There's no set beat, and no one right way to perform any given passage.

What makes conducting a recitative particularly challenging is that the singer often has instrumental accompaniment. Now this accompaniment typically consists of held whole notes (*recitativo accompagnato*) or short chords to punctuate the recitative, but still—how do the instrumentalists know when a new measure starts?

This is where the conductor comes in. It's the conductor's job to follow the singer and indicate to the other musicians where each new measure begins or where the next entrance occurs.

What you have to do is approximate the pulse of the measure—that is, to follow the soloist and prepare the instrumentalists for their next note. One approach is to treat the ensuing "measure" as a fermata—that is, you just hold your arms still and wait for the next note, then give a preparatory upbeat before the next beat, which represents the next whole note.

Another common technique is to beat quickly to the next entrance of the accompanying forces, then wait for the soloist to get there. Say the accompaniment plays a quarter note chord on beat one when the recitative starts, but then doesn't come back in until beat four of the third measure. The conductor would bring everyone in on beat one and then conduct quickly through three measures, going to beat three of the third measure and then stopping. When the soloist reaches this point of the passage, the conductor then brings the accompaniment in on beat four by lifting from beat three and striking beat four.

It's important to note that most recitatives are written out in standard metric fashion, with four (or however many) beats to the bar. The singer, however, freely interprets the notes and the beat, so that there's not a steady rhythmic pulse. Still, you can follow along with what the singer is singing, and thus be prepared for the next orchestral note.

> **FERMATA**
>
> Even though a recitative may be written in traditional rhythmic notation, that does not mean that you can or should conduct the vocalist through the passage. During a recitative, the conductor's job is to follow the soloist, not to lead her.

In some instances the orchestra plays more than simple whole notes. There may be a "stinger" placed somewhere other than beat one in the measure, or even short rhythmic patterns notated. Conducting these notes and patterns is more difficult, simply because it's more difficult to place these fixed notes within the singer's free-form vocal elaborations. This is why recitative conducting is a more advanced art, and one that requires study and practice.

Conducting Plainsong

You find *plainsong* in the services of many different religious denominations. I happen to go to a Lutheran church that, while relatively modern in most trappings, still employs a *cantor* singing the chant in various places of the service.

> **DEFINITION**
>
> **Plainsong** (also known as chant, as in Anglican chant and Gregorian chant) is a musical passage in which biblical text is sung with its natural, unmetered speech rhythms. In Christian and Jewish services, a **cantor** is a solo singer to whom the choir or congregation responds. (In some Jewish traditions, this is an ordained position.)

As you might suspect, the difficulty in conducting plainsong comes from its unmetered nature. As you can see in Figure 14.1, most chant is written with stemless notes, which means that there is no set rhythm; instead, the text should be intoned with the same rhythms of the spoken word.

Figure 14.1: *The notation for a typical plainsong or chant.*

What this means is that you need to figure out in advance just how the chant will be recited. In particular, you need to divide the notes into logical groupings of two and three. That is, there should be two or three notes or syllables for each pulse.

Using the chant in Figure 14.1 as an example, the first group of three consists of the syllables "A-ve Ma." The next group of three consists of the changing notes for the single syllable "ri." And the final "a" takes up two note placements, as it's a longer, held note, for another beat. So the groupings for this first section look like this:

A-	ve	Ma-	ri-	i-	i	a-	a
1-	2-	3	1-	2-	3	1-	2

Here's something else: the pulses in a chant don't have to be (and seldom are) of equal duration. That is, a three-syllable pulse is probably going to be longer than a two-syllable one; don't conduct a three grouping like a triplet. But that isn't always the case; a two grouping at the end of a phrase might actually be held slightly, and thus end up being longer than a three grouping.

If all these groupings and pulses seem a bit arbitrary, that's only because they follow the pattern of human speech, which is seldom conducted to a strict beat. Like any spoken phrase, a recited chant will have its own natural rhythms. The natural verbal stress informs the underlying pulse, which you conduct as individual beats.

Once you've identified the proper groupings for the text, conducting the chant is pretty much as simple as beating a simple up and down pattern for each pulse. You beat the pulse at the start of each pattern—the "1" in the 1-2-3 or 1-2 pattern. Don't use a fancy conducting pattern; just a simple one-beat pattern, conducted to the underlying pulse of the chant.

When conducting chant or plainsong, use a very gentle movement of your hand, nothing too forced or direct. You want to subtly guide the singers, not drive them forward.

Conducting Cadenzas

When it comes to cadenzas, there's not much to conduct. The orchestra or band stops, the soloist does his or her thing, then the ensemble comes back in again. The conductor is responsible for the starting and stopping, but not for what goes on during the cadenza.

Stopping the ensemble is easy; just conduct what's written in the score. Likewise, there's not a lot to do during the cadenza itself. Just stand silently, either on the podium or beside it, and let the soloist solo.

The challenge in conducting a cadenza is getting the ensemble back in. If it's a written cadenza, you know how the solo is supposed to go and when it's supposed to end. If it's an improvised cadenza, as is common in the jazz world, you have to pick up on the soloist's cues as to when things are coming to a conclusion.

At that point, you start up the ensemble much the same way you do at the very beginning of a piece. That means a big preparatory upbeat and a major downbeat. In many instances, especially at the end of a jazz piece, the cadenza is followed simply by a long held note; sometimes the soloist continues improvising over the held note. You should conduct this note as you would any fermata, with a big cutoff at the end.

> **THE CONDUCTOR SEZ**
>
> Watching the soloist is very important. The soloist will often give physical cues when they are about to finish. It's the conductor's job to pick up on these cues.

In other instances, the cadenza is followed with an *a tempo* section—that is, you return to the original tempo before the cadenza. This means you need to use a preparatory beat to set the tempo, and then keep keeping on through the balance of the piece.

Conducting Unmeasured Preludes

Conducting an unmeasured prelude is much like conducting a cadenza, except the prelude is at the beginning instead of the end of the piece. Common practice lets the keyboardist play the prelude, with the orchestra coming in at the end of the passage. Again, you need to judge when the end of the prelude is nearing, so you can mount the podium and prep the other musicians. From there, it's a simple preparatory gesture followed by the first beat, and the rest of the piece proceeds apace.

The Least You Need to Know

- Unmetered music consists of pieces or passages without a rigid tempo.
- When conducting a recitative, follow the singer and prepare the orchestra for their next entrance.
- When conducting plainsong, conduct the natural pulse of the chant.
- When conducting a cadenza, step out of the way during the solo, then prepare the band or orchestra for the downbeat following the cadenza.
- When conducting an unmetered prelude, wait for the soloist to finish and then start the ensemble normally.

Different Types of Conducting

Part 4

Conducting is conducting, to some degree; it doesn't matter whether you're leading a choir or orchestra or marching band, you still work the baton and use the appropriate beat patterns. But there are differences between different types of conducting, different issues you'll encounter, and it pays to learn a little more about each possible scenario.

To that end, I've interviewed more than a half-dozen conductors in a variety of musical styles—orchestra, marching band, big band, choir, musical theater, even studio conducting. These working professionals freely share their real-world experiences and advice—which you'll see when you read the chapters in this final part of the book.

It's good stuff, and exactly what you need to prepare for conducting in the real world.

Conducting Orchestras and Concert Bands

Chapter 15

In This Chapter

- Learn how to conduct an orchestra
- Discover how to conduct a concert band
- Find out how to conduct student bands and orchestras
- An interview with conductor Manny Laureano

General conducting techniques out of the way, let's turn our focus to the challenges involved in conducting specific types of ensembles and performances. First up are a couple of old warhorses, orchestras and concert bands.

Sometime in the life of almost any conductor, you're going to find yourself standing in front of a hundred or so instrumentalists, all waiting for the baton to drop. What do you need to know to be a successful orchestral or concert band conductor? It's all here, so read on to get the whole scoop.

Conducting an Orchestra

I'll be honest with you. All the conducting tips and techniques I've discussed up to this point in the book are based primarily on orchestral conducting. That's right, if you deem to read no further in this text, you'll know most of what you need to know to adequately conduct a symphonic orchestra, which is an instrumental ensemble consisting of strings, winds, and percussion, typically with 80 to 100 musicians in total.

Still, there are some nuances of orchestral conducting we have yet to address. Let's do so now.

Knowing the Instruments

A typical symphonic orchestra has somewhere in the neighborhood of a hundred musicians playing a couple of dozen different types of instruments. You need to know a little bit about how all of these instruments work.

The majority of performers are playing one of the four main string instruments—violin, viola, cello, and double bass. That means you don't just have one or two people playing violin; in most orchestras, you have 16 first violins, 14 second violins, a dozen violas, 10 or so cellos, and anywhere from 6 to 8 basses. You need this many string players to produce the smooth, dominant sound of the modern orchestra. With almost a third of your players playing some sort of string instrument, you need to have a good understanding of what they're doing. That doesn't necessarily mean that you need to become a string player yourself, but it does mean that you should at least be familiar with things like bowings, pizzicatos, mutes, and the like. You should be able to rely on your concertmaster to work through the details, but you still need to speak their language.

> **THE CONDUCTOR SEZ**
>
> It always pays to make good friends with your concertmaster!

The rest of the orchestra is composed of brass (four or more French horns, two or three trumpets, the same number of trombones, and a tuba), woodwinds (a piccolo, two or three flutes, a couple of oboes, a couple of clarinets, a bass clarinet, two or three bassoons, and maybe a contrabassoon), and percussion (a half-dozen players banging everything from snare drum to xylophone to timpani). There may be a few harps thrown in for good measure, and maybe even a piano or organ as well.

Note that with the exception of the strings, all other parts are played by only a handful of players—often just a single performer. That lone piccolo player has to hold her own against 60-odd strings. Keep that in mind when managing the troops.

You not only have to know a little bit about all these instruments, you also need to know how to read a score—that one piece of music that combines all the instrumental parts. Score reading is an art to itself; you have to be able to see the general shape of the music, while still paying attention to individual parts as necessary. That speaks to the importance of score prep, as I discussed in Chapter 3; you can't effectively convey your instructions to the orchestra if your nose is buried in the score.

Facing the Orchestra

Now it's time to face these hundred or so musicians. It's them versus you, and there's only one of you.

The good news is, you're the acknowledged leader of the team. (And it is a team sport, not a solo endeavor.) The performers are depending on you to show them the way; they want your instructions.

> **THE CONDUCTOR SEZ**
>
> Pros will see through an ill-prepared conductor. Know how you want things to go—and make sure your decisions are informed.

The bad news is, standing alone in front of that instrumental army can be quite intimidating. It takes a supreme amount of self-confidence to take charge of the troops; that self-confidence has to be based on a sense of your own skills and preparation.

When you step up to the podium, remember everything you've learned throughout the course of this book. Know especially that everything you do—every little gesture and motion—must be able to be seen by every single musician on the stage, all 100 of them. The podium has to be high enough and the music stand has to be low enough for everyone to see the baton. You must keep your hands in that tight frame between your waist and your head; you can't hide any motion from any quarter of the ensemble.

Make sure you can make eye contact with each and every musician there, and that they have a clear view of both your hands.

From there, it's all up to you. Raise the baton and take charge—it's time to play!

Mixing the Sound

One of the key challenges in orchestral conducting, and the one that most puts your personal stamp on a performance, is the ability and need to fine-tune the sound of the orchestra. I'm not just talking about dynamics and tempo here; I'm talking about the entire instrumental mix.

Let me explain.

As you know, an orchestra is comprised of 100 or so musicians playing two dozen or more individual parts. Most composers will take advantage of all those available parts to create lush and intricate soundscapes. But it's not within the ability of the composer to determine just how all those parts are mixed together—that is, which parts come to the forefront and which fade into the background. That's the job of the conductor.

> **THE CONDUCTOR SEZ**
>
> While it's the job of the composer to create instrumental and vocal mixes, the conductor balances the orchestration in performance based on interpretation informed by a host of variables—venue, size of the ensemble, audience, and so forth.

Consider this. At any given time in any given piece, you may have first violins, second violins, violas, cellos, flutes, clarinets, oboes, trumpets, trombones, French horns, and all manner of percussion instruments, each playing unique parts. Do all of these instruments play at the exact same volume level? Should one particular line have prominence? Which parts are more important than others?

Now you might say that it's obvious; the part carrying the melody should be dominant. That's probably true, but what about the other two dozen parts playing at the same time? Even if the melody is in the first violins, maybe there's a cool little line being played by the oboes; wouldn't it be nice if you could bring that part out a little?

And that's the role of an orchestral conductor—to function as the sound mixer. It's what a recording engineer does when mixing a recording, bring this part up and turn that one down, until you have the final mix that sounds best to your ears.

This is why one conductor's version of the Dvorak's *New World Symphony* will sound different from that of another conductor. It's a matter of picking and choosing which parts to emphasize and deemphasize. Every conductor has different musical tastes, different sensibilities, and different ears; how you hear a piece will be different from how other conductors hear it.

Your job, then, is to fine-tune the mix to your liking—informed by the composer's intent, of course. This is done to a large degree during the rehearsal process; that's where you tell the flutes to play a little louder and the cellos to play a little softer, and so forth. You can do this verbally, or you can do this with your left-hand gestures. Since you can't really speak up in the middle of a concert performance, you might as well verbalize your desires while you can, just so there are no misunderstandings about what you expect.

Once you get on the concert stage, you have more fine-tuning to do. That's because the acoustics of the concert hall are going to be different from those of the rehearsal room. (And every concert hall has different acoustic properties as well.) You'll need to use your left-hand gestures to bring up or down the sound in different sections during the performance, adjusting in real time to the acoustical characteristics of the hall.

> **WHOLE NOTE**
>
> It pays to learn the acoustic properties of a concert hall before your first performance. Have someone else take the baton during dress rehearsal so you can walk around the hall and hear how it sounds from different points—and then adjust the mix accordingly.

Conducting a Concert Band

Conducting a *concert band* is similar to conducting an orchestra, except without the strings—and with a lot more brass and woodwind players. In fact, it's that huge increase in wind instruments that contributes to one of the primary challenges in conducting a concert band.

> **DEFINITION**
>
> A **concert band**—sometimes called a symphonic band, wind ensemble, wind symphony, or symphonic winds—is a large instrumental ensemble with brass, woodwind, and percussion instruments, but no strings.

Understanding the Band

You can think of a concert band as a marching band without the marching, and with chairs. (That's the background, anyway; the first concert bands were indeed military bands assembled for concert purposes.) Or you can think of it as an orchestra but without the strings. In either instance, it's a unique assemblage of instruments that has its own interesting sound.

The instrumentation of a concert band is significantly different from that of a string orchestra. You have more different types of woodwind and brass instruments (saxophones and baritones or euphoniums, in particular), and more of each instrument. Instead of the two or three trumpets you find in an orchestra, a concert band is likely to have a dozen or more trumpet players playing three or more distinct parts. The resulting sound is much louder and, dare we say, brassier than the smoother-sounding orchestra.

As a conductor, you need to know a little bit about all the band instruments just as you do about the instruments of the orchestra. And reading a concert band score is every bit as important and challenging as it is in dealing with its orchestral counterpart.

Achieving the Right Tone

Because of the larger number of instrumentalists playing each part, and the inherent difficulty in keeping wind instruments in tune, intonation is a particular challenge for concert band conductors. Put simply, it's difficult to achieve a uniform section tuning when you have so many wind instruments playing together.

What you often get, especially with less experienced players, is a kind of circling around the pitch. One clarinet player may be a little sharp, another a little flat, and so on, throughout the section, making the resulting sound unpleasantly thick. You need to work with the individual sections, over time, to teach them how to achieve a more precise section tuning, or forever live with a band that just sounds kind of "off."

Beyond intonation, you have the challenge of creating an appealing overall band tone. Given the inherent tonal characteristics of the brass and woodwind families, it's common to have a band that sounds too harsh and brilliant. It's more challenging to achieve a rounder, more relaxed timbre, but worth the effort. Again, this is something that happens over time during the rehearsal process.

Finally, you as the conductor must fine-tune the mix of the individual instruments, just as an orchestral conductor does. Left to its own devices, a concert band will be heavy on the brass and a little light on the woodwinds. You need to bring up or down individual sections to achieve the overall sound you want.

> **THE CONDUCTOR SEZ**
>
> Intonation is a challenge for orchestras and choirs, too—it's not just reserved for wind ensembles. Bottom line, tuning is tuning is tuning. And if it's not in tune, it doesn't count!

Conducting Youth Bands and Orchestras

Conducting younger musicians presents unique challenges—but also unique joys. It can be frustrating dealing with student musicians, of course, but also great fun.

It's a Learning Experience

First of all, remember that playing music is always a learning experience, but particularly so for younger musicians. Every new piece you put before them presents new opportunities and challenges. You'll constantly be presenting them with things they haven't experienced before—and, hopefully, teaching them how to deal with them.

That means, of course, that you need to know what it is you seek to teach. In a school situation, you may need to be able to teach your student musicians how to play their instruments, at least on a basic level. When a trumpet player asks how to finger a given note, or a snare drummer has trouble with sticking on a given passage, you need to be able to provide the answers. That's a challenge.

Beyond that, you'll be teaching overall musical concepts. We're talking about playing in different styles, in different time signatures, and so forth. It's your job to expose youngsters to things they might not play or listen to otherwise; to me, that's the fun part of the job.

Dealing with Distractions

With the concept of teaching always in the back of your mind, you do need to realize that your band or orchestra is in competition with students' other activities. There are lots of distractions available these days—television, movies, iPods, video games, social networking, texting, sports, you name it. (Plus the age-old distractions of the opposite sex, of course.) You somehow have to make band or orchestra appealing enough to hold its own against these distractions.

Unfortunately, these distractions—especially the technological ones—often find their way into the rehearsal room. You need to hold the attention of your student musicians for the course of the rehearsal, which may mean forcing them to turn off their cell phones and cease from texting for an hour or two. They probably won't like that, but it's necessary.

Choosing a Repertoire

Whether you're leading a junior high band or conducting a city-wide high school orchestra, choosing which music you play is a big challenge. Not only do you have to represent various styles and eras, you have to select music that your student musicians are technically capable of playing.

It gets more difficult when you realize that not all the musicians in your band or orchestra are at the same level of musicianship. In any student ensemble, you're going to have some real virtuosos and a lot of players who are only marking time. Some players will exhibit technical mastery beyond their years while others will have trouble playing basic scales. That's just the nature of the beast.

The trick is selecting music that challenges your best players while not overly stretching (or stressing) the lesser musicians in the group. If you choose music that excites the more talented players, others in the band or orchestra will have trouble keeping up. If you choose music that even the lesser musicians can play, you're going to bore the bejeezus out of your talented players. It's tough.

As an example, when I was back in junior high, we had a percussion section that could play the pants off of anything put in front of them. (I was a member of that section, so excuse my bragging.) Unfortunately, most pieces our band director found that had challenging percussion parts also had more intricate brass parts, and our trumpet players weren't quite that advanced. The drummers were having fun, but the trumpets weren't cutting it.

Rather than programming for the lowest common denominator, the solution in this instance was to give the percussion section its own showcase outside of the normal band material. That is, we programmed a percussion ensemble feature in the middle of the band concert. That gave the more talented percussionists something to focus on, without tasking the rest of the band with something they'd struggle with.

That doesn't mean, of course, that you shouldn't challenge even your lesser players. You should. But there's a difference between asking them to stretch a little and trying to get them to play something that is simply beyond their reach. As the music director/conductor, you need to find the best compromise for all your players.

Conducting in the Real World: An Interview with Manny Laureano

All this conducting stuff is great in theory, but how does it play out in the real world? Well, to inject a little reality into the proceedings, I talked with nine different conductors in various types of music. My intent was to add some real-world perspective to the mechanics covered elsewhere in the text; you'll find these interviews throughout all the chapters in Part 4 of this book.

When it came to orchestral conducting, I wanted someone who had experience with both professional and student performers. I also thought it would be interesting to find a conductor who was also a performer, to look at life from both sides of the podium, as it were.

I found just the right guy right here in the Twin Cities, where I currently live. Manny Laureano is the co-Artistic Director of the Minnesota Youth Symphonies (MYS), and conducts the MYS Symphony Orchestra. In addition, Manny has conducted a variety of other ensembles over the past several decades, including the Metropolitan Symphony Orchestra, the St. Olaf Orchestra, the Calhoun-Isles Community Band, the National Suzuki Youth Festival Orchestra, and the Minnesota All-State Orchestra. He's also in demand as a clinician for young orchestras throughout the state of Minnesota. (For what it's worth, my grandchildren's favorite babysitter plays oboe with the Youth Symphony, and she says that Manny is "a fun guy.")

But conducting is just one thing Manny does. His main gig is actually Principal Trumpet with the Minnesota Orchestra. He's been with that world-renowned orchestra since 1981, and also served as Assistant Conductor during the 2005–2006 season.

When Manny and I hooked up, it was obvious that he really loves what he does—especially working with student musicians. We started out by talking about how he got started in conducting.

MICHAEL MILLER (MM): *What is your formal background in conducting?*

MANNY LAUREANO (ML): I don't have a formal background, that's the interesting thing. The very first time I got in front of a group to conduct I was in ninth grade. It was the day in junior high school where the teachers and the students got to switch roles for one day. The teacher in a given class would pick a kid, so I asked if I could conduct the ninth grade band rehearsal, and the conductor said yes. He had a lot of respect for me as a young musician; he said yeah, go ahead, take a stab at it. The bug bit me and I kept taking advantage of any possible situation where I could do that, as the years went by.

It always started out in an education position, always working with a small group of people. It eventually grew to working with community bands here, and then community orchestra, and then the Youth Symphonies, and it just kind of grew.

The point is that along the way, sitting in my chair as Principal Trumpet of a great orchestra, I got to see the best and the worst. I got to see the mistakes they made, I got to see what worked and what didn't work. It was a wonderful advantage to kind of learn vicariously, and not have any of the pressure.

MM: *Do other conductors also have a performing background?*

ML: A lot of them do. For example, Osmo [Vänskä] was a clarinetist when he was in Finland. Every so often he'll take a clarinet out and play a piece of chamber music, you know. Just recently, there was a piece of music that was written for him to do an improvisation in a kind of jazz style. So he keeps his clarinet skills up. He has that background.

> **WHOLE NOTE**
>
> Osmo Vänskä (1953–) is the current principal conductor and music director of the Minnesota Orchestra. He has also conducted the Lahti Symphony Orchestra, the Iceland Symphony Orchestra, and the BBC Scottish Symphony Orchestra.

MM: *Do you think that helps?*

ML: Oh God, yes, it's got to. It's got to.

First of all, you learn all the beat patterns. You learn what all of the situations might be. The actual physical act of conducting is not rocket science. If you can move your hands, and you can move them in patterns, and you have an internal sense of pulse, you can conduct.

Now this is the problem. Some people have great pulse, they can keep a beat very steadily. Some people don't. Some people are very sensitive to what they hear and what is necessary to be done in order to correct something. That's critical. That is absolutely critical, that when you hear something, not only can you identify what's wrong, but you know what to do about it.

So those are the two critical areas. And again, I learned a tremendous amount just by observation. What's the old Yogi Berra quote? "You can observe a lot by watching." I love that quote! But it is an apt quote. If you're interested at all in what to do, then you really have to observe and absorb. Observing and absorbing are the two critical elements for any person who is playing an instrument yet wants to conduct.

MM: *Obviously, as a performer, you've seen a lot of great conductors. And you've probably seen a lot of not-so-great conductors, too.*

ML: [laughs] Yeah!

MM: *So what are the key things that separate an average conductor from a really great one?*

ML: An average conductor will pretty much go along for the ride. Their stick technique is usually adequate, but they don't hear and have the ability to make the corrections that will make the difference between a good, solid performance and a really effective, great, memorable performance.

The guys that give you the memorable performances, these are the guys where I'll get a picture in my head and I'll remember, "Oh yeah, I remember when we did this piece, I remember when we did that piece. Man, that meant something when we played it."

Then there are others that I can remember, they just sort of got in front and let the orchestra do its thing. Which is not bad for us (the performers), but I think the audience gets a little bit cheated—unless they're people who aren't expecting anything terribly much other than just hearing their favorite little piece of music.

But here's what it is. Great conductors will take a standard piece of repertoire and suddenly make it a brand new piece. They'll bring out voices and tempos and things that you had never considered before, and you'll go, "Holy smokes, what a great idea this is! It's so effective. I never heard what the second clarinet was doing in the middle of this gigantic mess and it completely changed the piece."

That's the gift that a great conductor will give an orchestra or an audience.

MM: *Now how much of that comes at the time of performance, and how much of that is prep work?*

ML: You can smell that coming in rehearsal. With the great conductors, I swear, I think the rehearsals are the most enjoyable part, because that's where you learn the stuff. The concerts are just sort of gravy.

For example, Klaus Tennstedt was a favorite conductor of this orchestra. What we all lived for were his rehearsals, because that's where he would make this observation or that balance change. That's where he would bring all the nuance out. We loved his rehearsals. And the concerts were great; we remember his concerts very well, too. But I think most of us lived to hear what wonderful little pearls he would come up with.

> **WHOLE NOTE**
>
> Klaus Tennstedt (1926–1988) conducted the Swedish Radio Symphony Orchestra, the North German Radio Orchestra, Germany's Kiel Opera, the Toronto Symphony Orchestra, and the Minnesota Orchestra.

MM: *That speaks to the conductor really knowing the music beforehand, right?*

ML: Completely, completely. And it's a whole other thing when you're doing a world premiere. I tell you, the really great conductors can take a brand new piece of music and make it seem like something that you've played for years. They just understand what the music is about. They have made themselves into an eloquent voice of the composer.

Ultimately, we as conductors are advocates for the composers. We are their court-appointed lawyers who get paid to make the case to the public that this is a piece that is worth listening to. And the jury will decide whether we're guilty or innocent. We have to present our case. Like any good lawyer, we have to pull out any trick that we possibly can. Find where the voices are and do it.

I've conducted any number of world premieres, pieces I've had commissioned, for the Youth Symphony or the Metropolitan Symphony, when I had them. I've done a couple of world premieres for the Minnesota Orchestra, young people's concerts. And that was my job, to make sure that people really got something out of the music.

MM: *When you're doing a premiere, are you typically working with the composer? Is he or she involved?*

ML: The composer is there, and I have to come in with all guns loaded, knowing what I'm doing, all the beat patterns are there, all that stuff. And basically after a certain section turn around and say, "Hey, Dan, did you like that?" And he'll say, "Yeah, that was great. I need more second clarinet in section 34. I need the tempo to be a little bit slower."

A conductor has to be careful not to get too involved with the composer. They understand what they want, but sometimes they don't quite get the limitations that you have to deal with. There's got to be a good balance of how much you deal with the composer.

MM: When you're dealing with a youth orchestra, do you ever run into issues of the music just not being playable at that level?

ML: That should never be the case, because a good conductor needs to know the quality of his soldiers. You've got to know how big a hill you can take. So rarely is there, in our case, music that is too difficult.

Where a lot of youth conductors fall down is in how they prepare, how much time they take with a given section, and whether they're able to really explain what it is that the kids need to do. One of the things that I do is assign homework—every week. I just did it recently. For the second violins, I pointed out two passages from the Tchaikovsky symphony they're learning, and I said "I want this by next week. I need it on my desk, 8:45 next Saturday."

You have to impose those sorts of restrictions and those sorts of goals. I learned that lesson many years ago, when I was conducting four out of five movements of the Bartok *Concerto for Orchestra*. I told the kids, "You need to practice. You need to practice. You need to practice." Well, the problem was, and I didn't see it until the end, that the piece is just so gigantic. You tell them to practice but they need to know where, what, what do I do?

I realized the error of my ways at that point. And I said, "Okay, from now on we're gonna take this in chunks. Practice from number 34 to number 38, first violins. Brass, I need you guys to get sections B to C. I need that for next week. I want to hear it."

So you give them clear, stated goals and then they know how to prepare. Kids have to be guided; you cannot take anything for granted with them. You want to dance the dance of treating them like adults by never condescending to them and by expecting them to give you first class, all the time.

But you also have to understand that they are kids. They don't know the same things that the Minnesota Orchestra knows. You can't take anything for granted. You state what you want once, very clearly—twice, if there's any misunderstanding—and then you say, "Okay, here's what I want, go. Bring it to me next week." Or, "The passages that you know, I need it right now. Let's repeat it a few times, but you get the idea of what I want."

MM: How does the rehearsal process differ from a youth orchestra to a community orchestra to a pro orchestra?

ML: The Youth Orchestra typically meets once a week. So you'll have a program that takes ten rehearsals, because you're doing it over ten Saturdays. I could take the same program and prepare it, probably, in six or seven, if I had them one day after another.

MM: Because they lose something with the time going by.

ML: Yes. This is why we have the assignments that I say are so important. If you ask for the right things, then you'll have some continuity.

Normally, where youth conductors fall down is that they think that just because you correct it once in rehearsal, that they'll get it. You know, they'll have it in their pockets next time. That is not a guarantee. You have to rehearse something, tell them to practice it, and when you get back into rehearsal the very first thing you do is attack that thing that you did. Have that running, have that continuity.

MM: So how does that process differ when you're dealing with older, more professional players?

ML: Basically, it's the same process, to varying degrees with the professional level of the group.

Community orchestras are also usually a once-a-week endeavor. In a few lucky places they may be a twice-a-week sort of thing, but usually they're once a week—and it's the same problem. The dance is a little different, because now you're dealing with adults, you're dealing with some college kids, and maybe the occasional really talented high school kid. So you've got people of similar levels but different ages, and that's a whole other animal, in terms of the respect issue, but the demands, also. I'm happy that you're 80 years old and a grandmother to half of the people in this community, but if you are going to play in the second violin section, I need you to do this.

What happens often is you'll take a repertoire that gets a little more difficult. Sometimes grandma may choose to practice a little more, or she may say, "You know, I think I've had enough of this," and let somebody else do it.

Now when you get to the professional level, you have a Minnesota Orchestra, well, there isn't anything you can put in front of these people that they won't be able to play. Any great orchestra will just attack something and tear it to pieces.

One of the most amazing things that I've ever seen was when we did a premiere by a Finnish composer named Kalevi Aho. We did a symphony of his, it had to be about three seasons ago. I'm gonna tell you something, Mike, that reading session of a really difficult piece was almost a performance. It was fantastic. I've been very proud of the orchestra many times, but that was one of the times I was very proud of how phenomenally prepared everybody was.

MM: Pros relish a challenge, I've found.

ML: It is true. You are right, we love getting something that is just a little bit above our comfort level, and then tearing into it and presenting a beautiful concert experience for the audience.

MM: You ever have a problem with some professional orchestras being bored with some repertoire?

ML: Yeah, yeah. And usually it's a question of the conductor. You can take a piece like Beethoven's Fifth, which gets played so much. Well, we started playing all of these Beethoven symphonies with Osmo, and he brought an immense amount of new approaches to the table. Really, it's a question of the conductor, when you have standard repertoire like that, to make it interesting.

MM: Now, you've also conducted concert bands, in addition to orchestras. What are the differences there?

ML: Well, you have to have a lot of patience for intonation. A conductor in a concert band …. I can't say job one, but one of the big jobs is listening to pitch and really getting people used to a good sound when it comes to intonation. Bands tend to get into what I call the intonation of averages. You'll have people sound flat, some sharp, and then it just sort of becomes a sound all by itself.

MM: It kind of averages out.

ML: Yeah. It's the same thing when you have a large string section. So your clarinets will be kind of like your first violin section, and you get this sound, kind of this odd humming kind of sound. And you can either, as the band director, accept that, or you can say, "You know, this really isn't good."

This is something that, when these kids come to me at the Youth Symphony, a lot of them are accustomed to that sound of the intonation of averages. And I say, "No, you can't do that anymore. You guys have to have one A, one B-flat, that sounds all the way through. It can't be this kind of a constant, weird-type oscillation. You can't have that here." For many of them it's a revelation.

MM: *In terms of getting the musicians to do what you want, an orchestra has a hundred or so musicians in it and one conductor. That doesn't seem like a fair fight to me.*

ML: [laughs] Well, pity the poor conductor, because when it comes to practicing ….

I'll go downstairs in a little while and grab my horn and practice and improve. What does a conductor do? Call up the people in the neighborhood and say, "Here, each of you hold a drum?"

MM: *[laughs]*

ML: You know, the only time that they get to work is when they're able to find a pile of people sufficient in size for them to be able to work together.

There's that aspect to it. There's also the psychological aspect to it, where the conductor has to be part psychologist. You have to analyze a given situation, a reaction to something you have said or done, and be able to address it right away, in the most efficient way possible, because the clock is running and you can't sit there and allow time to fritter away.

So you've got to be a good musician. You've got to have good hands. And you've got to be a psychologist.

MM: *How do you practice that? Like you said, you can't just get a group of people from around the neighborhood. How does a conductor practice his craft?*

ML: You know, a lot of it is in solitude, I'm afraid. A lot of it is just learning the beat patterns, turning on the Victrola, and—just like somebody working out something athletic—get your moves together.

Then you might have a friend who plays piano, and you'll ask that friend to play something while you conduct them. You can make it into a game, saying "Today I'm going to do some things like slow down and see how you react to it." And you see how good you are at imparting the information. With any luck, you can expand that into a small chamber ensemble.

But it ain't easy, Mike, I'll tell you! You're kind of getting the idea here. It's the toughest thing for young conductors.

MM: *What's the worst thing you've had happen to you while you were conducting?*

ML: I've been pretty lucky, but I remember one time it was *I* who got lost. I was conducting the Minnesota Orchestra, one of my first times, and it was one of these things where the orchestra played for four measures and a little tag at the end. And I shorted them by a measure.

MM: *[laughs]*

ML: I cut them off a measure before. The winds, brass, percussion stopped; the strings kept going. I could make a little statement about that, but I won't. [laughs]

That's about the worst. I have never had a train wreck. I've had situations where a piece didn't get off to a good start. But you can cut them off and start again. And that has happened. That happens in professional orchestras.

Most of the time it's a technical issue. Something might have gone wrong with someone's instrument, or somebody in the chorus wasn't watching, something like that. If it's just a couple of measures, there's really no point in going on, because it just sets a bad mood for the piece.

You just kind of smile and say, "Okay, let's try that again." And everybody feels like, "Whew! Second chance," and it sets a much better tone.

MM: What sorts of things do you find most fulfilling as a conductor?

ML: In rehearsal, I would have to say that it would be watching the Youth Symphony do something for the very first time—and do it really well. Or something where they just haven't gotten it, they just don't understand one thing and then finally, finally the light comes on and they do something at an artistic level that is so high, just something you would have expected from the Minnesota Orchestra. You just go, "Thank you." Just something really, really special and elevated. Something that you just wouldn't expect young kids to be able to grasp—or you do expect them to grasp, but it's been so long in coming.

Usually those sorts of things, almost without exception, have to do with music that has lots of little tempo changes and then just that one little lift, and place it. When you get a hundred kids to all do that at the same time, you've won. You have absolutely won. The kids have suddenly gone from feeling like kids to adults. I have to say, that's probably what I enjoy the most.

And there you go, that's in the process of a rehearsal. It's not so much about the performance. I mean, the performance is wonderful, but when you're conducting a youth orchestra, It's about education. It should be about education, and teaching the kids the ropes. Teaching them the things that they will need to go on, should they choose to go on.

To know that one day that kid may be playing that same Mahler symphony that you did with them, and they'll be in a professional situation and they will remember. They will remember that time that they did it with their youth orchestra, the very first time. It's almost like revisiting a first love, they're thinking about that first girlfriend. I think providing students with that moment is one of the great joys, for me.

> **WHOLE NOTE**
>
> This is an excerpt from a longer interview I conducted with Manny Laureano. You can read the entire interview online at www.idiotsguides.com/conducting.

The Least You Need to Know

- One of the chief roles of an orchestral conductor is achieving a unique sound mix—deciding which parts to emphasize and deemphasize.
- One of the challenges in conducting any instrumental ensemble is achieving a uniform tuning and the desired overall tone.
- When conducting a student ensemble, remember that's a learning experience for the musicians.
- One of the challenges in conducting student ensembles is choosing music that challenges your best players while still being playable by the lesser ones.

Conducting Marching Bands

Chapter 16

In This Chapter

- Understand the modern marching band
- Learn the role of the drum major
- Discover different conducting patterns
- An interview with band director Glenn Northern

In the previous chapter we discussed conducting for concert bands. Well, you take away the chairs and get 'em moving, and you have yourself a marching band. (There's a bit more involved than that, but you get the idea ….)

In a marching band or drum corps, the conducting is done by one or more drum majors. Depending on the style of the band, the drum major may use the conducting methods I've discussed in this book—or do something different entirely.

Getting to Know the Marching Band

A marching band is a unique instrumental ensemble in that the musicians simultaneously play and march—often in sophisticated formations. It's a challenge, both for the players and the band director.

Today's Marching Bands

When I was in high school, during the groovy '70s, marching bands were a big deal—both in terms of importance and size. I went to Ben Davis High School in Indianapolis, Indiana, and the marching band there was a good 300 people strong, participated in (and often won) the yearly marching band contest at the Indiana State Fair, and often traveled out of state to march in major parades.

Things are a bit different today. First, a school's marching band finds itself in competition with an increasing number of other extracurricular activities; as a result, bands are typically smaller than they used to be. They are, however, often more professional, and participate in more structured competitions. Many states have sophisticated marching band contests that span multiple weeks of competition, and some multi-state contests exist.

Today's marching bands also do a lot more than march in parades—although there's still a little of that. Top-level marching bands focus on their field shows, which are performed at football games and in competition. These shows are elaborate displays of precision marching combined with challenging musical arrangements. The best marching bands rival quality concert bands, in terms of musicianship.

Equally important, the makeup of the marching band has changed significantly since my days in the line. Many bands now have a "pit" or *front line* of nonmarching instruments that lines up along the sidelines, in front of the band. This front line contains various mallet percussion instruments (marimba, xylophone, chimes), timpani, keyboards, and sometimes electric bass and guitar. The pit really enhances the sound and enables the band to play more sophisticated arrangements.

> **DEFINITION**
>
> The **front line** (or "pit") is a nonmarching section of a marching band, lined up at the front of the field. Most front lines contain larger and less portable instruments, such as marimbas, timpani, keyboards, and the like.

Of course, not all marching bands are created equal. Schools with a history and emphasis on competition will have strong field programs and do a lot of traveling; schools without the competitive history will do a lot of marching in parades and in half-time shows.

The size of the band (and the school) also makes a difference. A band from a small school might have fewer than 20 members; a "pep" band organized for high school basketball games might have 30 to 40 members; a monster band from a large high school or college might have 200 members or more. Naturally, the larger the band, the more sophisticated the music you can play and the field shows you can create.

Meet the Corps

Then there's the creature known as the drum and bugle corps—or, in most circles, just the *drum corps*. As the full name implies, the drum and bugle corps consists of drums and bugles, of various shapes and sizes. Think of it as a subset of a traditional marching band, but on steroids.

> **DEFINITION**
>
> A **drum corps** is a marching band that consists primarily of percussion and brass instruments, with a focus on competition.

The world of drum corps is both fun and demanding—and it's all about the competition, which is at a very high level. Most drum corps travel around a region (or across the country) in summer touring circuits, performing their meticulously rehearsed shows on football fields before large crowds and panels of judges. The corps are judged not just on musical performance, but also on visual performance and general effect.

It's All About the Show

Whether you're talking drum corps or competitive marching bands, everything revolves around the band's show, which runs around 10 to 12 minutes long. A drum corps may keep the same show for an entire competitive season, where a marching band might do several shows over the course of a year. The musical content can vary wildly both between and within shows, running the gamut from symphonic works to Broadway tunes to rock and roll to Latin and other ethnic music.

While the musical content is unpredictable, most shows share a common structure, consisting of multiple pieces connected together in a larger whole. For example, a typical drum corps show starts with an opener designed to grab the audience's attention, which then flows into a feature for the percussion section. This is, more often than not, followed by a ballad (typically featuring the horns), which then builds into a closer, which is the climax of the show. Naturally, other shorter pieces may be inserted into this general framework.

Understanding the Role of the Drum Major

The leader of the marching band or drum corps is called the *drum major*. This person—or persons, depending on the organization—functions as the on-field conductor, as well as the team leader.

> **DEFINITION**
>
> The **drum major** is the leader and field conductor of a marching band or drum corps. If a band has more than one drum major, the senior drum major is sometimes designated the *field major*.

A Short History of Drum Majoring

Just as marching bands themselves evolved from military bands, the position of drum major originated in the British Army's Corps of Drums, sometime in the mid-1600s. This musical organization was essentially a fife and drum corps, with the drum major being the chief drummer and leader.

During this period, the drum major was responsible not only for calling out the (short) pieces to play, he also had to help defend his fellow musicians on the field of battle. (It was a lot more dangerous being a drum major back then.) This meant that the drum major was as much a military position as it was a musical one.

That all changed over time, of course, as military engagements became less formal and the concept of using a drum and fife corps in battle faded into memory. Military bands became more popular in nature, marching in parades and playing public concerts, and the role of the drum major changed to that of a conductor, more or less.

Drum Majors Today

The role of the drum major today depends to a degree on the type of band being led. For purely marching bands, the drum major literally leads the band. He marches in front, carrying his *mace* and whistle, and tweets the band into one song after another.

> **DEFINITION**
> A **mace** is a large staff used by some drum majors that functions as a type of oversized baton. Marching maces run in size from 38 to 51 inches long.

The drum major serves a similar function in more traditional field marching bands. That is, he uses the whistle to start the performance and beats the mace in time throughout. For more competitive marching bands and drum corps, however, the drum major functions more like an orchestral conductor. The mace is typically forsworn in favor of bare-handed conducting, and the beat patterns more closely resemble the more elaborate patterns presented in this book, as opposed to the simple up-and-down patterns seen in military bands.

In addition, you'll often find more than one drum major in a band. Many competitive bands use two or three drum majors, positioned at different points along the sideline. In this type of multiple-major configuration, one drum major is assigned the lead role, and the others follow that person's lead.

As the on-field conductor, the drum major is responsible for everything a conductor is traditionally responsible for. That means starting and stopping the performance, setting and maintaining the tempo, controlling dynamics, phrasing, and other musical nuances, and signaling cues and accents.

Many competitive drum majors are also performers. Sometimes that's in a musical sense, as when a drum major picks up his instrument to play a solo in the middle of a routine. Sometimes that's in a visual sense, with elaborate conductive flourishes and such; a drum major or field major may toss his mace high in the air or execute flashy twirling maneuvers. It is a show, after all.

Finally, the drum major functions much like the captain of a sports team. He's the group leader, responsible for morale as much as anything else. For many outsiders, the drum major is the face of the band—which is a significant responsibility.

Learning Marching Conducting Technique

Given the focus of this book, we're going to focus on the drum major's role as conductor. How a drum major conducts depends entirely on the type of band being led.

Using Standard Technique

Most competitive or field bands and drum corps require their drum majors to conduct using standard technique. That is, the drum major stands in front of the band and conducts beat patterns with his right hand and gestures musically with his left.

> **THE CONDUCTOR SEZ**
>
> There is far more mirroring in marching band conducting than other types of conducting, with both hands doing the exact same thing. This is especially true with more traditional bands.

In this type of band, which is most common today, the drum major does not use a mace. While some may employ batons, most conduct bare handed. The reason for this is simple; it's virtually impossible for musicians to see that small baton across the width of a football field. It's a lot easier to see the drum major's hands, especially when he's wearing bright white gloves.

When conducting a marching band without a baton, hold your hands in a flat or slightly curved position. Make sure your fingers are held tightly together, not splayed.

> **THE CONDUCTOR SEZ**
>
> Not splaying your fingers is good advice for all types of conducting, not just with marching bands. A colleague of mine likes to say that when you splay your fingers, the music falls through them.

With the physical size of the playing field in mind, some drum majors will employ slightly simplified beat patterns in lieu of the traditional patterns we discussed previously in this book. Most common is the simplified 4/4 pattern shown in Figure 16.1—down, left, right, up. The thinking is that it's easier for far-flung musicians to see the beats in this pattern, than in the traditional pattern with more nuanced beats and rebounds. (Refresh your knowledge of four-beat patterns in Chapter 6, if you like.)

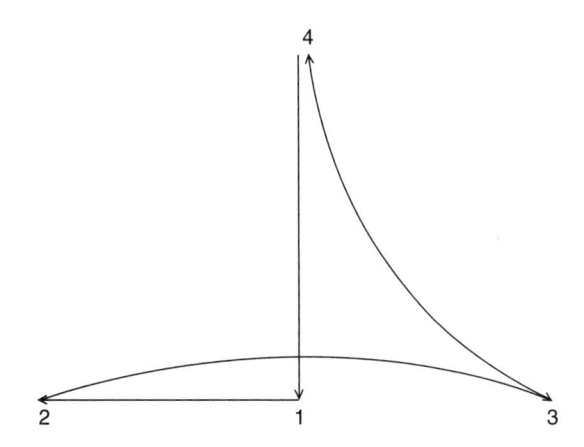

Figure 16.1: *The simplified four-beat pattern.*

Whatever beat patterns you employ, you'll probably need to make bigger gestures than is typical with concert conducting. Again, it's a matter of size and distance; smaller gestures just get lost at the far reaches of the field. Everything you do as a conductor needs to be a little bigger and more emphatic. It's traditional conducting, but outsized.

> **THE CONDUCTOR SEZ**
>
> Another popular four-beat pattern is one I call the "sideways V." In this pattern you come down and slightly out for one, in for two, back out for three, and back up to the starting position for four.

Using Military Technique

Then we have the more old-fashioned marching bands, what we'll call military bands because of their focus (or dependence) on tradition. A drum major in a military band typically uses a mace, and conducts using simple up-and-down patterns. In most instances, the left hand is used to mirror the right, rather than to indicate musical gestures; sometimes the left arm stays out of it all together as well.

What does a typical military conducting pattern look like? Really, it's just a series of up-and-down motions. Figure 16.2 shows such a 4/4 pattern—note that the actual beats are all in a straight vertical line, one on top of another.

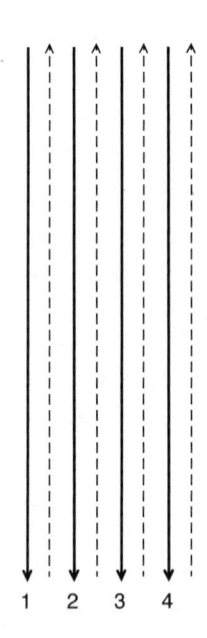

Figure 16.2: *A simple military-style four-beat pattern.*

There are variations to this, of course. Figure 16.3 shows a popular four-beat pattern where the upbeat after beat three moves out to the side before swinging back down to beat four. All four beats are still at the same point, it's the swing out before four that differs.

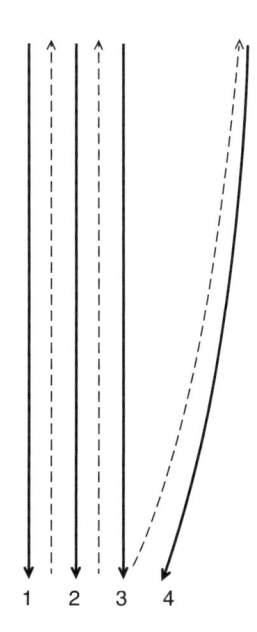

Figure 16.3: *A variation of the military-style four-beat pattern.*

In addition, some military-style conductors will use the traditional simplified four-beat pattern shown in Figure 16.1. Just remember that whatever pattern you choose, you'll probably mirror that pattern with your left hand.

> **WHOLE NOTE**
>
> Which conducting style and patterns you use will be determined by your band director and staff. Consult with them before you start practicing one way or the other!

Conducting in the Real World: An Interview with Glenn Northern

Penn High School in Mishawaka, Indiana, has a powerhouse marching band in a state long known for its high-quality marching programs. Penn's Marching Kingsmen have been finalists in the Indiana State School Music Association (ISSMA) Marching Band State Finals for 10 consecutive years, and were a top 10 finisher in the 2011 competition.

Since 2001, Glenn Northern has been the leader of Penn's marching program. As Penn's Director of Bands, Glenn also conducts Penn's Symphonic Band I, Gold Band, Freshman Concert Band, Freshman Advanced Band, and Pep Band. He has twice received the Distinguished Service Award from ISSMA, where he is currently president-elect. He also served as president of ISSMA during the 2004–2005 academic year, and has served on the executive committee of the Indiana Bandmasters Association (IBA).

I talked with Glenn the week before Penn competed in the semi-state level of the 2011 marching band competition. We started out by talking about some of the changes in marching bands over the years.

MICHAEL MILLER (MM): *How big is the influence of the drum corps stuff on the traditional marching band?*

GLENN NORTHERN (GN): It's pretty big, I think. You look back to the '70s, early '80s when a lot of marching bands were doing kind of a Big Ten style drill. That would probably mirror a lot of what you saw and still see in a lot of colleges. The drum corps' influence, I'm guessing probably in the '70s, started to creep into that.

I always hear stories about some of the bands in Indiana, some of the guys who were very cutting edge, as far as bringing in different designers and doing different kinds of drill things. Every time I hear those stories, it's always kind of an early to mid-70s timeline where that started to happen. Eventually everybody was doing it by the mid-80s, when I was in college and doing a lot of staffing with bands. That's pretty much what it was in Indiana.

MM: What all does it affect?

GN: Instrumentation is affected, especially in the contemporary movement of marching bands, to the degree of trying to create the best sounds outside. The quality of the instruments has changed.

When I was in high school I remember my high school having fiberglass sousaphones. Today that would be heresy to have a fiberglass sousaphone, because the tone quality wouldn't be good. You might have a brass sousaphone, that's what our band happens to use, but the idea of finding a better-quality instrument to create a really great sound—it's more about the quality of sound rather than the volume of sound, like it used to be then.

MM: Do you have fewer musicians, then?

GN: I think there are fewer musicians, but that's only because of the evolution of the activity in society. I always hear stories about bands in the '70s in Indiana that were just monstrous. Like little schools. One of my first teaching jobs was in a school that was like 600 students total, and at one point this little school had a band of over 200 students. That was before Title IX and before girls' athletics. For the girls, that was a major activity for them. When the doors were opened and they could have basketball and volleyball and golf and all these other sports, then it changed, the participation changed. I've heard stories like that around schools all over.

The other thing with the instrumentation that's changed is the percussion contribution is way different now. In the '70s you think back to having a bell or xylophone that was actually marching on the field, on a rack, on a harness. Or a glockenspiel that somebody was playing with one hand and holding up with one hand. Now you'll see a sideline percussion section that has $100,000 worth of equipment. Marimbas, multiple marimbas, multiple vibraphones, timpani, and chimes. And of course now you've got so much electronic stuff, you've got digital grand pianos in the pit section, the front ensemble section of a marching band. So that's a real change, too, because that changes the color of the ensemble and the quality of the percussion section sound. And, of course, the number of players is way different there, in that element of what we do.

MM: *I'd imagine it changes the quality of players, too. I was a drummer back then, and you had some very mediocre players playing very simple snare drum parts. I remember one year I lugged around these things, I don't think they make them anymore, called Timp-Toms …*

GN: A tri-tom sort of thing, yeah.

MM: Except I think they were made of solid concrete. [laughs]

GN: You know that back then there were groups that used marching timpani. There'd be four players out there, each carrying a timpani. Those things are back breaking. Finally, somebody started putting those things on the sideline and that became the evolution of the front ensemble.

MM: So the quality of the music you're playing has improved, right?

GN: That's true. You always see groups doing serious music. Even back then you'd see groups playing Mussorgsky or Shostakovich or Tchaikovsky, some big composers, great music. They still do that, but it's probably circled around. Now there's a mindset of being true to an original work. Of course, as the quality of the bands got better, the arrangements got better, too.

Now I see a push toward what I call effect music. You can take a classical piece, but you turn it into a marching band or drum corps moment, usually with some different chord structure, and that's more about the highs and the lows of the music. If you're designing a competitive marching band show now, you're thinking about I need a really high musical impact moment here in the first 45 seconds of my show. Then I need a real down, soft, pretty moment. And then I need to come back to kind of a big hit moment, within another minute.

There's such an ebb and flow, it's almost like a short attention span composition. You're trying to create a lot of moods but not bore or lose the interest of your audience.

MM: Where do you get your arrangements?

GN: It varies. There are a lot of people around the country who pretty much do nothing but arrange music for marching bands and drum corps. Some of those guys probably write music like concert band pieces, or write for other groups. Some of them are people who compose for film scores and do that kind of work in Hollywood. It varies a lot. And some of them are just teachers who do a lot of writing or arranging themselves. It kind of varies. But there are a lot of good people who pretty much just do that as their living. They write for 20 groups or something a year and charge each one a few thousand dollars. That's how you make your living.

MM: With the increased emphasis on the quality of the music, then, it seems to me that the importance of the conductor has increased also.

GN: That's right. Certainly, you look at the evolution of a marching band drum major, it's very different than it used to be. You go back to the old mace and whistle, those drum majors might not even have been on the podium. They were just on the field, doing whistle commands, starting the tune with four whistles. The mace was basically just a prop at that point. Of course, the mace finds its origins back in the Middle Ages, when they would literally take a stick and beat it on the stage floor to keep the time.

Now, our best high school drum majors look like they could be conducting a symphony orchestra. The nuance and the technique that they have is so refined. They don't all look like that, but the very good ones certainly have a refined training that probably a lot of the high school band directors don't possess.

MM: Let's start at the beginning. It doesn't start on the field. You're starting with rehearsals in the rehearsal room, right?

GN: Yep. If you're talking about marching bands, there are a lot of drum major camps around the country. Good ones, where students will go and learn. There are always several parameters to the training, they'll learn some student leadership techniques, they'll do a lot of conducting and learn the actual technique that they're going to need to have.

And they vary. Some of them are still very old school, kind of military. If you sat through the semi-state contest tomorrow at Ben Davis and watched 20 of the Class A bands in the state, you'd see people who are very traditional in the way they look as a drum major. They'll be having heavy subdivisions of the beat in their hands. Then you'll see other people who look like they're conducting a symphony orchestra. It's such a different style. It's probably appropriate for the music that band plays.

But sometimes it's not. I always marvel when I watch a drum major who conducts with a lot of subdivision, and they might be playing a piece that's kind of pretty and soft and even kind of slow, but they still have so much subdivision in their hands. It's just the style that that band uses and that drum major uses. It might go back to the camp that that drum major was trained in, or just the way that that band does that.

MM: Now when you start out in rehearsals, I'm sure it's you doing the conducting, right?

GN: Usually it's the staff, and drum majors are kind of learning their way through and conducting along. A lot of times the staff in our band will start telling students, kind of instruct them, "I want you to do this here, I want you to do this." We'll get our drum majors together and we'll conduct to some music. And we'll conduct in a mirror where they can see.

Most large groups will use multiple drum majors, so there's certainly a unity of style you want them to have. For ours, we use four. We have a dance studio kind of room where we've got mirrors, where they can conduct at themselves and see each other and see themselves. And we'll talk about matching style, we'll be very specific about whether it's a smooth flowing thing or if it's more staccato, more rigid in style, and what that necessitates from them, what they need to do to make that happen.

MM: How would you describe the difference in conducting a marching band versus conducting a concert band?

GN: It varies. It could be almost nothing. When I watch our drum majors conduct, I think that they could be conducting a concert ensemble. And I've seen some great drum majors from other schools that I think the same thing of every year.

The ones that are very different are these drum majors that we've been talking about, who kind of conduct with a different, more military band style. Usually there's a lot of subdivision in what they're doing. And there's a lot of mirroring of hands. A serious conductor is going to conduct mainly with his right hand and do a lot of shaping and gesturing with the left hand, trying to give musical cues to the ensemble, not time keeping. Typically a military style drum major is going to be doing a lot of mirroring and probably giving almost no kinds of cues with their left hand.

MM: Thinking back to my days in marching band, one of the challenges is just the distance. You're covering a football field, and you have the issue of physics, where the speed of sound is slower than the speed of light. How do you deal with that?

GN: That's really a band training issue. Some groups will have more than one drum major across the front sideline. I've seen schools that will have four across the front sideline, some that'll have three, like maybe one in the center and two on the outside.

In our band we have two, we'll put 'em around the 40 yard lines. So we don't have a drum major in the center, but have two kind of off center. One of those drum majors is in charge of the pulse, and the other front drum major is doing nothing but watching the first drum major. Then the back drum majors are watching which of the front drum majors is in charge of the pulse.

In most bands there's one drum major who's the primary and everybody else is watching him to make sure that he's keeping the same pulse. In that way you can get the beat spread around the ensemble.

The other issue is kind of a back-to-front issue. When you're dealing with the timing of the band, we talk about this with our percussionists all the time, trying to anticipate the pulse of the drum major's hands. What our drum majors end up doing, is most of the time, our drum major who is in charge of the beat is watching the feet of the center snare player. The pulse really starts with that center snare drum player. He's in charge of the battery, the marching percussion, so they stay together. The drum major's watching his feet to make sure that his pulse is right there with that drum major, and then the band follows that. So a lot of times the pulse starts in that regard.

MM: *Do you have issues keeping the band on the field in sync with the pit?*

GN: You easily could. The pit is usually in the front, so their instructions are also to listen back to the pulse, and not watch the drum major. Which is kind of funny, because if you watch the pit, they're all very physical, there's a lot of drama to it. There's some acting involved in that. A lot of times you'll see them looking up at the drum major and playing this really gorgeous thing. In reality they're probably looking at the drum major but they're really not watching the drum major for the pulse. It's kind of like, I should look up here to sort of look engaged. We'll tell our pit all the time, look up but don't watch that, just listen back to the pulse you hear behind you.

Of course, the staging of the band, where the band is, always creates different issues. If the drum line gets too far forward in the form, and there's brass or woodwind players behind the drum line, suddenly they have a different responsibility to the pulse. They may not be able to listen to the battery like they were able to when the battery was behind them. So the pulse gets kind of driven and moved around the field.

MM: *It seems to me that one of the challenges when you're dealing with any student ensemble is you have to get music that's easy enough for them to play but still also challenges them, then also take into effect that you have players of various levels in the band, right?*

GN: That's right. And one of the issues, at least in our marching band, is for us it's an extracurricular activity. We don't play our marching band music during school, so it needs to be music that's attainable to us with that parameter. Most schools are probably playing their marching band music some during classes and some are probably doing nothing but playing their marching band music at this time of the year.

For us, we almost want the music to be quite easy for our advanced players and we want it to be pretty easily attainable to our younger, middle-range players. And then a few players are probably struggling to get to it. So picking music of the right technical ability is really important. If you go too far one way or another …. If you play music that's too easy it may sound too easy, and even a good band is disadvantaged; you may not sound as good because, frankly, your music's not as good. You're trying to walk that line of picking something of substance and something that sounds good but not something that goes over the heads of everybody, or at least the younger bands.

We've done that. We've picked music that's been too hard for us, we've picked it with the older players in mind, and then struggled because the other players couldn't keep up.

MM: Going beyond the marching band, what are the challenges you're facing leading a high school band program these days?

GN: The challenges probably haven't changed much. Most people would probably say the most urgent thing is just the change in society and the change in students. In a lot of schools there are more options for students—including options away from school. A lot of students would just go home and play a video game all evening, if somebody would let them, and not really put time or effort into some kind of a team activity, like an athletic team or a band. I think you fight that battle in trying to keep students engaged and give them a home in their school, some kind of an activity that's comfortable and safe for them, and fun.

Certainly in most cases where education is being so challenged financially, we're seeing programs being cut or downsized to the point where they're not offering as many things, or there's less staff teaching. So the program's not able to be as active or offer as many things to its students. We see a lot of that in Indiana right now. Education's kind of under fire. We're seeing it directly because our state government seems to have this sense of there's a lot of fluff and a lot of pork in public education. They're kind of waging war on it, is the way it feels.

MM: I've never quite understood when teachers became the bad guys. I have a sister-in-law who was teaching music in Indiana and her program got downsized to the point that she left the state. She's teaching over in Ohio now.

GN: Man.

MM: So I'm looking at the band program. You have the salaries of the staff, and you're buying a lot of equipment. Especially for a marching band today you have a lot more equipment than you did 35 years ago. Where does the money come from for that?

GN: That's the other game with the marching band stuff, it kind of becomes a rich man's game, because everybody ups the ante. The really strong programs up the ante by hiring staff that are really great, and of course they're expensive to hire. That's separate from your school corporation teachers. Most marching bands use many good staff members from outside who might be really good experts, either percussion experts or color guard experts. You kind of create this culture where in order to compete, you have to do that to some degree.

Most schools do a student fee kind of thing. In our school, I think we're pretty typical in that our students pay a fee just to be in marching band. And then all that fee is turned around to expenses just for the marching band—which is mostly staff, but even the show, we purchase the drill and we purchase the music, we're purchasing the percussion arrangements. Then you've got the equipment and the travel and the food expenses.

Like you said, when you put that much percussion equipment on the field, or try to have really good brass instruments on the field, it can get really expensive. Especially if the school's not supporting it. Some bands probably do that on their own, just with their student fees.

MM: Seems like there's a lot of parent fundraisers going on, too.

GN: That's right. The band booster organizations are still as strong as ever. That probably comes from people your age and my age who had great experiences there and their kids are part of that, so they understand how important it is. They work so hard in some ways, the band booster organizations might be working now at their highest level, in terms of how many educated, highly trained parents putting their personal expertise to work for the band, and just the number of volunteer hours that you get.

You look at any [big school]. They all have that kind of support. The directors probably see it as doing what the school corporation can't or won't do.

MM: Personally, what do you find most fulfilling about your job?

GN: The best thing is just working with the students. It's funny because sometimes that gets clouded, there are so many things you do in the job, it's easy to get distracted. But that's the real best part of it. Literally just being around them and seeing them work and seeing them achieve something and seeing them grow as people and as musicians.

Anybody who's been in an organization, especially in a marching band–type organization, you know that most of what you learn really isn't about the music. It's teamwork and the dedication and the work ethic and the time management and all those things.

It's no surprise when you hear corporate CEOs talk about that kind of training, how valuable that is for their employees. That's what they need in their employees, the problem-solving skills and those kinds of things.

It may be that the student is a really, really smart student but if he's not involved in those things in his school that are teaching him those things, it's hard to do that on your own. It's hard to grow those kinds of skills on your own.

> **WHOLE NOTE**
>
> This is an excerpt from a longer interview I conducted with Glenn Northern. You can read the entire interview online at www.idiotsguides.com/conducting.

The Least You Need to Know

- Today's modern marching bands and drum corps are focused on competitive routines, and feature a front line of nonmarching instruments.
- The drum major (or sometimes the field major) is the leader and field conductor of the marching band.
- Military-style drum majors conduct with a large mace using simple up-and-down motions.
- Drum majors in competitive bands conduct without a baton, using the same beat patterns as concert conductors—but more exaggerated.

Conducting Jazz Bands

Chapter 17

In This Chapter

- Learn what a big band leader does
- Find out why some band leaders are also performers
- Discover how to conduct a big band
- An interview with band leader Mark Buselli

Call it a big band, a jazz band, a jazz ensemble, or a jazz orchestra, it's trumpets, bones, saxes, and a swingin' rhythm section. It's the music of Benny Goodman and Glenn Miller, of Count Basie and Duke Ellington, of Buddy Rich and Maynard Ferguson, of Gordon Goodwin and Maria Schneider. It's jazz, jazz, and more jazz—and one of the more unique conducting opportunities you'll find.

What Does the Leader of the Band Do?

Here's the deal. Big bands sometimes have conductors, and sometimes they don't. There's always a leader, but there isn't always a guy standing up front waving a baton.

Why is that?

A jazz band, unlike "serious" concert bands and orchestras, is kind of a groove band. That is, most of the tunes are straight ahead jazz or rock, in a constant time signature and tempo. The band gets started, kicks into a groove, and keeps playing until the tune's over. There aren't a lot of tempo and time changes to navigate; it's pretty much a start it and forget it kind of deal—except when it isn't.

There's actually quite a lot of nuance that a conductor can bring to a big band. There are lots of accents (we call them "hits" or "stings") throughout most pieces, lots of changes in dynamics, and even the occasional odd time signature to deal with. Then you have the issue of bringing the whole band back in after an extended solo, and the inevitable fermatas and cutoffs at the end of a piece. In other words, there's work there for a conductor, if you want it.

Whether or not a big band uses a conductor depends a lot on the experience level of the band. Student ensembles, in general, benefit from having a conductor/band director up front. Younger players often need the reassurance of a conductor keeping time for them, as well as the cues a conductor provides. Chances are, if you're leading a high school or college jazz ensemble, you're standing up front and waving your arms around. (But probably not using a baton; jazz conductors typically don't use batons.)

A professional-level big band, on the other hand, often makes do without a full-time conductor. There's normally a band leader, of course; someone has to program the music and lead rehearsals. But there's less need for a conductor to keep the beat and cue every entrance. At most, the leader will signal post-solo entrances, tempo changes, and end-of-tune cutoffs.

Here's what you have to keep in mind. The biggest big bands throughout history have had leaders who played in the band rather than stood in front and conducted. Think Benny Goodman (clarinet), Glenn Miller (trombone), Count Basie (piano), Duke Ellington (piano), Woody Herman (clarinet and saxophone), Stan Kenton (piano), Buddy Rich (drums), Maynard Ferguson (trumpet), Gordon Goodwin (piano)—all band leaders who play(ed) in their bands and didn't conduct full-time.

In all these cases, the band leader is the leader of the band—and a player in the band, too. The band leader chooses the arrangements, decides who solos where, counts off the beginning of each tune, cues in the band after solos, and cuts everybody off after held notes at the end. He also plays in the band, takes his own solos, and blends in with the other musicians. His conducting is done with a nod of the head, a briefly raised hand, maybe even a gesture with his instrument. It's double-duty for a professional big band leader, but that's the way the job works.

Conducting the Band

Whether you're standing in front of the band as a full-time conductor or conducting from your place in the band itself as a player/leader, there are quite a few things to pay attention to. We'll address them here.

First of all, forget the baton. Few if any modern band leaders conduct with a baton; instead, bare-handed conducting is the norm. That's especially true if you're a player/conductor; it's impractical to both hold your instrument and a baton at the same time.

During rehearsals, the leader is responsible for achieving the right tone and instrument mix. It's your job to determine how the saxes blend with the trumpets, and so forth. Even though you're only dealing with 15 to 20 musicians, achieving the proper mix determines the sound of a particular band.

> **WHOLE NOTE**
>
> You'll probably need to do a bit of on-the-spot sound adjusting during performances, especially with student ensembles. The sound of the room affects the sound of the band, so you'll need to bring things up or down accordingly.

Starting a tune is more often done by counting than by a single preparatory gesture. That's kind of a practical thing, too, especially if you're conducting from within the band. But even dedicated big band conductors find it useful to get a feel for the tempo and groove beforehand, counting off a few measures before the band comes in. Take a moment to fix the tempo and then count the band in, ready to groove.

Once the tune starts cooking, you may not need to keep pounding out the beat patterns. If the band's in a groove, there's little you can add by beating one two three four over and over again. Get out of the way and let things simmer, if you can.

That general rule can be broken if you're working with a student band that needs the visual reassurance a conductor provides. It may also be necessary to conduct the beat if you're playing an odd time signature piece, like something in 5/4 or 7/8 that's more difficult for the band to count and groove to.

If you do choose to conduct a beat pattern, consider going with a simplified pattern instead of a traditional one. For example, if you're in 4/4 (and you probably are, most of the time), consider using the down-left-right-up pattern shown back in Figure 6.5. Big band conducting isn't that fancy; you just have to get the point across without interfering with the groove.

> **THE CONDUCTOR SEZ**
> A big band is really about tempo and groove, isn't it? Not one of looking for rebounds.

Whether you're conducting a beat pattern or not, you probably need to step in when there are a lot of hits and stings going on. These syncopated accents are part and parcel of most big band music, and you may need to cue in the players to make sure everyone hits the accents at the same time. Use your left hand to cue the hits while maintaining a simplified beat pattern with your right.

You'll also need to step in to conduct changes in dynamics, bringing the volume level down or letting the band scream when called for. In addition, you'll need to signal the band back in after extended solos; in many arrangements, the soloist is encouraged to go for as many choruses as he wants, accompanied only by the rhythm section. When the solo peaks, it's your job to bring everybody back in as necessary.

Finally, the conductor is necessary to end each tune. If it's a stinger ending, you need to signal the sting. If it's a held note, you need to indicate how long it's held and then signal the final cutoff.

Actually, it's kind of fun conducting a big band. The energy level you get from that particular combination of instruments can take your breath away. One little gesture of your hand and you can blow the roof off the joint.

> **THE CONDUCTOR SEZ**
> You may have an instrument in your hand while leading a big band. Get used to it if that's your bag!

Conducting in the Real World: An Interview with Mark Buselli

Leading a big band is a big task—and it goes well beyond conducting. For this chapter's interview, I turned to a guy who leads both professional and student big bands, so he knows the ins and outs at all levels of conducting.

Mark Buselli is a talented and versatile musician and educator. He co-leads, with trombonist/composer Brent Wallarab, the Indianapolis-based Buselli-Wallarab Jazz Orchestra, one of today's premiere regional big bands. He's also leader of and plays trumpet with the Midcoast Swing Orchestra, the BWJO Sextet, and the Mark Buselli Quartet and Quintet.

Mark also happens to be Director of Jazz Studies at Ball State University in Muncie, Indiana, where he leads the school's two student big bands. He graduated from the Berklee School of Music in Boston, and received his MM in Jazz Studies from Indiana University.

I've known Mark for a number of years, from when I used to live in central Indiana and caught Mark and his big band at Indianapolis' premiere jazz club, The Jazz Kitchen. Back then, Mark was gracious enough to serve as technical editor on my companion book, *The Complete Idiot's Guide to Solos and Improvisation* (Alpha Books, 2004). His website is www.markbuselli.com.

We started out by talking about the role of the conductor in a big band.

MICHAEL MILLER (MM): *So let's deal with the basic question: Does a big band really need a conductor?*

MARK BUSELLI (MB): You know, that's a really good question. Now, most of the work in a jazz ensemble is done in the rehearsals. The conductor is up there, but most of the time when a conductor is conducting beat patterns, no one's watching him, because it's more of a groove music. The director or the conductor serves a purpose calling in backgrounds on open solos, and calling in cues.

Mainly, I like to think of the conductor in a big band as the chef in a kitchen. I know that sounds a little weird, but here's why.

When you're up there conducting, you're trying to get the right texture at the right time. You're mixing ingredients. In other words, every room you play in is going to be a different sound than you're used to in your rehearsal room.

The pros, because of their experience, usually know how to deal with new rooms really quickly. When you get to the college level and high school level, they don't have as much experience and they're not used to hearing the sound like that coming back at them differently. So you're up there making sure that the texture between the saxophones is right, calling for dynamics to push this down a little bit, pull this up a little bit, giving downbeats at beginnings of sections. And, especially for endings, cutoffs, holds, cadenzas, all that kind of stuff is where you're mostly needed.

Now, there are some kinds of music, like, take Maria Schneider, for instance. Yeah, she needs to be up there. Because her music, call it mixtures of classical and jazz, some parts slow down and speed up and for that you definitely need a conductor.

> **WHOLE NOTE**
>
> Maria Schneider is a big band leader, composer, and arranger. The Maria Schneider Orchestra is one of the more innovative modern big bands playing today.

But for the most part, for high school jazz, when you're talking about young kids, they need to see somebody up there. They need to see somebody giving them a downbeat.

For me, to tell you the truth, I'm always, always thinking about the sound and the texture of the band. As the sound is coming toward me, I'm mixing it. I'm like the mixer on a mixing board. The sound knob. You know, the controls, on what I want to hear. Because it's my responsibility as a director to get the sound that I have in my head to the audience.

MM: How does your role change from rehearsals to the live performance?

MB: Well, rehearsals, we get to the nitty gritty. We get to all the hard passages. And, especially in rehearsals, I like to make sure everyone knows who they're playing a passage with.

For instance, let's say that it's an alto saxophone, trombone, trumpet *soli* line. Well, everyone's got to know that they're playing with those three people. They also have to know how that's supposed to blend. Most of the time, they're in tune. But if they get out of tune, who do they listen to, to get back in tune? Who is the primary focus? Who's got the lead? Who should play a little louder? Who should play a little softer?

> **DEFINITION**
>
> In big band music, **soli** refers to an entire section playing in harmony.

It's that sort of thing. Then you get into the soli stuff, working out sax solis, or trombone or trumpet solis. And dealing with the rhythm section, especially the drummer. Young drummers like to slam the drums. With the drums, yeah, they keep time but they're also a coloring agent. They help provide all the nuances that the music needs. Let's face it, a good drummer is a musician. Regular drummers really aren't.

MM: [laughs]

MB: But for me, the rehearsals are the big point. The rehearsals are where you say, "Okay, this is going to be open. I'm going to cue this in."

Now in a professional band, people will be writing automatically on their parts. In a college band, people will be sitting there like with lobotomies, looking at you. A lot of times, not all the time. Not my band. They know that if they don't bring a pencil, they're gone.

Kids think that they're going to remember all this stuff. And when it gets to a concert and the lights are different, there are people out there, you can't even remember your own first name sometimes. So I make sure that everything in rehearsal is written down and is very clear. This is when we're looking up. This is the beat we're gonna cut off on. We're gonna *crescendo* here, everyone's gonna *crescendo*. That's the way the music is shaped in the rehearsal.

MM: What do you do, as a conductor, when you're dealing with a student band and you get into a live performance and—it's going to happen sooner or later—something goes wrong?

MB: It just happened last night, Mike! It's funny you say that.

Last night we had a drummer who tried to fill a little bit too much, and he got off and was too stubborn to get back on. I just said, "Horns, here's where we are, here's where we are." Finally I looked at the drummer and gave the drummer a downbeat, "This is where we are, right here." For about 15 seconds it was really shaky.

I tell every student in my jazz techniques class, you're not ever going to be a conductor unless you've survived a train wreck. I mean, when something goes wrong onstage and panic sets in, you have to remain calm. Or it might even grind to a halt! I've been in three or four of those in my life. And they're not fun. You learn how to deal with that situation.

MM: *Now, a conductor can also affect the energy level of a performance, right?*

MB: Absolutely. A lot of times, when I conduct, if it's an open solo section, I'll walk away. If the band is swingin' and it's a big soli section, I'll walk away. I'm not gonna stand up there and conduct beats.

But I will get up there sometimes and conduct dynamics. They may think they're going to a certain level on their *crescendo*, and I'll want more. I'll make it visibly where I want it. And that particular attention to dynamics I think a lot of times makes the excitement happen.

Look at the Count Basie band. They're going along, [softly] "Ding ding da ding ding ding ding ding [louder] BA POW!" Everyone's head goes off, you know, "WOW!" That, to me, is where a lot of the excitement comes in, when the people reach dynamics.

MM: *In a pro ensemble, often the leader of the band is also a player in the band. I mean, you're a player in your own band. And you think Basie, you think Woody Herman, you think Buddy Rich. What are the challenges of trying to lead a band while you're also playing in it?*

MB: That's a great question, man. It's challenging. Let's put it this way: I used to stand up in front of the band. Not anymore. Now I just want to go and play in the trumpet section. Brent Wallarab gets up in front of the band, he doesn't even play anymore.

You're spending so much time listening to the band and paying attention to details, the last thing you want to do is play a part, standing up front. Now, you might play a solo standing up front, which is a lot different. But if I'm going to be a band leader up front, I'm not going to go up and play third trumpet from the front of the stage.

MM: *You're not going to blend with the section. You've got all sorts of issues.*

MB: Exactly. So most leaders who do will just play solos. And most successful leaders will play few solos.

I think it's very important, especially in these days, this economy, when people come out and have to play for $20 on a gig in a big band, the reason they're coming out is not to listen to you up front playing your solos. The reason they're coming out is because they're getting a chance to play good music and they're getting a chance to solo. So I make sure, in a professional situation, that everyone who wants to blow gets a chance to blow.

MM: *That brings up another issue. A big band's a smaller ensemble than an orchestra or a big symphonic choir, and you've got guys who are both section players and soloists. You're dealing with some egos there.*

MB: [laughs] You're asking the questions today, my friend! Yeah, you're dealing with a bunch of egos.

I guess the one thing that professional players have to realize is that when they walk in the door there's a coat rack over there, and it's not only for your coat, it's for your ego. You gotta check it at the door, man.

For instance, this one guy in the trumpet section was criticizing the chart because of the *Harmon mute*, the way a Harmon mute was written. And I leaned down the section, and I said "When's the last time you wrote a chart? In fact, I never remember you writing a chart."

> **DEFINITION**
>
> A **Harmon mute** is a type of trumpet mute designed to elicit a particular sound from the instrument.

MM: [laughs]

MB: Everyone's an expert.

That's the toughest part about leading a band, a professional band. College bands, you don't really get that. Professional bands, most of the time, don't get that. But every once in a while you deal with these egos that are just too big for the room.

MM: Another role of the band leader is choosing the charts, choosing the music. How do you approach that these days?

MB: Programming is very important. I like to have a variety of grooves. And, to tell you the truth, I don't like to put two tunes together, back to back, in the same key. I think variety is the spice of life.

The other thing is, programming is an art in itself. A good opener, the middle should build, and then it should drop off for a nice slow song, and then it should build again. There should be a couple of climaxes within a program. And you should have a strong closer. Most of the time people are going to remember that last tune the most as they walk out.

So I pay particular attention to programming. And I like a lot of different types of music.

When I'm programming my college ensemble, I like to expose them to a lot of different kinds of music. I'll have different themes for the concerts. Modern Big Bands. Music of the Thirties and Forties. Salsa. The Music of Bobby Watson. The Music of Maria Schneider. By exposing the college kids to many different kinds of varieties, they're going to be able to meet the demands when they get out into the professional world, because they've been exposed to so much.

In a professional band, especially the one I lead, we do a lot of our own original music. It has its own merits and it has its own curses. A lot of people haven't heard of it.

We've been very fortunate to have eight recordings and our name all over the place. We've been on NPR a lot. We've been on the jazz radio charts, getting up to number four. We've had a lot of exposure, thanks to our record label. So we're able to play a lot of our own music at concerts, while other big bands have to play repertoire music, of other bands.

MM: I was going to ask you about that. We've got 80 years or so now of repertoire in big band music, how do you get that mix between new stuff and old stuff?

MB: Here's how. We used to do a concert series, and we'd have a theme. Themes work great in today's world. You know, like The Music of Gil Evans, specifically *Porgy and Bess*. Another concert could be The Music of Duke Ellington, of a certain time period. The Music of Count Basie. All themed music. Or you can even have a particular slice of years that you're gonna do with different bands from those years.

Because of our CDs and our recordings, we can actually go out and say the Buselli-Wallarab Jazz Orchestra is going to play here, we're going to play the music of Mark Buselli and Brent Wallarab, and we'll get a crowd. Because people know this music, especially regionally now. Or the music of David Baker, which we put on our last CD ("Basically Baker," 2007, G.M. Recordings).

> **WHOLE NOTE**
>
> Dr. David Baker is a leading jazz composer and educator. He is Distinguished Professor of Music and Chairman of the Jazz Department at Indiana University School of Music, as well as conductor and artistic director of the Smithsonian Jazz Masterworks Orchestra.

A lot of bands have these themes and they have guest artists to lure the people in. When it comes down to it, in a big band you have to make money. Everything has to make money.

MM: *Or you have to be supported somehow. Up here in Minnesota we have lots of big bands, one of them is the JazzMN Orchestra. It's a publicly supported organization. They sell subscriptions and they put on a four-concert series each year. They're doing themes, they're doing guest artists, stuff like that. And they fill the house.*

> **WHOLE NOTE**
>
> The JazzMN Orchestra (www.jazzmn.org) is a nonprofit, community-supported big band in the Minneapolis/St. Paul area. In addition to their annual concert series, they conduct an educational outreach program for local high school and middle school students.

MB: We did that, too. We had a board of directors. We had people raising money for us. A lot of cities now have their own jazz orchestras.

Here's another thing, Mike. A person comes up to me and says, "I want to start a big band." He's 20 years old. I tell him, "Look at my hair. I used to have a full head of hair. See my hair now?"

Just the logistics of trying to organize things. Which makes me so amazed at these old big-time band leaders, without email. They have to put stuff together on the phone. Wow!

MM: *[laughs] Well, they did that or they had a contractor or something. But that speaks to another issue: You probably don't have the same personnel from gig to gig—or do you?*

MB: That's another great question. It depends on the depth of the city. Minneapolis is a lot bigger than Indianapolis, which would lead to more big bands, because there's a higher pool of talent. I'm sorry, but in Indianapolis there's an "A" pool of players I like to play with. After that, it drops off considerably.

MM: *You get a lot of good guys leaving town, or it's just not a big enough town, anyway.*

MB: When we have all of our "A" players, we can compete with any jazz orchestra around. When we have to get a couple of subs here and there, it dives.

MM: *Are you getting much new talent?*

MB: Yeah, there are kids coming up. There are some good jazz programs around the state. And we, as educators, try to use these kids. We try to bring 'em up.

That's met with support from most of the educators. And sometimes it's met with a lot of resistance from some of the pros who don't teach.

MM: *They don't like the competition, or what?*

MB: No, they don't feel that they should be there with students.

MM: *But if a cat's got talent, what's it matter?*

MB: Yeah, there are two different ways to look at it. So that's another thing that we deal with.

MM: *Back when I was playing, 35 years ago, there was kind of a big band resurgence in the '70s, with Woody Herman, Maynard Ferguson, Buddy Rich, Stan Kenton. So there was a lot of interest in the program then. How has the interest maintained over the years?*

MB: I'll tell you the truth, the interest has maintained through all these college programs.

MM: That's great.

MB: The college programs, to me, are the savior of the big band. As well as they should be. The big band is an integral part of American music. And in a big band, in a jazz orchestra, especially with all the great writers today, the John Hollenbecks, the Maria Schneiders, I'll put Brent Wallarab in that category, too. These people are such great arrangers and orchestrators that they can get so many sounds out of 16 pieces.

I'm mainly drawn to the new textures of sounds. I'm more of a modern big band person. I consider Ellington a modern big band. I mean, I love Basie, I love the blues, I love that whole feel and I think that kids should be exposed to it. I make sure that my second band at Ball State learns how to play that type of music, that they're exposed to it. But in my top band, I look to challenge them a little bit more, with different textures and rhythm and time. Especially time. Most big bands play in 4/4 all the time.

How has it changed? I take my hat off to the people who lead a big band. I take my hat off to them, because it's one of the hardest things to do and to keep it going, keep the morale going. One of the big things in morale is to have good music. Because everybody knows the deal, that's a musician. They know when you get called for a big band, hey, you're gonna have great music but not good pay.

Somebody a long time ago told me there are three things that can happen in music. You can have good money, good music, and a good hang with your friends. Now, if you have two of those, it's a great gig. If you have three of them, it's nirvana. It doesn't happen a lot.

MM: Most times you're lucky to have one.

MB: Exactly.

MM: So all of the different things you do, from the teaching to playing in the big band, different types of music, what is it you find most fulfilling in leading the big band?

MB: Oh, boy. It's when you're leading the big band, and you have 17 musicians on the same wavelength. For instance, if I play in a five-piece combo, that's pretty cool—especially when we're improvising and the band's together. Now you take that energy, you take that improvisation, you put it with 17 pieces. You can go from that five-piece combo to an incredible high. If the writer who knows what they're doing can shape music like that, it's a feeling that once you get done, it's like a drug. You want more.

When it's done right, to me it's the most exciting musical event in jazz. A great big band.

MM: I agree with you. That's why I love big bands. Always have. There's no more fun thing to play in than a big band.

MB: I mean, you go as a spectator and you've got 17 people you can watch. You never get tired of watching something. Then you have your soloists, then you have your lead players, and then you have your people blending. It's a team. It's like a big sports team.

> **WHOLE NOTE**
>
> This is an excerpt from a longer interview I conducted with Mark Buselli. You can read the entire interview online at www.idiotsguides.com/conducting.

The Least You Need to Know

- The leader of a pro-level big band is often a player/conductor, conducting only starts and endings.
- Student big bands often benefit from having a full-time conductor in front of the band.
- A big band conductor counts off the beginning of a tune but doesn't always do beat patterns throughout.
- You can also conduct cues and accents, cue in the band after solos, and conduct holds and cutoffs at the end of tunes.

Conducting Choirs

Chapter 18

In This Chapter

- Discover the basics of choral conducting
- Determine whether or not to use a baton
- Learn how to conduct youth choirs, community choirs, church choirs, and professional choirs
- An interview with choir conductor Dr. Eric Stark

So far we've looked at various types of instrumental conducting. Now it's time to turn to the vocal side, and look at the world of choir conducting.

Of course, there are a lot of different types of choirs out there—we like to sing. You may find yourself conducting a student choir, a church choir, a community choir, or a professional choir. Your choir might only have a dozen members or may have a hundred. It might be an all-women's choir or an all-men's choir, or a full SATB ensemble. You could even be conducting a children's choir.

Whatever type of choir you're conducting, you need to know some basics. That's what we'll examine in this chapter.

Conducting Differently—or Not

Here's a common question: Should a choir conductor use a baton?

Some vocal conductors say no. They feel that the baton is too rigid, and keeps the music from flowing as it should. Other vocal conductors say yes, for the same reason orchestral conductors use a baton. The baton helps define the beat, better than bare-handed gestures do.

Most conductors, however, say that it really doesn't matter. A good conductor can get results with or without a baton. Using a baton doesn't necessarily translate into a more rigid or staccato performance, just as not using one doesn't necessarily result in sloppy beat patterns. It's all a matter of what works for you.

So you can't define a choral conductor by whether or not she uses a baton. Choral conductors do not have to conduct bare-handed; use the technique you like best.

> **THE CONDUCTOR SEZ**
>
> I concur that it doesn't matter whether or not you use a baton. Good technique will inform your gestures and allow you to be expressive with a baton or precise without one. I will say, however, that if you're having issues with clarity, using a baton can keep you honest.

Learning Proper Choral Conducting Technique

I recently attended a choral concert at my local Lutheran church. (We have a lot of them up here in Minnesota.) The music was well chosen and well played, which speaks well to the choir director's talents. But as a conductor, she looked like some sort of demented butterfly in heat, with both arms flapping wildly in mirrored motions describing large, uneven circles in the air. I have no idea how the performers followed her; I certainly couldn't tell where "one" was.

Regrettably, this type of "untraditional" conducting is not unusual in the vocal world. Because a disproportionate number of choral conductors tend to be nonprofessionals (this is especially true in the ranks of church and student choirs), a certain laxness in conducting technique is common. That's unfortunate; choirs at all levels deserve and benefit from professional conducting. There's nothing that says a choir conductor shouldn't follow the same guidelines as an orchestral conductor.

That means using your right hand (baton or not) to conduct proper beat patterns. Not simplified beat patterns, like the down-left-right-up 4/4 pattern, but the full patterns where every beat has its own ictus on the horizontal plane. (Refresh your knowledge of beat patterns in Chapter 6.)

It also means using your left hand for more musical gestures—dynamics, cues, phrasing, and the like. It is not good technique, even in choral conducting, to mirror your hands.

What's different about conducting a choir, as opposed to conducting an instrumental ensemble? In terms of mechanics, they're pretty much the same. But there are unique issues involved with vocalists you'll have to deal with, especially during the rehearsal phase.

For instance, the choir director often functions as a vocal teacher, especially with student and even community choirs. Not all the singers in your choir will exhibit proper vocal techniques—a good stance, breathing, resonance, and so forth—which means if you want to achieve the best possible sound, you'll need to train your choir to sing properly.

Speaking of breathing, it's the conductor's role to instruct the choir when to breathe during a piece. It's all part of establishing the desired phrasing; you want everyone (or at least everyone in a section) to breathe at the same time, not wherever they feel like doing so. This is definitely an issue to address during rehearsals.

> **WHOLE NOTE**
>
> Good posture is part and parcel of proper vocal technique. The best way to encourage good posture in a choir is to exhibit the appropriate stance yourself while conducting.

The overall tone of the choir is also your responsibility. This relates to some degree to vocal training, but even properly trained vocalists may need instruction in developing the proper ensemble timbre.

You also have influence over the choir's diction—that is, how they shape their vowels and consonants, and pronounce the words they sing. At the most basic level, this requires a knowledge of the various languages texts are written in, but you'll also need to direct the attacks and releases inherent in producing vowel and consonant sounds.

> **THE CONDUCTOR SEZ**
>
> Good diction is defined as a combination of proper pronunciation (correctly sounding a word) with clear enunciation (pronouncing with great clarity).

Finally, and this probably goes without saying, you're responsible for everybody singing in tune—or, more accurately, encouraging all your singers to be responsible for tuning. Intonation is a challenge even for professional choirs; it's a real bear when you're dealing with students or part-time singers. It pays to spend a decent amount of rehearsal time working through intonation exercises, and to make intonation awareness an active habit.

> **FERMATA**
>
> Avoid the temptation to sing along with the choir while you're conducting. If you do so, it'll be difficult to hear the choir over the sound of your own voice—and thus distract from your ability to conduct.

Conducting Youth Choirs

Let's take a specific look at the topic of conducting youth and student choirs. Whether we're talking a school choir or a community youth choir, the challenges are similar.

Probably the most important factor in conducting young singers is knowing the abilities of your singers—which will vary wildly by age. You need to pick music that's appropriate for the choir's age level, and that can be successfully sung by your particular singers.

Conducting Elementary School Singers

When you're conducting at the elementary school level, it pays to keep it simple. We're talking kids with little or no formal training as yet; they may not even be able to read music. In addition, they probably don't have the attention span to tackle pieces that require a lot of individual practice.

To this end, you should avoid choosing songs with complicated rhythms and large leaps; stick to easy step-wise lines. Most elementary-level choirs have just one or two vocal parts—a boys part and a girls part, perhaps—and the younger the choir, the more likely they are to sing (or attempt to sing) in unison.

Conducting Middle School Singers

When you get to middle school (grades six through eight), the singers have a bit more training under their belts—but now you have to face the challenge of changing voices. And it's not only the boys' voices that change; the girls' voices are maturing as well.

Boys whose voices have not yet changed will sing what may be labeled a "tenor" part, although the actual voice is in the female soprano or alto range. Boys whose voices *have* changed don't quite graduate to bass status just yet. Instead, they're more apt to sing in the baritone range, notated on the bass clef.

Girls' voices at this age are starting to mature, but still tend to fall in a generic middle—they haven't yet separated into true higher (soprano) and lower (alto) ranges. You're likely to find girls' parts in the low soprano range, though typically in two parts.

This adds up to a three-voice choir comprised of soprano I, soprano II (sometimes labeled alto or tenor), and baritone. This lets you choose slightly more challenging material, although you should still watch out for anything too complicated.

Conducting High School Singers

By the time you get to high school, most of the singers' voices have changed, so you have traditional soprano, alto, tenor, and bass voices. However, high school vocal ranges are not quite as wide as the fully developed adult ranges, so you need to watch out for pieces written in the extremes.

Here's another reason to avoid music with extreme ranges for high school singers. Youthful voices pushed to the extremes not only tire easily, they sound thin, strained, and dynamically weak. For the best tone, you want music that stays in the beefy part of each range, and doesn't veer too much into the zone of passage from the singer's lower to upper registers.

> **WHOLE NOTE**
> Whatever age choir you're conducting, choose songs that are appropriate for the abilities of your choir. For example, if you're conducting a relatively young children's choir, choose music written in unison or two parts. Move to three- and four-part arrangements only when you're working with a more experienced choir.

Conducting Community Choirs

The community choir is a common but odd beast. Every town and community seems to have one or more, so most choir conductors have had community choir experience at some point in their lives. The challenge comes in the typical mix of trained and untrained voices; it's not quite an amateur choir, but also definitely not professional level.

This mix of trained and untrained singers makes for a unique challenge both in programming the music and conducting rehearsals. You have to pick music that challenges the more talented singers in the choir, while at the same time keeping in mind the limitations of the lesser-trained singers. In addition, you need to keep in mind the size of the choir; music meant for large, professionally trained choirs will be difficult to pull off if you have a smaller, less-capable group of singers.

Rehearsing a community choir is especially tricky, as you're typically dealing with adults doing this in their spare time. You can't be *too* demanding, or they won't show up at the next rehearsal. On the other hand, you need to encourage the necessary amount of work to achieve the sound you want. It's a management issue.

> **THE CONDUCTOR SEZ**
>
> It is a fine balancing act, challenging your singers yet allowing them to succeed immediately with "bulletproof" pieces, moving fast but finding moments to really teach difficult sections. It takes time to develop a sense of things in this world.

Because some singers will be stronger than others, you may find it difficult to achieve a pleasing blend with a community choir. It's the danger of individualism; strong singers will stand out like a vocal sore thumb, and not blend in with the rest of the choir. Blending gets easier the more singers you have, but you may need to have an aside with any singer who's just a little too good for the overall ensemble—but not quite good enough to recognize the blending issue.

You can also achieve a better blend by stressing the importance of listening during rehearsals. Ask singers to listen closely to others in their section and try to match the sound they hear. Encourage uniform pronunciation of vowels and consonants, and work hard on group phrasing. Then just work, work, work on blend and balance during the rehearsals; good results take time.

> **THE CONDUCTOR SEZ**
>
> One of the dangers with avocational choirs is a lack of rhythmic precision. Never settle for sloppy rhythms. It's a fine choir that sings with precision!

Conducting Church Choirs

The church choir is a unique form of community choir. Like a community choir, you're typically working with a mix of trained and untrained singers of various ages. You also have the challenge of infrequent rehearsals, typically after work during the week.

With a church choir, however, you have the added challenge of choosing from acceptable nonsecular repertoire. You can't just pick any old song for the choir to sing; it has to carry the message of your church, and perhaps of that day's sermon or scripture readings.

And it goes without saying that the music you choose has to be achievable by the singers in your choir. If you're weak in the men's voices (which many church choirs are), don't choose music that requires a powerful bass presence. The worst church choirs are those where the choir director's ambitions don't fit the choir's abilities; the best are those where the music matches the available talent.

> **THE CONDUCTOR SEZ**
>
> Many publishers put out quality repertoire for just this situation. SAB (soprano, alto, baritone) pieces allow for more women than men yet provide balanced voicing for a choir with a weak men's section.

When in doubt, simpler is better. Avoid music with notes that are too high or too low. Be wary of arrangements with lots of fast-moving notes, difficult syncopated rhythms, or lines with too many wide skips. With new music being performed every week or so, you simply don't have time to tackle overly challenging pieces. Of course, this is just a safe place to start; as your group improves over time, you can try more challenging repertoire.

In addition, many church choir directors are responsible for choosing and leading the hymns sung by the congregation. In some churches, this duty is shared with the minister, or even assumed by the minister. What you have to watch out for in this situation is a minister choosing hymns that reinforce the message of that day's sermon, but that are not musically suited for the amateur singers in your congregation. (I can't tell you how many times I've sat through a service with absolutely unsingable music—but with words that fit that day's sermon.)

In this situation, you have to gently nudge the minister one way or another. Maybe you can suggest some alternate hymns, or provide a list of on-topic hymns for the minister to choose from. Even better, many denominations have resources available that list hymns suitable for the day's readings or current liturgical season.

If worse comes to worst, use your prerogative as music leader to limit the number of verses that a congregation has to muddle through when the tune is too tough. You can also have your choir learn the melody and sing the first verse alone to help the congregation learn the new tune.

> **THE CONDUCTOR SEZ**
>
> I have always maintained that the job of the church choir director is threefold. There is a triangle to balance—musical aspects (obvious; know your art!), professional aspects (show up on time, etc.), and spiritual aspects. Unfortunately, this last one gets frequently left behind. While not required, the church choir director often serves as the "shepherd" of the choir and ensures that they are spiritually fulfilled. To many of these folks, singing in a church/temple choir is a big part of their personal worship. Be sensitive to this.

Conducting Professional Choirs

If all goes well, you'll eventually find yourself conducting a group of professional singers. This is a real joy; you get to spend less time on basic vocal techniques, and more time on tackling more challenging music.

Of course, you face the same issues as you do with other types of choirs, just at a different level. You still need to focus on blending voices and achieving the overall choral tone, on breathing and phrasing, and on choosing the appropriate repertoire. But you can quickly move beyond these issues and get the most out of your choir; a new world of sophisticated choral music is now within reach.

Conducting in the Real World: An Interview with Eric Stark

When it comes to conducting choirs, few conductors have the breadth of experience as Dr. Eric Stark, Artistic Director and conductor of the Indianapolis Symphonic Choir. Eric also serves as Associate Professor of Music at Butler University's Jordan College of Fine Arts, where he conducts the Butler Chorale and Chamber Singers, teaches courses in conducting and choral literature, and serves as coordinator of the school's vocal and choral areas. Eric also served as chorus master for Madonna's half-time extravaganza at Super Bowl XLVI in Indianapolis—a once-in-a-lifetime opportunity. He blogs about his musical experiences at the Indy Sings blog (www.indysings.blogspot.com).

I've known Eric for a number of years. He was the technical advisor on another of my books, *The Complete Idiot's Guide to Singing* (co-written with our mutual friend Phyllis Fulford, Alpha Books, 2003), and I thought he could provide some good insight to budding choir conductors in this book.

We started the interview by talking about how choir conducting differs from orchestral or band conducting.

MICHAEL MILLER (MM): *You conduct both choirs and orchestras, in the course of things. How different is conducting instruments versus conducting people?*

ERIC STARK (ES): On one level, not very. You know, the conducting patterns are the same and a lot of the gestural vocabulary is the same from one to the other. However, there are things that instrumentalists respond to more than singers, and vice versa, that kind of fall into the realm of the music psychology, if you will. You know, things like posture.

Good posture from a conductor's standpoint is important for everybody to see because it helps them remember how posture is important for them, whether they are playing an instrument or singing. But particularly with singers who are using their bodies as their instruments, we want to model good, upright posture, so that they can have maximum, effective use of their breath, their physical apparatus, their abdominal muscles, that sort of thing. So stuff like that is important because singers make sounds so differently from how instrumentalists do.

I think that particularly the role of the hands is different in front of singers, as opposed to when you are in front of instrumentalists. I sometimes envision that I'm forming the words with my own fingertips and imparting that instruction to the singers I'm in front of—which is obviously different than with an orchestra.

Then there's a whole realm of rehearsal techniques that work with instrumentalists that don't work with singers—and vice versa. Just because the instrumentalists I work with are professional musicians, they've got advanced degrees in music, they've been studying their instruments for a couple of decades or more, and oftentimes the singers I'm working with are either young people at my university job or dedicated volunteers with my adult chorus who may have had some voice lessons or some music study but very likely have not had as an advanced level of that. So you use a different vocabulary when you are talking with them.

It's kind of a yes and no answer to that question, depending on what is actually being communicated and what you are trying to accomplish. Some things are the same and some are really different.

> **THE CONDUCTOR SEZ**
>
> I agree with Eric that the musical vocabulary is the largest difference between instrumental and vocal conducting. I certainly use much more imagery with singers (especially young singers) than I do with professional orchestras. Pros only want to hear "louder … softer … faster … slower." Student singers and avocational singers often want more color.

MM: Now, rehearsal is key in conducting. Just how do you approach a choir rehearsal?

ES: That's so true. I know some people who tell me that they enjoy rehearsing more than they do performing. I certainly enjoy the rehearsal process a lot. But I always try to leave something there for the performance that we haven't experienced before, so that performance can be the truly special thing.

I always try to set some goals for myself and for the group when I'm starting a rehearsal. Sometimes I'll write these down on a notepad, you know, the approximate amount of time that I'll spend on each piece and what I want to do, are we just reading it for the first time so we want to hear what it sounds like and get it on its feet, or are we nearing the performance date and we're polishing and refining. So what I do in the rehearsal varies a lot depending on where we are in that process.

Sometimes I'll know what I want to hear before I walk in. And other times I want to hear it in the choir before I make some final decisions, so I'm listening and evaluating and responding to what the singers bring. And I'd like to think that the singers have interpretive, artistic ideas themselves and if they, as a choir, present something to me that maybe I hadn't even thought of, that I could be open to that offering and possibility and respond in a way that allows that to take place. In other words, I'm not so set in stone as to whatever my own ideas were that I wouldn't consider doing it perhaps another way. I think that's the best kind of aesthetic process.

MM: Well that's an interesting concept; we all know that different conductors can make the same choirs sound different. What you are saying is that having the same conductor doesn't mean two choirs will sound identical, either.

ES: Yeah, I think that's true. You know, the whole process of performing music and making music is so mystical, in a way that we never can really fully describe what is happening.

But to your first point, I teach conducting, so I have a class full of 13 students. They all get up and conduct the same thing with the same people playing it or singing it. But it sounds different every time because of the subtle cues that they emit and the musicians pick up on. It's really fascinating, that's a fascinating concept to see. It's as different as fingerprints, in a way.

MM: When you are teaching conducting classes, what are the key things that you try and get across to your students?

ES: In my basic conducting class, the students are learning for the very first time how to conduct. So we're doing basic patterns and kind of a basic gestural vocabulary, and also working with them to feel physically comfortable in front of a group.

It can be a little like public speaking for some of them, you know, to stand up in front of one's peer group and lead them in a way that you've never really done before. It can be intimidating and frightening for some. Other students love it and have no trouble with it, but, I want to break down the emotional or psychological barrier to their comfort, because in order to be an effective conductor we have to be comfortable being up there and being a leader. Then giving them some basic rehearsal techniques when they're working with voices or working with instruments.

It's likely that the name of every instrument on an orchestra stage could appear in the score in English or in German or in French or in Italian. So somewhere along the lines you've got to study a vocabulary list that has all of those foreign language terms in it, so that doesn't throw you when you see it in the real world.

Then, with my graduate students, we presume that they've had a year or two of conducting study already and probably also have had some professional experience conducting a school group or a church group or an orchestra. So we can work more on some advanced concepts, like recitative conducting, which we find in opera or oratorios. This is really very challenging and it's kind of where the proof is in the pudding for conductors. If you can conduct recitative, you should be able to conduct everything. So with my advanced students we'll often do little recitatives from Mendelssohn's *Elijah*, or from a Mozart opera, or other kinds of things to get them experience with that.

I tell my students that anybody can be a song leader, anybody can stand up in front of a group and say "Okay, one, two, ready, go," then the piece starts and the tempo doesn't change until you get to the end and then it's over. Anybody can swing their arms to that. But to effectively conduct recitative, you have to really accompany the singer or soloist; stop, start, change tempo and give cues and cutoffs and all that sort of thing, kind of on the fly. So that stuff we don't get into in the basics—not for the first year, certainly.

MM: *About the personality of the conductor. I mean, if you're really, really shy and you stand in front of a group of people, it's going to be difficult. Just how strong willed do you need to be?*

ES: We talk about a concept in my class called "impulse of will." I didn't coin that phrase, it came to mind, it's in the textbook we use. But that's the evidence that the conductor has a way he or she wants it to go and it's obvious to everyone in the room. So that's kind of the vision that's guiding. And we've all seen conductors who do that very effectively and we've also seen, unfortunately, sometimes conductors who don't have a clear idea of what they want. In my experience, those are often very frustrating rehearsals because you end up chasing something that nobody can identify with in person. You never achieve that goal. It's that sense of vision that the conductor has in mind, and either speaks about or shows in the gesture that I think all of the musicians want to rally around and support and arrive at.

MM: *You know, the worst situation to me, as a player, is when you have the conductor kind of being led around by the players, as opposed to the other way around.*

ES: Yeah, if the conductor doesn't know what she wants to hear, it's impossible for it to be successful. Because there are so many decisions and, you know, if you're a string player you want to know, is this note long or short, is it on the string or off the string, or is this a *legato* phrase or *staccato*, how do you want it? And if they haven't made those decisions, then you're going to get kind of a Heinz 57 instead of an interpretation that's true to one person's kind of vision of the piece.

MM: *Some of that confidence and knowing what you need to do really speaks to prep work. How much prep work does a conductor need to do?*

ES: That's an issue that I struggle to impart with my own students, and the importance of it. Because, really, there's no finite number that tells you, okay, you spent this many hours on it, you should be ready. I never really feel ready to conduct a piece until I've performed it. I think I'm a pretty dedicated score studier, but no matter how much time I spend, I always feel like there is more I want to learn.

I had a teacher who told me that it should be clear to everybody in the room that the conductor is the person who knows more than anybody else about the piece, about the composer, about the contents, about all of those things. So it's not just knowing what's on the manuscript page, the dots and the rhythms and all that, but it's knowing the history of the piece, when it was written in the composer's lifetime, what else was going on that might have impacted how it came to be. If there is text, where that came from.

That's just hundreds of hours of research on a major work that can take a long, long time. When I'm preparing myself to conduct a major work, something that's an hour in length, of course an orchestra or larger, I'm studying the piece usually a year in advance—and sometimes longer and farther out than that, if I'm really scared of it.

MM: *This speaks to knowing the score but also knowing the parts, the instruments or the voices. How good of a singer does the conductor need to be?*

ES: That's a good question, and probably you can find a variety of opinions on that. For years there was a kind of an old school philosophy that conductors needed to be virtuosos on something before they would be entitled to the podium, because they need to have the chops and the musicianship that will allow them to earn the respect of the players. There are still some conductors who feel that way, and I think that's a valid and interesting perspective.

But more recently, since the '50s and '60s, there is the rise, really in this country, of doctoral level conducting scholarships. There is another philosophy that says somebody who has a Masters and/or a Doctorate in conducting from one of the leading institutions has demonstrated their scholarship, their skill, their intelligence, musicianship that way. So maybe they have taken piano or voice or another instrument along the way and they're pretty good at it, but they wouldn't be a soloist necessarily, as a professional, on that thing, but they understand how it works.

I was a piano student and a voice student, myself. I never soloed on either of those, in terms of a recital, nor would I. But I understand how the voice works, I've studied voice a lot. I studied vocal pedagogy and I can teach voice through the choral rehearsal for singers who are amateurs. And I can give instructions that get a group of voice majors, my university group, to all sing in the same way.

You know, I'm a big fan of a choir shouldn't sing Bach the same way it sings Rachmaninoff, the same way it sings George Gershwin. A different color should be used for each of those, so that requires a skillful kind of operation of the voice, to give those colors. The same can be said about instruments. So the more technical you can be, the more effective, I think you can impart your ideas to an ensemble. And especially singers, because unlike, say, the violin, we don't see what the larynx is doing when you are singing. It's inside the body. So you have to often talk in imagery and sensations and that can be a little loosey goosey at times. You want to choose your words carefully so people have the right concept in mind.

MM: *It seems to me that, especially when you're conducting student level choirs, part of your job is being a teacher, isn't it?*

ES: Sure. I think every choir rehearsal, in a way, can be a voice lesson. I am very eager that all of my singers sing in a way that is healthy and that helps the voice grow and thrive. I would never ask a singer to do something that could physically harm the voice and I feel like I can teach good voice management to beginners, intermediate, and advanced students, and that's part of what I'm expected to do. So there is an ongoing lesson plan at work, especially with singers.

MM: Now, you conduct both student singers and older, more adult singers in the Indianapolis Symphonic Choir. How does that differ?

ES: I wonder that myself sometimes, when they surprise me. The adults who sing in the Symphonic Choir are there because they are choosing to do that as their avocational pursuit. So they are very, very dedicated. They rehearse three hours every Tuesday night, and weeks that we have a performance, more than that. Usually every night we will have a rehearsal for three and a half to four hours.

MM: I should probably explain for the readers of the book, the Symphonic Choir has singers of all ages. Some of them are college students, and some are, well, who's the oldest person in the choir, someone in their 60s or 70s, probably?

ES: Yeah. Actually, I have a soprano in the choir who has been singing for almost 40 years and she's just turned 81.

MM: Oh man. I know my wife sang for the Symphonic Choir back when she was a college student at IU. She did it for a year or so.

ES: Yeah. We re-audition the group every year so everybody has to pass an audition year after year to maintain their membership in the choir. The group gets better and better, and each year I end up having to cut some people, which is never enjoyable but, if you want to be good, that's what you've got to do.

MM: So what are the real challenges in, I wouldn't call it a community choir, but it's a group of people who come together once a week to do this, what are the challenges in conducting that kind of group?

ES: I think for me the challenge of knowing the music and having a vision of what I want to have happen with the piece and a rehearsal, is the first challenge.

The next one is communicating my ideas clearly through the gestures. I sometimes tell people jokingly that I got a doctorate in nonverbal communication. Because that's really what it is, the body language, the facial expressions, and the arms, communicating with the singers and my accompanist and an orchestra when we are doing something together like that.

And then the next challenge is not only having a rehearsal plan but also being able to depart from it if you sense that it's not working. If a better idea emerges in the midst of a rehearsal and you don't pursue it because it's not what you wrote down the day before in your rehearsal outline, that's pretty stupid. If folks will work faster than you thought they could, then you should pick up the pace and work with them.

I also find it a bit of a challenge to challenge the singers to work quickly and efficiently. I hate wasting time and I want to reward my best singers by keeping them challenged and stimulated, even if it means the singers who are less experienced might be a little bit frustrated. Because my philosophy is that the frustrated ones either will work harder and try to learn and come along and move up in their own skill level or they'll drop away and maybe go sing at a church or something like that, which would be fine. I'd rather satisfy the best singers that I have and keep them challenged and engaged, even if it means risking losing some of the bottom. I'd rather do that than work toward the bottom of the group and frustrate my best vocalists because I'm not going fast enough.

MM: Yeah, you don't want to lose your best performers.

ES: Exactly.

MM: Do you have any rehearsal tricks that you like to use?

ES: With the Symphonic Choir, I spend about 15 minutes doing vocal exercises at the beginning of every rehearsal, to get the body and the voice and the brain ready for singing. Some of that is a little trickery, I would guess.

You know, I think all conductors have to be psychiatrists a little bit and understand group dynamics. Especially when amateur singers get together, you want to pull them out of their shell a little bit and you want them to sing heartily and without worrying about what other people will think. So part of what I do in the warmup is loud and really crazy sounding, because I know if I can get them doing that comfortably then they'll do their best without being sheepish or shy during the actual rehearsal.

> **THE CONDUCTOR SEZ**
>
> Unlike with instrumental groups, when you make a mistake as a singer, you can't look at your instrument and blame it for the error. With singing, it's all you! As a choral conductor, you must create a rehearsal environment that allows hearty mistakes—an environment that respects effort and the journey toward perfection, not just the destination.

Then, during the rehearsal, some of the tricks I use are count singing, which is a technique that Robert Shaw developed where you take the text away but you just sing on numbers—one, two, three, four. I'm sure you are familiar with that.

Or taking pitches away and singing rhythms and texts on an open fourth harmony where the basses might be on an F and the tenors on a B-flat or the altos on a B-flat and the sopranos on an A-flat. So harmonically it doesn't really sound like anything, but it allows them to really concentrate their efforts on rhythm and text and articulation, that sort of thing. Taking away certain elements so that we can focus on the element that needs it the most is a really helpful way to break down a complex issue at hand when you are trying to sing a big piece.

And then gauging the energy of the room, when would it be a good idea for them to stand up and sing a little bit and get a boost of energy that way. Or, if they have been standing a while, maybe they need to sit. When can they stand to work in a very detailed slow pace polishing, or when do they need to just sing through and let their hair down. And when do they need to hear a joke, or a funny story or something.

In a three-hour rehearsal, especially in that last hour, they kind of need that. And if you can get them laughing, of course that's good for the singing muscles first of all, because it gets everything moving and energized. But it kind of lightens the mood and it'll mean that they can hunker down another 15 or 20 minutes and give you good effort right there at the end.

MM: So after you have done all of your rehearsals and now it's the night of the performance, what changes from the rehearsal to the performance?

ES: I feel like it's not really me leading the performance. I try to leave the window open for the muse, if you will, to pop in and whisper some sort of a divine or artistic inspiring thought as we're standing there on the stage. So I don't make hard and fast tempo decisions. Or take dynamic level, if it occurs to me in the moment this would be really nice if it were something much softer than we have ever rehearsed it. I try to prepare my singers to be ready for that.

I think the performance that goes exactly the way it was rehearsed can feel a little stale sometimes. I really like there to be a sense of spontaneity and inspiration and fresh newness on the stage, because I think the audience picks up on that and it can be a really exciting, very special thing.

So I feel like I'm kind of like a cook, you know. I spend all my time preparing the ingredients and making sure the oven temperature is right, that everything gets mixed together, but I don't put it on the table until that night and we'll see how it goes.

MM: *So what, personally, what do you like most about conducting?*

ES: It just feels like it is perfectly made for me. I love leadership. I love rallying people around a common cause. And that's different from bossing people around, that's not what it is. But I think I'm good at that.

I love music. I love musicianship. I love working on a phrase to get its inner beauty or specialness to come out. I love sharing that with people and I find that in the rehearsal and concert stage. It's really a priceless kind of a thing. And it's really gratifying to be a person that helps nonprofessional musicians experience that.

You know, this is my bread and butter. This is my nine-to-five, and I love it. But this is what many of my volunteer singers do after they have worked a 40-hour week. And they love it, it becomes super important in their lives, as important as relationships with their family in some cases. So that's really gratifying and special to be a part of something like that.

And the pieces that we get to perform and I get to conduct are very special to me. They only live if somebody chooses to perform them, you know, they are not like paintings where you put them on the wall and they're always there. It's only when you open the book and work and get the dots off the page that Beethoven comes alive, or Bach, and it's pretty special that we're entrusted with that responsibility.

MM: *Any final words for the person who aspires to be a conductor—or, in some cases, just kind of has it thrust upon them?*

ES: That happens a lot, you know. It's like in a church setting, where somebody studied violin and we need a church choir director and you had violin lessons, so why don't you do this? As far as I'm concerned, it's not so much about what you're like when you're conducting and where your arms go, as what's in your head and your leadership skills.

So my advice for those people would be to pick music that you are passionate about and that you're excited to share with people, and then bring them to your understanding of that piece. And I think, almost no matter what you do with your arms, you'll be successful.

> **WHOLE NOTE**
>
> This is an excerpt from a longer interview I conducted with Eric Stark. You can read the entire interview online at www.idiotsguides.com/conducting.

The Least You Need to Know

- Choir conductors can use a baton, or not.
- Choir conductors should use the same beat patterns and left-hand gestures as instrumental conductors.
- Choosing appropriate repertoire is important for conductors of all levels of singers.
- Conducting younger and untrained singers involves a degree of vocal coaching.
- Conducting community and church choirs is challenging because of the mix of trained and untrained voices.

Conducting Musicals and Shows

Chapter 19

In This Chapter

- Learn how to conduct musical theater
- Find out how to conduct opera
- Discover how to conduct other types of live shows
- Interviews with Broadway conductors Dave Hahn, Larry Yurman, and Eric Stern

We've covered conducting orchestras and other instrumental ensembles. We've covered conducting choral ensembles. But there are a few points where the instrumental and choral worlds meet—and they represent unique challenges to a conductor.

In particular, I'm talking about the world of the stage—musical theater, operas, and other live, in-concert shows, where you have to conduct both an orchestra and vocalists. There's fun stuff here.

Conducting Musical Theater

Let's start with musical theater—conducting musicals. This is a unique challenge, in a number of different ways.

First, you're in a pit—actually, in *the* pit. This is a recessed area typically in front of and sometimes a little beneath the stage itself. The musicians sit with their backs to the stage; you, the conductor, face the musicians and the stage. (Your back is to the audience, of course.)

The pit is a rather confined area, dark and a bit claustrophobic if you're so inclined. In a typical musical you have a couple of dozen musicians crammed into this dreary space, and the sound kind of echoes around and around before it goes out and up. You'd think that, given the small space, visibility wouldn't be an issue, but it is; given how musicians are crammed into every nook and cranny, it's often difficult to achieve a good line of sight with all the players.

> **WHOLE NOTE**
>
> The number of musicians in the pit differs with the type of organization. School and community musicals tend to have more people in the pit; Broadway musicals have fewer; regional productions have fewer still. In some instances, certain parts are played on synthesizers or via prerecorded tracks.

The challenge here is conducting both the musicians in the pit and the performers on the stage. And it isn't even that simple; you have to both follow and lead the stage performers. What they're doing is keyed on the music from the pit, but also cues the music. It's a bit of a puzzle getting all the pieces to fit together.

And remember, you're conducting both singers (on stage) and instrumentalists (in the pit). You have to have strong vocal and instrumental conducting fundamentals to work with both these worlds.

In terms of conducting technique, the basic stuff works—standard beat patterns in your right hand, musical gestures in your left. You definitely want to use a baton, but be careful about using a longer one; given the confined space, you may end up poking the nearest players if your baton is too long, or if your gestures are too extravagant.

In some instances, you have to work with either a click track or prerecorded instrumental tracks. That means you need to wear headphones and somehow mix what you're hearing in the phones with what you're hearing from the live musicians. It also means you have to follow the click or prerecord, while still following the action on stage. Tricky, that.

Some situations call for the conductor to also play in the pit. Typically this means a dual role as conductor and keyboardist. This is a little tricky, although helped a bit by the smaller size of the ensemble and the amount of practice you get in rehearsals—and in just performing the same show night after night after night. Still, playing two roles can be challenging.

In many productions, conductors actually serve as music directors. That is, conducting is just part of the job. As the music director, you're also responsible for rehearsing the stage performers, working through arrangements, editing things during the rehearsal process, and so forth. You interface with the director of the show, of course, as well as the choreographer and the stage manager. It's a group production, and you're just one (very important) cog in the machine. As such, it helps to have some orchestration chops in your bag—especially when you're working on a new production. Songs and arrangements evolve over the course of rehearsals and tryouts, and you may be called upon to change the music on the fly. You have to be able to adapt.

The challenges don't stop there, of course. You have to deal with an ever-changing cast of musicians, the egos of stage actors, the vagaries of audience reaction, you name it. The actual conducting may end up being the lesser part of the job—even though that's the one thing that's relatively constant from night to night.

Finally, the role of the conductor is different in musical theater than it is with traditional orchestral, band, or choral conducting. In the types of music I've discussed previously, the conductor has significant influence on how the music is interpreted. Not so on the stage; while the conductor is equally important to the production, his role is to accurately reproduce, night after night, the intent of the show's composer. When a couple goes to see a Broadway musical, they don't want to see a particular conductor's interpretation of the score; they want to see the show as it was designed to be seen. The conductor works in service to the composer (and the book writer, of course).

Because there's so much involved in the production of a stage musical, I interviewed three Broadway music directors/conductors to gain their input. Their interviews are at the end of this chapter; you should find them highly informative.

Conducting Opera

Musical theater is a popular entertainment. More serious in nature is its close relation, the opera—which itself was the popular entertainment of its day.

Conducting opera is similar in its challenge to conducting musical theater. You have to possess both vocal and instrumental conducting techniques, and manage both singers and instrumentalists.

The orchestra for an opera is placed in a pit in front of the stage, similar to but larger than a typical musical pit. The size of the orchestra is similar to that of a traditional symphonic orchestra, so you're working with a lot of musicians—including the soloists and chorus on stage.

As with musical theater, you have to conduct both the on-stage singers and the pit musicians. You also, to a degree, have to follow the on-stage performers—with one particularly unique conducting challenge.

The big thing that's different in opera is the use of the recitative. I discussed recitative back in Chapter 14, so I won't repeat myself here. Suffice to say that a recitative is a passage for a solo vocalist, typically with limited instrumental accompaniment, that can flow outside standard tempo. Literally, the text is sung or recited in a kind of speaking pace, predominantly set by the singer.

Your job as the conductor is follow—and lead, just a little—the vocalist through this passage, while also leading the orchestra through their accompanying parts. It's one of the most challenging forms of conducting out there, definitely not for beginners.

> **THE CONDUCTOR SEZ**
>
> The recitative is typically used to present narrative material at a fast pace, so the emotion of the moment can be expressed in the arias. Story in the recitative, reaction to the story in the arias.

Conducting Live Shows

Then we have what I'll just call live shows—concert performances where you're conducting some combination of instruments and singers through a selection of songs. There are all sorts of live shows you may encounter—the backing band for *American Idol*–type shows, the accompaniment for a local beauty pageant, the orchestra for a big-time awards show, you name it.

What all these performances have in common is that you're conducting a group of musicians (mostly instrumentalists, sometimes backing singers) that accompany one or more lead singers on stage. You have to lead the orchestra or band while following the singer(s)—while also providing a little leadership for the singers as well. Typical musical theater stuff, really.

It gets dicey when you consider how quickly put together most of these shows are. Unlike a stage musical or opera, each of which go through weeks or months of rehearsals, a typical live show might have one or two rehearsals—if you're lucky. I've participated in several of these things where you have just a single dress rehearsal the day before or afternoon of the performance; I've even done a few where there was no rehearsal at all, and everyone involved was sight reading.

That's flying on the edge, folks, which carries with it a certain level of excitement. (Or fear, depending.) As the conductor, everyone involved is depending on you to tell them what they need to do—and you get to do it pretty much on the fly. It's a lot of thinking on your feet, a lot of adapting in real time, a lot of hoping and praying you all get through this together.

When it works, it's exhilarating. When it doesn't—well, you just hope not too many people remember those moments. The focus is on the performers on stage, after all; your job is to make them look and sound as good as possible.

> **THE CONDUCTOR SEZ**
>
> When dealing with events that are broadcast live, you know there's someone in the production booth who cares more about timing than quality. You want to keep that person happy by sticking to the timetable—an important skill for any conductor leading live, televised events. Hit your mark or they'll find someone else who will!

Conducting in the Real World: An Interview with Dave Hahn

In preparing for this chapter, I had the good fortune to interview three—count 'em, three!—successful conductors of Broadway shows. Each had a unique personal perspective to add to the discussion.

My first interview was with David J. Hahn. Dave is an upcoming pianist, songwriter, and conductor in New York. He conducted the Broadway production of *Priscilla, Queen of the Desert* and the North American tour of *Wonderful Town*, and is currently serving as Associate Conductor for the Broadway revival of *On a Clear Day You Can See Forever*, under Music Director Larry Yurman. (I interviewed Larry, too—that's the next one coming up.)

I first became aware of Dave and his work through the Musicians Wages website (www.musicianswages.com), of which he is the co-founder and frequent contributor. His own website is www.davidjhahn.com.

As someone who's had the unique experience of working with both Broadway and touring productions, I wanted Dave to comment on how conducting on the road differs from conducting on Broadway itself.

MICHAEL MILLER (MM): *Conducting in a touring experience versus on Broadway, how does that differ?*

DAVE HAHN (DH): Well, the conducting is pretty much the same. You know, a show is a show; an orchestra is an orchestra. You do the same thing on the road that you do on Broadway.

But, you know, the lifestyle is a lot different. When we were on *Wonderful Town*, it was a bus and truck tour, which means you're on a bus and the set is on a truck and you go from one town to the next. Usually on bus and truck tours, you have one nighters, which on split weeks means you're a half week in Memphis and the other half the week you're in, like, Texas. So that can be grueling.

MM: I would imagine. What do you do with your days?

DH: Most of the days are spent on a bus. In nine months we drove 25,352 miles!

MM: Eeps.

DH: In nine months! That's three times around the earth, or something like that. So you spend a lot of time on the bus.

MM: Yeah.

DH: That is its own thing, that's a tough job, because you never really leave. On Broadway you have the luxury of going home after the show is done, sleeping in your own bed. I know none of this has to do with conducting, but in the end it does a bit, because it's a different job, as far as management goes.

MM: I was reading on your Musicians Wages blog, which I love by the way, at one point you wrote a post where you were talking about the difficulties of being on the road and associating with the other people on the tour. Because you're their boss and yet you're on the bus with them every day.

DH: That's right. Well, I go back and forth on that. I mean, I should preface all this that I don't necessarily have all the right answers and I'm learning as I go, too. It is problematic. In the theater, the conductor or music director is typically a middleman job. The producer and director are above you. You're in charge, you're responsible for the management of the music department, but also the musical aspect of the show. So you're dealing with the stage management and the actors as well.

Having a management position is difficult because you have to manage and sometimes that's easy, and sometimes that's hard. When you're living with the people 24 hours a day, it's difficult. And I'm not sure I ever found the right way to do it. I don't think there is a perfect answer.

I felt that I had to be a little separate from the people I was going to manage. You can't party with them one day and the next day be upset with them for showing up to the gig hung over or something, because you were there, too. That kind of thing. That's a challenge, for sure.

MM: Are you dealing pretty much with the same musicians the whole tour, or do people ship in and out?

DH: On the tour I was on, which may or may not be a typical tour, we traveled with a 16-piece band or orchestra. There was only one town where we picked up musicians, in nine months. So for about eight months we had the same musicians. We had some personnel changes while we were on the road, which is pretty typical. You have people where the road isn't for them, or they have family trouble back home, or they get a better gig. So there's some turnover, but for the most part it was the same musicians for about nine months.

MM: Well, that's going to be the same even if you're on Broadway. People will ship in and out over time, right?

DH: The thing about Broadway, though, is there is a culture of subbing on Broadway. That changes things up a lot. According to union rules, you're required to play 50 percent of the shows a month, which means you cannot *not* be there half the time. It's your job. You can sub out and have someone else in, half the time, but most people don't sub out that often. They want to make some money. On the road you don't have that. You have eight shows a week for six weeks in a row, you have the same musicians.

MM: *You mentioned to me previously about having some gigs where you were both conducting and playing keyboards. Talk a little about how that works.*

DH: Piano conducting positions have become more prevalent in the last 20 years, as orchestra sizes have gotten smaller. It's really a function of amplification. In the '40s and '50s they didn't amplify the orchestra, so you had to have a big orchestra if you wanted to fill the theater with sound. But as amplification got better, you could have smaller orchestras that made more sound.

Now, here on Broadway we have nine-piece bands for *Priscilla, Queen of the Desert.* That's a very small band for that space. That space used to hold 24 musicians for shows, decades ago. Producers find it very appealing to be able to combine the piano player with the conductor.

In practice, for people like me, it may not be ideal, but it's definitely possible—especially if you have a smaller size band. And speaking of *Priscilla, Queen of the Desert,* I've conducted *Priscilla* on Broadway, and that's a piano conducting position—you're playing *key one* and also conducting the band. Of course, that's problematic because you only have two hands and two feet and they're mostly occupied. You conduct with a lot of head nods and if you have a free hand, you conduct with whatever you've got.

> **DEFINITION**
>
> In musical theater, the first keyboard chair is often called **key one.**

It's not really so uncommon to have a music group without a conductor. Even in the classical world you have chamber orchestras with no conductor and they get along fine. And what ends up happening, in the piano conducting position, is it ends up being a lot more like a chamber orchestra situation, where you as the piano conductor are more like the role that the concertmaster takes in the chamber orchestra situation. So you're leading, but you're all playing together as musicians as much as you can.

It's easier for some shows than it is for others. There are some shows that have a lot of cutoffs, a lot of tempo changes, and a lot of difficult areas. It's hard, hard, you know. It's not like a rock show that you start the song and then you end the song. It's a little easier to do that.

MM: *You mentioned that the size of the orchestra has been getting smaller over time.*

DH: Yes, smaller and smaller, and that's something the union is having to fight more and more. Because producers, especially with rock shows, don't need [as many musicians]. Minimum is 18 musicians and if it's a rock quartet show, and they only need 4, what are they supposed to do with the other 14?

MM: *Have five people playing tambourine or something. [laughs] But by shrinking the orchestra, does that negatively affect the quality of the sound?*

DH: Oh yeah!

MM: *So what do you have? Do you have synthesizers replacing certain instruments, or do you have prerecorded tracks, or what?*

DH: Synthesizers replacing entire string sections and horn sections. Yeah, it definitely affected the industry in a negative way, but I also don't see the alternative, especially in regional theatre, where this is a lot more prevalent. Broadway has its own problems, but at least the union rules are protecting it. And when someone goes against the minimum, there are repercussions through the union. On nonunion jobs there is no way around it.

Producers are trying to move more and more toward technology, and technology is moving more and more toward us. It's getting better and better. Some of these string sounds are awesome. They sound great; they're never out of tune.

> **WHOLE NOTE**
>
> This is an excerpt from a longer interview I conducted with Dave Hahn. You can read the entire interview online at www.idiotsguides.com/conducting.

Conducting in the Real World: An Interview with Larry Yurman

I mentioned that Dave Hahn was Associate Conductor for the revival of *On a Clear Day You Can See Forever*, starring Harry Connick Jr. Dave's boss on that production is Music Director Larry Yurman, and Dave suggested I talk to him, too—so I did.

Larry Yurman is an experienced Broadway music director, orchestrator, and conductor. He has conducted a number of well-known Broadway productions, including *Grey Gardens*, *Marie Christine*, *Raggedy Ann*, *Roza*, *Swingtime Canteen*, and the Nathan Lane revivals of *Guys and Dolls* and *A Funny Thing Happened on the Way to the Forum*.

I talked to Larry in mid-October 2011, during the *On a Clear Day* rehearsals.

MICHAEL MILLER (MM): *As the music director, what are your specific roles in the process?*

LARRY YURMAN (LY): Teaching the music. I've got two hats, really, as the musical director and the arranger. But in the day to day, once rehearsals begin, you are teaching the music, you are maintaining the music, you are adapting and changing it as needed—creating scene change music and utilities and underscoring. It's fortunate to be the arranger as well. So I'm here, and they're killing two birds with one stone, it's all happening at once.

Basically, the music director's job is to teach and maintain the music, and then ultimately once the show gets into the theater, there's a time just prior to the show's opening where you meet the orchestra. You rehearse the orchestra—which we will have 18 pieces in this particular band. And then you conduct the show, and you run the show, musically, every night.

MM: *At what point do you bring in the other musicians, bring in the orchestra?*

LY: We're in the theater on the 31st (of October) for three days, just the actors and again, just myself, my associate, and the drummer. That's just getting used to the stage, sort of feeling things out, trying to map things out on a larger plane and with the actual set pieces now beginning to be a part of it. November 3rd, 4th, and 5th are our orchestra read-throughs. We have about six hours on the 3rd and 4th, and we have three hours on the 5th.

And then we have what is called a *sitzprobe*, where the actors will come to the rehearsal studio where the orchestra is, devoid of any distractions that are stage related. You're in a rehearsal studio with 18 musicians and you are there to sing the songs with them. It's very thrilling, usually, that kind of situation is the first time the orchestrations have been heard by the actors. Suddenly it's as if you're being lifted by way more than a piano. It's usually a wonderful day when all that finally arrives.

> **DEFINITION**
>
> A **sitzprobe** is a seated rehearsal in a musical production where the singers first sing with the orchestra.

Then, on the 7th, the orchestra comes and joins us in the theater. And we have about four or five days then, the actors are there all day with me, my associate, and the drummer, and the orchestra might be there three hours a day, or three to five hours a day.

Our first preview is November 12th. So when you count backward, the orchestra is there about nine days before we begin.

MM: *How do you go about getting the orchestra? Who takes care of that?*

LY: There's a gentleman or woman, usually in the hierarchy of these things, who is referred to as the musical coordinator. The old school word for that would be the music contractor. So we have a contractor in our midst and he, months ago, was responsible for the hiring of players.

MM: *Do you have a say in that, do you get to pick musicians you want to use?*

LY: Yeah, trying to be aware of certain strengths. You have to kind of project a bit, because nothing has been written, other than the piano score at that point, which is still in evolution. We don't know that, oh, we're gonna have an incredible flute part so we need this guy. We don't know any of that yet. There's a list of great players here in New York that have a reputation, so you're sort of staying to that list whenever possible.

Then there are the occasional new people who creep in. And they creep in, which is a whole other scene of how musicians get into pits. Usually by subbing and getting known by a conductor. Making an impression, and then they stay in your head. So you might recommend them for the next job that comes up.

I do have a say. But I like the contractor doing the job that he does, because it kind of eliminates worry on my part. If it's somebody that you actually respect and trust, then you know you're going to have a great band.

MM: *You've been in the business for several decades. How has the music, the orchestra changed on Broadway?*

LY: It's become smaller. [laughs]

You know, you're less assured of having the complement of players that created the sound that people are familiar with. It's all generational, you know. People grew up with a certain kind of style of sound, of limitless possibilities in terms of orchestra color.

When I first started out, all the larger theaters in town had had 25-person minimums, which was a wonderful complement. It's not always the perfect answer, for all shows, but it was a great thing to be able to rely upon when it came to anything that you wanted. Just a full palette of color.

Over time, that has been whittled away, except for something like *Follies*, which becomes the exception to the rule. There producers allowed the original orchestration, and that was orchestrated and originally done when those minimums were in place, the larger ones. So that has like a 27 man band in there. That is the exception to the rule.

Now the larger theaters will have minimums that are designated at 19. And then all the smaller theaters, everything's sort of relatively gone down from there. But everything used to be more.

We were commenting on this with my orchestrator, talking about how even 19, which sounds like a great number, that's 18 and me, the conductor. It's 18 players in the pit, it's still lacking some elements that he would like to have to create. It's the difference between having three reed players in the pit, versus five. The standard for decades used to be five. Now you could decide to have five reed players but maybe you'd not have any string players in there instead. You have to rob Peter to pay Paul.

That's how things have changed. You always get a little anxious when the discussion turns to moving a show that has been somewhere to a Broadway house, and then what do the producers have in mind. How do they view an orchestra's worth? They're practical, they're crunching numbers, so I understand from their point of view. But in what ways are we going to have to limit our possibilities when it comes to playing.

MM: *One other thing I wanted to ask you, since you've worked with guys like Nathan Lane and some other dynamic performers. You're interacting with these folks in the rehearsal process. How do you deal with the actors' and musicians' egos and personalities during the process?*

LY: Carefully. [laughs]

MM: *[laughs]*

LY: I like to think of myself as a diplomat. I'm looking for the common ground. I don't like to throw my weight around in a way that is "It has to be my way or the highway."

Fortunately, I do have allies. I have potential allies in that world and I will rely on them as well. If there's really some issue that comes to the forefront, then it needs to go past the director. Because music directors, even though they're musicals, music directors certainly are not the most powerful people in the room, even when it comes to things like this.

You know, "carefully" is my response. I think I'm sensitive to who people are and how they want to be seen and be dealt with. It becomes a little bit of that kind of negotiation, that you figure out who people are and you try to play to how it's going to work. That expression, drawing the flies with honey?

MM: *Attract more flies with honey, yes.*

LY: That's how I've survived. [laughs] You know, sometimes there's a little internal combustion that comes along with it, how you have to tamp down feelings of your own. But it's a collaborative medium and at times there's a hierarchy that you become very aware of. People that want to throw around power in a certain way, it's like okay, let me not get in the way of you. That's my philosophy.

MM: *I would assume, on Broadway, when you're talking the big draws, these are folks who own a room when they walk into it, right?*

LY: Yeah, right. [laughs] That's the other thing, when you actually assess it all. In this case, Harry Connick is a very lovely person to be around, so there are no issues. But were there to be, you'd say he's basically the reason I've got a paycheck from now until next July. Because the advance is good, people are excited to see him, people are coming to see him. You want to make it all right for that person who's helping put food on your table.

MM: *Any advice you'd give to someone who aspires to be a musical director on Broadway or regional theater or whatever?*

LY: The way it all happened for me, is I bode my time a little bit. You keep your ear to the ground, you network the way you feel is comfortable for you. Some people are very aggressive in networking and I was never that person.

It seemed like I had a commodity in my playing. All egos aside, when I first started out, my playing was noticed by people and that's what got me from one place to the next and got me my first Broadway show. I was in a room playing material for actors in auditions. If you have a commodity you need to know what it is. Hopefully it is true, it is a true thing, you're not making it up and you're not trying to inflate your abilities. But I always think that that will prove itself and that will eventually pay you dividends. If you just quietly express who you are and show who you are, then the people who understand that will experience it and appreciate it and something good will happen eventually. And that is the way it happened to me.

So I only say, in terms of other people, not to try to rush it. I think people sometimes push hard. I don't know if that's because they're really great operators and they're lacking something underneath in terms of technique, but they know how to get their foot in the door. It should be a talent-based craft, and I think people should just bring their worth into the room and let the chips fall. Because it's that kind of a business. It's kismet and coincidence and happenstance and being in the right place at the right time.

MM: *But ultimately talent wins out?*

LY: I think so. I think so.

> **WHOLE NOTE**
>
> This is an excerpt from a longer interview I conducted with Larry Yurman. You can read the entire interview online at www.idiotsguides.com/conducting.

Conducting in the Real World: An Interview with Eric Stern

Finally, I had a nice talk with Eric Stern, another veteran Broadway conductor and arranger. Eric has more than 15 Broadway musicals to his credit, including revivals of *Xanadu, The Music Man, Follies, Candide, Carousel, The King and I, Sunday in the Park with George,* and *Gypsy,* as well as *Shrek, The Musical.*

Eric has also built a reputation as a concert and broadcast conductor. He's led many major orchestras, including the Boston Pops, the Chicago Symphony, and the Cleveland Orchestra. He has conducted recordings for Mandy Patinkin, Dawn Upshaw, and Audra MacDonald, and he won an Emmy for his work on the television special, "Broadway Sings the Music of Jules Styne" for PBS. Eric's website is www.ericstern.net.

We started with the basic question—what does a Broadway conductor do?

MICHAEL MILLER (MM): *You conduct both musical theater and traditional orchestras. How do you approach each one?*

ERIC STERN (ES): Well, the biggest difference is when you're conducting a show, you're basically driving in tandem with the stage manager who is calling the show. The two of you are sort of driving this theatrical event together. The way the scenery moves, the way the light cues are called, the way the music moves, this is something that the two of you do together. I don't know a stage manager who calls shows who doesn't know immediately who's conducting a performance.

Likewise, I think conductors know exactly, from the very first light cue, who's calling the show that night. It takes a deft touch from both parties.

You are, after all, ultimately telling a story in a much less abstract way than you are even if you are conducting a Strauss tone poem, which is supposedly a story. But it's much more abstract.

You're also dealing with so many elements as a theater conductor and I'm including opera in there, too. There are so many things that you have to work with in order to make a performance seem seamless. It's not just you and your musicians. There's a lot in play. There are actors who are in a spotlight, in a scene, and you have to take in account the fact that there are instincts and emotions and all, I don't know what, hormones flowing, or whatever it is, there is just a lot going on. You have to learn to be sensitive to it. I find that really good theater conductors also make very good concerto conductors, because they learn to breathe and think like a soloist at work.

I can't really name specifics because I don't want to, but I've actually seen a couple of big names in American serious conductors, people who have had to take on a theatrical job for special occasions, and I sort of feel like they're not attuned to a singer the way that most theater conductors are. That they're uncomfortable doing a lot of dialog, the amount of dialog. These are techniques that we tend to just assume because we do them every day; doing a lot of vamps, what that means in terms of what you're doing with your hands, guiding off of dialog—which again, is something that most concert conductors never have to consider. It's just a slightly different skill set.

The other thing that you have to add to the mix is that when you're conducting a show eight times a week, it's an entirely different discipline than conducting theater and orchestra programs three times and then doing something else. First of all, the maintenance of a show over a long period of time is a very complex and difficult job. Making it fresh and making it new for yourself, for your audience, and for your players, is an interesting job. Knowing that you're conducting basically the same product and yet the elements are different. An understudy is on for an actor, or there is someone in your second reed chair that has never been there before, or you find an interesting, difficult mix between a drummer and a bass player that shouldn't happen again and you'll see to it that it doesn't happen again, but there you are stuck with it that night. There's just a lot going on.

MM: [laughs]

ES: I also tell students and people that come to me for advice, I always say that there is nothing that you can do in school, there is nothing you can do in life that can teach you what a long run is like, except to do it. It's a real education.

First of all I love conducting theater, because I love the idea of telling a story. It's exciting to me. Every time I start whatever production it is, I think what it must be like to be sitting in that chair and experiencing it for the first time. You kind of have to trick yourself that way.

But I tell people who ask me that the real danger is that after, I don't know what, after a couple months, after whatever, you have to be careful you don't find yourself conducting the beats. One, two, three, four, cue, two, vamp, two, three, dah, dah, dah, tempo change, *ritard*, and beat. Because it's easy to sort of let your body take that over. It ceases to become music. That's what I think I'm most happiest about is learning how to never let that happen.

MM: *How do you do that? I mean, after a hundred different performances or whatnot, how do you keep it fresh?*

ES: Like I said, it's an ever-changing parade of people, up and on and below the stage. You've got that going for you. Also, frankly, you know having a podium on Broadway, after you've played the first six months, basically, it's then you get away for a while. You do something else for a couple weeks, you take a brief concert tour, you take dates overseas, and you come back. You come back refreshed.

And the same, by the way, is true of musicians. I mean, for every musician in the pits, there are at least five approved subs by a conductor. The old school way of thinking was, no one should ever take off, ever; it's a terrible thing. But the fact is that when your best players come back refreshed, they play better. Better than having a second rate player who never leaves his chair and remains uninspired or actually goes downhill. So being able to get away for a little while is very helpful.

But as I say, you find ways, you empathize, you put yourself in the position of someone who has paid $120 to see that ticket. Sometimes it's hard to face it. But any job sometimes is hard to face. And I just think I manage to find life in the moment and hope that that carries you.

Sometimes, I tend to think of performances as one long rehearsal. You know, like this Friday night I'm going to get that little *ritard* that always can't quite get the harp to meet me here, I'm going to perfect that moment. Or, gee, this thing is sort of out of whack, it's been out of whack for the last few weeks, in terms of the theatrical propulsion from point A to point B. It's not quite as exciting as it was. Why is that? And you find yourself solving problems like that over the long term. That may sound very bizarre or arcane but you do find yourself trying to perfect, trying to constantly discover new things.

One of the most fun things I like is, once you've been on the podium or show for, I don't know, two, three months, you don't even pretend to turn the pages anymore. You know it. And a guy will come in playing for the first time, you know, the fourth reed book or the cello book and you say, "Okay, tonight I'm going to conduct every entrance, every curve of the road, for that book. I'm going to see if I can do it." And I'm going to make this player go, "Oh my God, you were wonderful!"

MM: *[laughs] You do have a plethora of substitutions throughout the run of a play, in the pit. Does that make your job more difficult?*

ES: As I said, it's kind of a tradeoff. It does make your life more difficult. But which problem would you rather have—breaking in new subs or trying to motivate someone who would rather stick pins in his eyes than be in that chair another night?

MM: *[laughs]*

ES: You know, the fact is musicians all need, we all need, other things to infuse us. You can't do the same thing and nothing but the same thing day in and day out. What kind of diet is that for a starving man? You need to replenish the soul. And it needs to be done in many different ways.

There's a very orderly process for getting subs into a pit. Every conductor, music director, or music supervisor sits down with a music contractor—they call them fixers in Europe—and determines the best way to do this. For instance, we may decide that the rules are, on any given night, only one new person can be in the reed section or only one first-time person can be in the strings. Only the people who have the original chairs in an orchestra are immune from any kind of firing or disciplinary action, you know. You really have to screw up badly to get fired from a Broadway show if it's your chair.

MM: *Okay.*

ES: But subs have no such rights. Subs can be summarily dismissed and thanked for their time, at any time during the tenure of their service. So subs are very prone to doing a good job. There are a lot of people who really basically make a living subbing in the pit.

Talk about one of the most interesting jobs, it's being a sub drummer. Because there you are actually leading and following at the same time. It's a very tricky job. Some guys are really, really great at it and I used to go, "How did you do that? You followed me every step of the way and yet you drove the orchestra."

By the way, that's another difference—the technical difference between concert conducting and pit conducting. That is in the pit, you have a rhythm section that's basically an engine for your show. Certainly my experience conducting Mozart has not proven to be the same! You're sort of dealing with a different dynamic in terms of where the engine and the rhythm comes from. It's a slightly different style of work as well.

MM: *Obviously the musicians in the pit follow you as the conductor. When you're dealing with the musicians, the actors, the performers on stage, do they follow you or do you follow them? Or is it a little bit of both?*

ES: It's a little bit of both, in the sense that there are, as in opera as well, certainly there are discretionary moments where a singer does have the discretion to linger on a *fermata*, or to play a *rubato* according to the scene, or Lord help you, you both have to cover for the fact that the scenic element hasn't arrived at the split second it was supposed to. You're always making adjustments. But yes, there are times where the singer on stage has license.

I know that some people marvel at a concert conductor and say, "My God, how does he get all of this information to them? How do they play so well just with that tiny little stick?" They seem to overlook the fact that we spent a week rehearsing it.

In a Broadway show, you spend months rehearsing it. It is my goal, when teaching a show to a cast, that it can be done conductorless. It's not always feasible but that's what you hold as your ideal. It's that this cast has been trained well enough to know that this is how this core goes, this is how this *ritard* is handled, this is how this is negotiated, this is where the climax is, and I don't have to conduct the *crescendo* for the cast, they know this is where it goes. In a sense you're not micromanaging every minute, although you are in control.

There are nights when a singer just doesn't want to go at the tempo that you've agreed on, and sometimes there's a little prodding. I mean, it happens. Let's face it, I can't deny it, there are some people of star magnitude or more marquee value whom you actually don't push because they're the 600-pound gorilla in the room. But I've worked with a lot of stars and the fact is you can usually find accommodation with people. You can usually find a place where the two might meet. I've heard legendary stories of people who absolutely could not be conducted and could not be controlled. But I've never experienced it myself.

MM: These days, as scores change, are you working with any prerecorded tracks or click tracks or anything like that?

ES: Increasingly you do find yourself conducting to a click, for a couple of reasons. If you have to sync up with multimedia elements which I think is what you were alluding to before, then you certainly do that. And there are some composers and/or music supervisors who want the show basically on a click, because they want it to vary.

The most important thing, when a click is being designed for a conductor, is to make sure the conductor controls the in and out of the click. Sound designers will say, "We'll trigger the click from the back of the house." I'm going, "No you won't." Because it never, never works well. But if the conductor has the button, off of his left hand, and five, six, seven and push, and controls the click himself, nine times out of ten, you'll be better off.

MM: Obviously the musicians you work with can affect the energy of the performance. The performers on stage can affect the energy. The house can affect the energy, too—the audience, right?

ES: Oh, absolutely. You have to train yourself to not let that affect you the wrong way. I mean, it would be very easy in certain circumstances to say, "Oh, this is a dull crowd. They don't seem to be enjoying it and I'm just going to relax." It's an easy thing to allow yourself to do, but I've had enough experiences where you've had a quiet crowd or a crowd who doesn't seem to be following it as well as you want them to. And then you get to the end of the act and suddenly there's this huge roar and you realize, "Well, they just enjoyed it the way that they enjoyed it."

You know, you just can't assume. It's your job to deliver the best thing you can in the moment and not to let that affect you too much. You know, certain matinees are notorious for the audience often being a little on the older side, or every show has a "Oh, we hate Thursday nights," or whatever it is. But you really can't take too much stock in that. On the other hand, there is nothing more exciting than when the room is with you. The room feeds the band, the band feeds the stage, the stage feeds the room, and it all becomes this very exciting thing. And that's undeniably pleasant, to say the least.

MM: Any time you're dealing with live performances, anything can happen on stage or in the pit. What kinds of things have you dealt with, and how do you deal with them?

ES: I can't honestly tell you how I get out of what we call train wrecks. A singer will just forget where they are or somehow an important person in the orchestra will miss a cue and sort of derail the whole thing. I just know that you get out of them. Sometimes people don't even know how it happened. You either call a measure number or enough people knew what went wrong to fix it.

It's one of those things where I look back and say "What, how did we get out of that?" He says "Eric, you were brilliant there" and I have no idea how it happened. But, you know, those kinds of things you can pull yourself out of.

If you have a heavily automated show and the automation breaks, there's nothing you can do. You stop. The stage manager gets on the horn and announces to the audience, "We've had a momentary technical problem" and then I have to fight the urge to turn around and do ten minutes of my stand up—which I can no longer do. Tell a few jokes, you just don't do that.

Sometimes something will happen on stage during a fluid moment of the show and you don't have enough music to cover it, and it's like something strange is happening. And you signal to your pianist, and the pianist plays something, or improvises around what you've done, until you're back on track. It doesn't happen all that often, frankly. I mean, in previews, Lord knows that happens.

MM: How do you deal with new people stepping into established parts later in the run?

ES: You do have to make special provisions for some people coming into a show, when you replace actors with another actor. Keys change sometimes, routines change, or dances are changed to suit a different set of abilities. Funny things happen on the first put in of a new person. Stepping into a role in an existing show is different from rehearsing the show for eight weeks.

MM: Do you have rehearsals for new people? Or when a person steps in, do they kind of step right into the deep water?

ES: Well, you are stepping in to a piece of intricate machinery that is already running, if that's the analogy that you are drawing. But you do have rehearsals. Even for ensemble members who are going on for the first time, or even swings who are going into a track that they've never played, you know because swings cover many tracks. You still have either a full put in the afternoon, for say, a star going into a major role, or you do mini quick little put ins a half hour before curtain, or you do an afternoon's put in for a couple hours with understudies. No one's ever put in the machine without a helmet.

MM: It sounds like you really enjoy your job. What part of it do you find the most fulfilling?

ES: I love the first orchestra rehearsals. I love it when a score is first being shaped. We do what I'm sure you know is called a sitzprobe, where the cast gets to hear the orchestra live in a room. It's probably the only time they will ever hear an orchestra, the accompaniment to their show, in optimum condition. Because on stage you hear what's pumped up at you. It's such a thrill to see a casts' eyes just widen and glow hearing an orchestration for the first time. Something they have been hearing on rehearsal piano or piano and drums for a few weeks. I love the first orchestra rehearsals without the cast where you literally explore a new orchestration, you look through it and alter it if need be and find where an orchestration grooves, where its sweet spot is. It's so much fun. That's a great thing.

I love musical rehearsals, obviously. I love that first week where you're teaching, especially the choral stuff which I love to do. I love finding an ensemble singing personality for a show. Every show has a different personality in terms of what kind of choral sound should be rendered. Is it a colloquial or street sound? Is it a cultured upper class sound? What does the chorus sound like? I love doing that. Discovering what kind of diction works for a show.

It's all pretty exciting. You know, when you have a show that first opens, you're caught in a maelstrom of activity—publicity appearances, television shows, making a cast recording, being in the Macy's parade. It's one thing after another where you're just living and breathing this brand new thing.

And the other thing is to see a show that you've worked on, that you even care about a lot, to see it succeed and actually have a life is not all that common. It's been my experience that things that I actually love most dearly, that had a place in my heart of hearts, generally didn't have a long life. And sometimes something runs for a long time and you go, "Eeew, this could have been so much better."

So to have something deserving reach the public and get a fan base and live, that's what you live for. I love that first moment where you're in auditions for a new show and people come in and they're singing songs from your last show, that no one had even heard of a year ago, and they're now part of the audition repertoire. You go, "Yeah, that's what it's about. That's great, we've contributed to the literature. We've created something that's lasting."

Like I said, it's not all that often.

> **WHOLE NOTE**
>
> This is an excerpt from a longer interview I conducted with Eric Stern. You can read the entire interview online at www.idiotsguides.com/conducting.

The Least You Need to Know

- Conducting a musical involves leading both instrumentalists in the pit and performers on stage—and, to a degree, following the action on stage.
- The role of the conductor in a musical is not to put his own personal interpretation on the music, but rather to faithfully reproduce the music as composed.
- Conducting an opera is similar to conducting musical theater, with the added complexity of conducting recitatives.
- Conducting other live shows involves helping the orchestra or band accompany the on-stage singers—but often with very little rehearsal or preparation.

Conducting in the Recording Studio

Chapter 20

In This Chapter

- Learn how to conduct movie soundtracks
- Find out how to conduct TV soundtracks
- Discover the world of conducting video game soundtracks
- Interviews with studio conductors Tim Davies and Pete Anthony

Our final look at the various worlds of conducting takes us to the West Coast of the United States, into the hallowed world of the recording studio. These conductors are responsible for recording soundtracks for your favorite movies and TV shows.

Conducting in the studio is much, much different from conducting on the stage, as you'll soon discover. It's a high-pressure atmosphere with a lot of people involved—not all of them musicians.

Conducting Movie Soundtracks

Studio conductors have an interesting job. They're involved in the very back end of the movie business; they do their thing after the film has been shot and edited. In fact, film scoring and recording (along with sound effects) is the last thing that happens before a film is distributed to theaters.

The process works something like this:

The movie director shoots the film. (That's a simplification of a very complex process itself, of course.) After the film has been edited into its final form, the director brings in a composer, who writes the music for the accompanying soundtrack. That music is in somewhat rough form, and then goes to an orchestrator, who decides which instruments play which parts. (Sometimes there's even an arranger in between the composer and the orchestrator, who fleshes out the composer's rough concepts.) The orchestrator then sends the final arrangement to a music copyist, who copies out each of the individual parts for the musicians.

> **THE CONDUCTOR SEZ**
>
> Often, directors or editors will want to use existing music (typically popular songs) for various scenes. This is true of both movie and television soundtracks.

At this point, a music contractor schedules time in the recording studio, musicians are hired, and a conductor is brought in. This point, by the way, is typically the night before the recording session. That's right—the conductor has, if he's lucky, a whole evening to prep the score before recording begins.

The recording session itself is rather time constrained, in that only a certain amount of time has been contracted for. (Plus there's the looming deadline for the movie's theatrical distribution, of course.) The conductor and musicians must nail the entire soundtrack in one or two takes, essentially sight reading the entire thing—while the conductor watches the rough cut of the movie on a giant screen behind the orchestra. (He has to sync the music they're playing with the action onscreen.)

Now that's a challenge!

It gets even more challenging. The conductor is not there to put his own personal imprint on the music; he's there to accurately reproduce what the soundtrack composer envisioned. So the conductor is essentially working for the composer—who is, in turn, working for the film's director (who is, in his turn, often working for one or more producers or studio executives).

All of these folks, from the composer on up the line, are typically sitting in the recording booth, listening to what's being laid down. For these nonmusician members of the team, this is typically the first time they've heard the music, at least in its fully orchestrated form. That means that changes are often in order; not everyone always likes what they hear. (Plus, mistakes can creep into the process when everything is done so quickly.)

> **WHOLE NOTE**
>
> Most composers these days will run a rough synthesized draft of the score by the director in advance, but that's not at all like hearing it played by a full orchestra.

The conductor, then, is responsible for leading the musicians through an unfamiliar piece of music (multiple pieces, actually), making any necessary changes on the fly, and satisfying the composer, the director, and anybody else who matters. No pressure there.

In this environment, it helps if the conductor has orchestration skills to facilitate making changes in the studio. In fact, many conductors also function as the film's orchestrator; it's a common dual role that often helps speed the process along.

It's not a job for everyone, and certainly much different from other forms of conducting. Yes, you use the same beat patterns and gestures, but the entire intent of the thing is different. It's like conducting musicals, in that the conductor serves the music, rather than the other way around. But the time pressures are unique, which means not every conductor can or would want to do the job.

Conducting TV Soundtracks

Conducting music for TV shows is very similar to conducting movie soundtracks, but with even more time pressure. Consider that most TV shows are on a weekly schedule, and you see the issue—there's a new mini-soundtrack to be composed, orchestrated, and conducted every seven days. If anyone in the chain is just a little bit late, it all goes to hell.

Granted, there's less music in a typical half-hour or hour TV show than there is in a two-hour movie. But still, that's a lot of work to be done on a very short schedule. This is why many TV shows reuse the same music cues over and over. Some shows don't even use live orchestras; instead, they use the sampled and synthesized parts the composer creates with his music notation program. At the end of the day there's a hard deadline, and the show's producers have to do anything possible to meet that deadline.

Conducting Video Game Soundtracks

There's a relatively new outlet for studio conductors these days, in the form of the video game industry. Today's video games are sophisticated mini-movies, with full orchestral soundtracks for each of the game's many levels and variations. It's actually a big business.

Conducting a video game soundtrack comes with the same issues and pressures of conducting a movie soundtrack. If anything, there's more music involved; it takes longer to play a complete multi-level video game than it does to watch a movie. The schedules are just as tight, however, and the music is always the last thing to be added. So the same pressure's there, if not more so.

Conducting in the Real World: An Interview with Tim Davies

How does one get involved in the wild world of studio conducting? What skills do you need to play the game?

To answer these questions (and a few more), I interviewed two very talented, very busy conductors in the Hollywood studio system. My first interview was with Tim Davies, who is more than just a conductor—he's a composer, arranger, bandleader, and drummer. A native Australian, Tim now lives in California and makes his living conducting, arranging, and orchestrating music for movies, TV shows, and video games. He has conducted for several major Hollywood composers, including Christophe Beck, Stephen Trask, Deborah Lurie, and Steve Jablonsky.

Tim's conducting credits include the movies *Couples Retreat*, *Date Night*, *Footloose*, *Despicable Me*, and *The Muppets*; the TV shows *House*, *Pushing Daisies*, and *No Ordinary Family*; and the video games *Monsters vs. Aliens*, *God of War 2 & 3*, *The Sims 3*, and *Batman: Arkham City*. In addition to his studio work, Tim leads the Tim Davies Big Band, which plays regularly in the Los Angeles area. His website is www.timmusic.net.

We started out by talking about some of the nuts and bolts of the job. It's a much different challenge than conducting for concert performances.

MICHAEL MILLER (MM): *Talking about conducting another composer's soundtrack, who typically makes the call? Is it the composer who calls you? Is it the director? Or what?*

TIM DAVIES (TD): It'll either be the composer or the contractor who's putting together the orchestra. So I've got composers who I have relationships with. Some I'm just a conductor for, like Christophe Beck, we just did *The Muppets* the other week.

> **WHOLE NOTE**
>
> Christophe Beck is a well-known composer of movie soundtracks. His credits include music for the movies *Starstruck, Bring It On, Under the Tuscan Sun, Elektra, School for Scoundrels, Charlie Bartlett, The Hangover, Date Night, Tower Heist,* and *The Muppets.* He won an Emmy for his work on the television series *Buffy the Vampire Slayer.*

MM: *Oh, that'd be a fun one.*

TD: But there are other composers that I sort of do everything for. They just send me something over the internet, and then I show up to the sessions with all the orchestrations. My team has done all the copying and then I conduct it. I'm sort of like a one-stop shop for all the music production.

MM: *So you're working primarily with the composer, as opposed to the director of the movie?*

TD: Yeah, I'm working with the composer. And the composer deals with the director.

MM: *Is the composer typically there during a session?*

TD: Yeah, 99 percent of the time the composer is there. And I'd say 75 percent of the time the director is there.

MM: *How does a typical job work?*

TD: I'm basically sight reading, so I get the scores the night before or the morning of and then take it through that. Then I get to liaise between the composer and the orchestra when they want to make a change.

Normally how it works is, we play it down once and see what happens. Then I will work on things that I have noticed, like phrasing and bringing the orchestra together—because we're sight reading. When people are doing repertoire, the orchestra knows it already, you know; they could make it through the piece. And my orchestra could make it through, too, without me, but they don't know where things are.

Like you have to explain to people, "Okay, Charlie, you're with the French horns there and the French horns need to breathe at the end of bar four, so you guys need to lift there." All these little things that when you play the piece 50 times, things just come naturally—or when you've heard it your whole life. But we're going to try and play it three times and make it sound like we've been playing it our whole life.

MM: *Now, you're getting pros here who have done dozens if not hundreds of sessions, right?*

TD: Yes. Their job is to play what's on the page and listen around them, but not to make bold decisions about who's going to play, who's taking the lead here, and how we're shaping this phrase. That's the conductor's job.

So on the first listen I've got to come up with a whole pile of things in order to shape this piece. Once I've said my bit and tweaked the dynamics a little bit, and just warned people that, no, that's not the melody—the trumpets sometimes think that they always have the melody, so they're going to be loud.

MM: [laughs]

TD: So once we have done that first run through, the composer and/or the orchestrator who are in the booth with me will have their notes with them, what they would like to do or change and bring out. Sometimes it's the exact thing I said. And sometimes it's another thing. Occasionally they say the opposite, I'd play this soft and they want it loud. And that's fine. And sometimes they really don't know what they want.

The reason they don't talk to the orchestra a lot is because they give terms in another language, it's not orchestra language. You know, it can be very confusing to the orchestra. So I get these crazy descriptive words of how they want something phrased, from the composer and the director sometimes. And then I have to put that into ten words or less in orchestra language. Sometimes I get that wrong, but I think that the job, with being in front of other people, is to be assertive and lead them down a path. If it's the wrong path, you find out pretty quickly, and then you just backtrack. But if you don't lead them down together as a whole, you won't find out what it is.

MM: Once you start recording, do you record the piece as a whole? When we're talking about recording for a film, you could just be recording a couple measures here or a couple measures there and patching in. How does that normally work?

TD: A bit of everything. Some composers like to get everything in one take because you get a more real sound—for example, when you get to the end of a big *crescendo*, but then you hit another massive section. In the real world the brass has to stop for a breath. And there's going to be a little pause there that you don't notice in the concert hall, but you might in the studio. So sometimes we will record right up to the end of the eighth bar or something, and then we can stop without going on, then let everyone have a breath, and start recording again and just cut it in.

> **THE CONDUCTOR SEZ**
>
> This is a wonderful reason why studio conductors have to be human metronomes (or be able to lock into a click track) and be incredibly consistent with tempo. It makes cutting in work very well.

The other thing is because the music is not being dictated by good musical phrasing, it's being dictated by picture or the energy level of the game. Sometimes there are impossible leaps that players have to do—like the strings might be screaming high on their E string, and then all of a sudden they have to play a riff in perfect time on their D string. It's impossible without a gap.

Also it's very hard if they're coming out of a tremolo or something, where their bows are just flailing away and then all of a sudden in one beat they have to play very precise and lock into a rhythm of some sort. That's near impossible to get the tightness we need. So in those cases we'll always start and stop.

So part of my job is looking ahead and working out, okay, here is where we start and stop to get the best performance out of the players.

MM: *Do you often—or ever, even—have the orchestra playing along with anything that is prerecorded?*

TD: Yeah, all the time, because a lot of scores these days are hybrid. There may be synthesizers or sound design elements, so we're always playing along to the stuff. Or rhythm section tracks, you know we don't do that all at the same time. It's done beforehand or sometimes after. In that case we're playing along with the composer's mockup.

But in most cases the players don't listen to that stuff. They really don't want to hear it—it's distracting—they have enough to worry about playing on the click track. So they just want to read their part and play on the click track. Only if it's a funky rhythm and there's a groove track do we sometimes put it in very softly.

You know, I'll play the track to them often so they'll know what they're playing against. But then they play when they are just playing, they don't listen to anything, just the click track.

On the really loud stuff, it's often impossible to record everyone at once. So you have to overdub the brass because it doesn't matter how many strings you've got, the brass is too powerful. We're writing for the picture and not what's practical, so if we need a massive brass theme, we'll do that. We call it striping. We rehearse it all together and then we do the string part, then woodwind, then brass after that. That way they can be turned up or down and not affect the strings because they won't be in their microphones.

MM: *So just the general setup of a session, is everybody wearing headphones at this point?*

TD: Yeah, unless we are doing what we call "free time," which is where there are no headphones and the stream is going across the screen, and they are following me and I'm following the stream. So on a romantic lush cue, we can do that, if there are no tracks that we have to line up with. We'll just do that and then if there is no click track, then they can take their headphones off.

And when you tell them to take their headphones off, there is a massive sigh of relief. Even though they do this every day and they love it, playing with something covering one of your ears and ticking in your head the whole time gets fatiguing. And it does take away a little bit of the musicality when you've got that distraction. You're not listening as much, and you can only listen to so much, especially when you're sight reading. They are listening to the click track, to themselves, and to the sounds around them to try and work out where they are.

But when you take the click track out, they are then only listening to themselves and around them, so you're going to get a slightly more musical response quicker—especially when tuning, often when we are having trouble with pitch, and again when sight reading and they've only played this thing once or twice. They don't know where they are in the chords sometimes.

And tricky harmony and stuff, the best way to solve that is to rehearse it without any tracks and let people hear it and play for the sake of playing. And 99 percent of the time that fixes it, especially with the players we are dealing with—you don't have to tell them they are sharp or flat, you know, you just play it so they are hearing.

Also, when you're doing that, it's kind of code for we're out of tune. Sometimes someone in the booth will say "Let's take an A," and that's code for "Well, the tuning sucked on the last one and we need to do it again."

MM: *I've always admired studio musicians, the challenges that they have to do. But being a studio conductor is challenging also, because you're not just conducting the musicians, you're listening to click tracks and you're watching the film go by in front of you, too, right?*

TD: I think on most of it, when using a click track, it's not about how your arms wave around. That's important—they do need a downbeat because they're sight reading. You've got percussionists running around between instruments, and the timpanist has his back to you half the time because he has ten drums. I had lunch with some of the percussionists the other week and they were saying they really like it. You're just clear. It's not a show; it's just give the downbeat and give them confidence, give some cuing, give shape to a phrase. You can add some expression, up and down, but remembering that they all have their heads buried in the part because they're sight reading.

So on the first run through you're kind of limited on what you can do anyway, because they're out of the corner of their eye looking for that downbeat. The goal is to give them the downbeat and stay out of the way.

But the big thing comes from when there is a problem, or you've got to relay changes. Because that's something that a normal conductor doesn't have to do. When the word comes down that bar 24 needs to be "darker," you can't just tell them to play softer or louder or something. You have to work out how do I change the harmony or voicing or playing styles to make it darker.

MM: *Sounds to me that having an orchestrator background is going to be a benefit to you.*

TD: It is. Successful studio conductors are all orchestrators or composers, because you need to be able to give those fixes. Sometimes you have an orchestrator or composer who knows the exact fix and you just translate it. But they might just say, "French horns, just do this" and that has a consequence for other parts and you have to be the one who checks all that.

MM: *So you're doing a lot of thinking on your feet. The average person is going to be amazed at how time compressed this all is. How much prep work do you get? What do you get in advance? How do you do that?*

TD: If I'm lucky, I will get the scores of some of them the day before, because they're not always ready, so I can go through and mark them up. But there is always some stuff that's just appearing while we're there.

I might pull something out of order and quite often I will hear the next number from the booth and I pull the score out of the pile and it's something I hadn't seen yet. So I'll quickly mark it up with my tempo changes and if there are some double bars I'll quickly pile a whole bunch more guide posts in and then mark some phrasing so I don't have to have my head buried the whole time. If it's four-bar phrasing I'll put some fours so I can look up and know that in four bars I can look down again and find where I am.

> **THE CONDUCTOR SEZ**
>
> Marking measures is useful for any conductor. I actually number measures in reverse for phrasing. So rather than marking the first bar of a four-bar phrase with a 1, and then a 2 in the next measure, and so on, I will start with 4 and then 3 and then 2 and 1. This makes it very easy to see phrase structure quickly.

I'll mark major cues. They've got to come in, I don't have to give them a cue, but obviously if you have a solo coming up, and you look that person in the eye, he's going to play better, because he knows where you are and he knows you know where he is. That's the same anywhere. They're not going to hold it against you if you miss it. There are just too many cues going on. You just can't get everyone.

MM: How long does a typical session go?

TD: In a day, it's normally two three-hour calls. In the studios here, we have a ten-minute break every hour, so it's actually only two and a half hours of recording in the three hours. It's pretty stressful; it's high stress, so it keeps everyone fresh. It's just a little break and everyone appreciates it. They run out for a quick cup of tea or coffee. Often I have to run into the booth to talk to people and all that.

I'm usually pretty tired and wasted after a full day of conducting because the whole day you're on. There's no time off. Sometimes at lunch you're sorting out things or marking up new scores and you've always got people asking questions. And then definitely when you're on the podium, you're the focal point. If you just pause for a second, then the whole thing pauses for a second. You can't. It's quite fatiguing.

Sometimes we'll do triple sessions where we'll do strings all day and then do brass in the evening or choir in the evening, or percussion or something where we're adding stuff in layers. Doing triple sessions is really tiring, but it's always fun. Beats having a real job. [laughs]

MM: You do scoring for film, TV, video games. I think the one that's going to be unique to most people is video games. How does that differ from a movie session?

TD: The music is more full on, because there's no dialogue most of the time. There are cinematics in the game, which is a little movie. So they're scored like a movie, but even then they're a bit more dramatic and compressed, so there's a lot more music. But there are no real love themes or underscoring.

You know in a movie you have a couple of big action cues, and then a lot of underscoring and little short pieces to just fill in some holes set in an emotional time. So in a typical movie you could have 60 stops, 60 different pieces to record, to make up 45 minutes to an hour's worth of music, ranging in length from 10 seconds to 4 minutes. In a game, everything tends to be a minute and a half to two minutes. Everything has to be loopable. And it's a lot more intense and a lot more full on.

So part of my job is to be the manager of [the musician's] lips. You've got a producer and composer saying "Go, go, go. We've got to record more music," and I have to say "No, no, no. If we do this, the poor French horns are going to die." I have to be the one who looks around the room and they're all about to fall on the floor, so then I'll say we have to let them breathe for a second. Or otherwise they start yelling out that they're getting tired, it gets worse. Just physically, for them to play full on the whole time ….

Video games, because of this volume issue, we tend to do them separate a lot. We'll actually do the strings first and then add the brass. Which means, in normal music, the brass sit there and count bars for 15 to 20 bars and then they play for 4 bars, etcetera. Whereas, when you're skipping all the rests, you say "Okay, bar 25, here we go, one two three four play." And then they play their 8 bars and then you skip the 8 bars and they don't get a rest.

So I have to be really mindful of not wearing them out. And I've also got to look and see, okay, here's a patch that's just going to be a problem. How do we deal with this? And also thinking ahead when we're doing the strings and I have to then look at the brass phrasing and then go okay, are we going to have the strings breathe now with the brass, or are we going to play through it, or, okay, I know the strings are going to play this rhythm this way but the brass will want to play it that way so I have to match it all up because they're not going to hear each other.

MM: *Hmmm.*

TD: The other thing I should mention, too, is that we are very spread out when we record. The percussionists are a mile back, and the French horns are miles over in the brass. You can basically walk between the strings and the brass.

MM: *You're doing this for better recording separation, right?*

TD: Yeah, just for recording separation. But it means you need to be wary of that. So when you do go to free timing it is tough, because everyone is so spaced out. Whereas a normal orchestra is set up nice and tight, they are all on top of each other, the poor French horns are miles away, sometimes they can't hear the cello naturally. So you have to think ahead, alright, this bit you need to hear the cello in your headphones so you can tune with them.

You say to the horns, "Can you hear the cellos there?" And that's just a nice way of saying that you guys weren't with the cellos. Or, you say "Would you like some more click track?" And that's code for that was out of time. So you say all these things. I'm known for just being direct, and saying that was out of time or that wasn't good at all. I don't beat around the bush with them. And most of them appreciate it, but it takes some of them by surprise the first time they hear me tell them that they suck or something like that. But it gets the job done quicker if you don't beat around the bush.

MM: *And they are pros. They do this day in and day out.*

TD: There are a lot of egos and half of them think they can do your job better and think they should be doing your job. But everyone in the room knows the situation, that we're not doing just our musical thing.

MM: *Right. Any advice you would give someone who is interested in getting started in this kind of studio work?*

TD: I think you have to know your orchestration; you have to know every instrument. Because sometimes you're dealing with orchestration that might not be the greatest, or it might be just done in a hurry, or it could be that there needs to be a change, so you're going to have to make those color changes. You're going to have to go, oh, why does that sound terrible? Because it's too low; that should be the English horn. Or, that's not working on the French horns, because it's in their low register and it's not going to be focused, so you put it in the trombones—knowing things like that and being able to predict where every section is going to breathe.

That comes from knowing orchestration and knowing the orchestra, knowing how every instrument works. You have to have played in an orchestra to know how they work, and how they look at the conductor and what they're looking for and all that. Definitely, to be successful, knowing orchestration [is important]. I know that I get my gigs because they know I can fix things and make them happen, without wasting time.

> **WHOLE NOTE**
>
> This is an excerpt from a longer interview I conducted with Tim Davies. You can read the entire interview online at www.idiotsguides.com/conducting.

Conducting in the Real World: An Interview with Pete Anthony

I also got the chance to talk to Tim's colleague Pete Anthony. Pete has been working as a conductor and orchestrator of feature films since 1988. He's worked with a number of famous composers, including James Newton Howard, Danny Elfman, Marc Shalman, Christopher Young, John Powell, and Christophe Beck. Pete's conducting credits include the movies *Bolt*, *Tropic Thunder*, *Hancock*, *I Am Legend*, *Live Free or Die Hard*, *Spider-Man*, *Pirates of the Caribbean: Dead Man's Chest*, *X-Men: The Last Stand*, *The Village*, *The Bourne Supremacy*, *Terminator 3: Rise of the Machines*, *Wonder Boys*, and *The Sixth Sense*.

Pete is a graduate of the University of Southern California (USC) Scoring for Motion Pictures and Television Program, and now teaches conducting and orchestration at USC part-time. His website is www.peteanthony.com.

We started by discussing just how studio conducting differs from concert conducting.

MICHAEL MILLER (MM): *Just how do you view the difference between concert and studio conducting?*

PETE ANTHONY (PA): As a concert conductor, you are the one whose vision is being realized. That dynamic is not the case in studio conducting. That's where a composer's vision is being realized, and the conductor is just the conduit toward that end.

For that matter, the composer's vision may not even be being realized; it's really the filmmakers who are driving the bus. So composers are trying to please the filmmakers, and the conductors have to help the composers do that. And the musicians are all there kind of on the same side as the composer trying to help the composer look good for the people that he was hired by.

MM: *The readers of this book might be surprised that composers don't always or even maybe often conduct their own work. Why is that?*

PA: Well, there are two reasons.

The lesser of the two reasons is that they're not familiar with conducting. Most guys are; some guys who don't conduct are perfectly capable of conducting their own works in the studio. But because of the way the business is—okay, this is a multi-part answer here.

The way that music scores have evolved, they use a lot of prerecorded samples and synth parts that go into making the whole cue. When you're playing the music for the first time, the composers often want to be sitting next to the filmmakers, who are their clients, so that they can share in that experience with them. The filmmakers are hearing the music for the first time with all the components together—they've heard samples, they've heard mock ups, they've heard realizations of what it might be, but they've never heard the whole thing. And so oftentimes, composers want to be close by where they can actually help mix it and present it with the best possible face on it, if you know what I mean.

MM: *Right. And it's fair to say that most filmmakers probably don't have a music background; they're not capable of extrapolating out from a score or from a sample, right?*

PA: Most of them don't have a music background, yes. For filmmakers this is the one part of the process where you're really handing over the creative reins to their project. What composers do is mysterious to most people in the filmmaking process. And the directors, since they can't write the music themselves, are relying on that composer. You have to talk to the filmmakers, but I think for them it's the one time in the process where they're really handing it over to somebody else. And then they come back in the loop when the composer is done with his creative stuff and they ask for changes and so on and so forth. Composers do whatever is necessary to get to where the filmmakers want to be with the score for their film.

So there's a technical element that the composer wants to make sure the guy is hearing the piece with all the right parts. This is prerecorded stuff and oftentimes no one really knows the whole mix the way the composer does. So he wants to be there, to be in the booth, making sure that the guy is getting everything.

In other words, you can play something back and if you got it wrong, if there's some wacky part that's way too loud, the director may go, "Wow, this isn't what I thought it was," not realizing there's a technical problem with the mix. And then from that point on, once their noses start squinching up, you've got a problem.

You know, when the winds of doubt blow through the creative side, on that side of the glass, that's a problem. Composers want to make sure they're in there to say, "No, I'm going to have to fix this, stop everything. Let me adjust this mix. Okay now, listen to this. This is the way I want you to hear it."

In other words, the composer for technical reasons wants to be close by to what the director is hearing, so he knows.

Now, there are also other reasons. The composer may want to just be there to experience what the director's feeling. You know, there's usually a team of people involved, and sometimes there's just 1 person; sometimes it's 3, sometimes it's 20. He wants to be involved in that, he wants to see what their first impressions are. He wants to be sitting there watching them. That's an important part of this whole business.

You know, it's understanding how people are responding to creative product. And if you're not there, if you're out conducting, and the director is in there, again with a squinched nose, and they're not sure, you want to be there right away to understand and dissect the problem. You don't want to be out conducting the orchestra and you're only going to find out about it 10 minutes later.

MM: *That makes perfect sense.*

PA: Because then all these conversations can happen that would unravel some of the creative choices that the composer made—and now he's got a problem. Whereas, if he had been sitting there next to the guy, he could have said, "Okay, we can solve this by putting it on the shelf for a moment. Listen to this part, there's a reason for this." He could have explained it rather than all the doubt going all over the place. So it's a lot about client management.

There's a technical aspect and there's a creative aspect as reasons to be by the director, producer, filmmaker, editor, whoever is kind of directing, making the creative decisions about the music that is going to be recorded with an orchestra. You know, it's a really expensive time, if you've got an orchestra playing. You've done all this work to provide mock ups and try to explain to them what is going to happen. When everybody shows up and you've got 70, 80, 110 people, playing music, it can be great and glorious. But if there is doubt about the creative direction, it turns from great and glorious to a nightmare because it's so expensive. Every minute that you spend fixing, changing, and so on and so forth, the pressure builds because it's very expensive time, by the minute, by the hour, and so on.

MM: *Essentially, you have to satisfy the composer and the filmmaker, as well as be the bridge to the musicians.*

PA: The conductor's job in the studio is much different than the concert hall, it's to be the center of the information universe. He's the bridge, as you said, the liaison, the translator sometimes. He has to speak in music terms to musicians, and he has to be on the same page as the composer.

> **THE CONDUCTOR SEZ**
>
> This liaison role also happens to an extent with premieres of new pieces in concert halls. When the composer is present, you wind up with a similar situation.

There is no doubt about that; he is working for the composer. He wants to make the composer successful. The composer is working for the filmmakers. The composer wants to please the filmmakers. That dynamic is incredibly important to understand. That's the difference between the studio and the concert worlds. In the concert world, the buck stops at the conductor. The conductor's vision is what's important. And in the studio, the vision of the filmmaker is what we're serving. Whole entirely different thing.

MM: *Now, how much rehearsal is there—or is there any rehearsal time? Or is it pretty much everyone goes into it cold and the first take is it?*

PA: There's some of that. With digital recording, it allows us to use a lot of the original performance, and so oftentimes we record our first take, our first run through. If something is particularly difficult, you know, virtuosic in the way it's written or presented, or particularly difficult for all the wrong reasons, particularly "left-handed," I may say there's no point in recording this, give me a second to play this through under tempo. We try to locate where the train wrecks are before they happen.

And it's under tempo or whatever, and then we put it together and then the second that it's anywhere close to being performable, the red light goes on and we record it. Then they end up taking the second or third time through, that's usually the best. If the budget allows, we'll rehearse it without recording it and comment and then come back and play it and then the performance may evolve. The filmmakers may respond and then it's not about the music, it's about what works for the film.

MM: *With all the changes in the industry, with all the sampling and notation programs and all that, has this affected the work? Or are some films skipping the orchestra and just using samples now?*

PA: Well, there are cross-cutting trends that are in place. Sometimes crazy scheduling makes it almost impossible to have a live session.

It happens in TV all the time. For example, I was involved on *The West Wing* for the first season. And they would deliver the reels to Snuffy Walden, the music composer, I forget if it was a Monday or Tuesday. Anyway, he would have Tuesday and Wednesday to write, and then we would have a session and we'd be orchestrating like crazy Wednesday and Wednesday night. Thursday we would have a [recording] session. And they would dub the thing Friday. Well, then they decided to give him the reels on Tuesday afternoon ....

MM: [laughs]

PA: And he'd write Wednesday, and we'd be orchestrating almost the same moment he's written it. Then it would be copied and we were having a frantic session. And then they were giving him the music on Wednesday and we could no longer even have a session. So as his schedule got tighter and tighter, whatever he composed in his composing process used samples to play orchestra mockups.

He's actually that fast and that good that he could do that. But it got so the schedule didn't allow an orchestra. What happened was they cut pieces from previous seasons to make the music they needed.

MM: Hmmm.

PA: But don't forget that in the film world, everybody can buy a $200 5.1 surround system, so there's demand for high production values. As your time gets shorter, it gets harder and harder to make the samples sound good. In other words, given unlimited time you could make samples sound almost as good as an orchestra. But with tighter schedules, that becomes impossible.

MM: And why not use an orchestra anyway, then?

PA: That's why I'm talking about these cross-cutting trends. One trend is crazy scheduling creates the necessity for another trend which is live scoring. But you don't have time for the live scoring music preparation. You have to get all these notes written down on music paper and they have to look right. So there is all this stuff going head to head. It pushes the pendulum back and forward, to the right, to the left.

One thing for sure, post production scheduling has gotten very tight. That isn't going to change. I used to [orchestrate] a film in four to six weeks with a composer. Now I don't even see music sometimes for eight to ten days before the scoring session. So instead of there being one of me working for six weeks, there are four of me working one and a half weeks.

MM: So they bring in multiple orchestrators?

PA: Yeah. So I work on more films and I do a smaller part in every film. Instead of an entire film by myself, now it's me with an entire team of four, five, or six guys.

MM: Time management is definitely part of the job. Do you have the luxury of going over into an extra session or do you just absolutely, positively have to get it all down by two o'clock or whatever the end is?

PA: Obviously, it depends on the budget. What was the schedule on this budget? There are many times where we are absolutely hard up against the wall, where we absolutely have to stop it at the hour or whatever. We have hard stops, must be done at this time.

I deal with it all the time, more and more lately. Part of the reality of filmmaking is that money up front is scarcer and scarcer. And it's not just a music thing, it's all aspects of a production. Whether you're making costumes and special effects or even doing electricity, whatever your job may be on the production, they expect you to do more for less. More for less, that's the mantra of production. They want more for less. And we just have to do it. They want us to use fewer players, unfortunately. They want us to record more in less time. They want us to do more for less.

MM: So what do you find most fulfilling about the conducting?

PA: Believe it or not, it's that challenge of doing more for less, it's actually fulfilling. You know, when you're really operating, hitting on all eight cylinders in terms of efficiency, in terms of the players understanding what you want, in terms of getting a good performance as quickly as humanly possible—that's fulfilling. That's one kind of fulfillment. There's sort of a thrill that comes with that, out of being shot at and missed.

There's also the music, believe it or not. I don't want to sound overjaded, but you know at times the music is uplifting. At times I really do love the music, and that's fulfilling.

MM: I've always thought the soundtrack, movie music, is the classical music of our time. And when you realize that it's done not over a period of months, but of weeks or days, it's incredible really.

PA: That's exactly what I say, Michael. It is the classical music of our day.

I recently conducted an orchestra of my kids' school district's annual celebrating the arts. At one point I had an orchestra of 150 kids, and we're playing stuff that I had worked on. After the fact somebody said, "While I completely respect what the transient others and the film and television industry bring in, we should focus our efforts on the classical repertoire." My immediate response for that was, "Where do you think the classical repertoire came from?" You know, Bach and Mozart didn't write because the muse visited them, they wrote because they had a deadline and a job.

MM: Bach had to turn out a piece every Sunday morning, right?

PA: Exactly. You can go to the library and find that he had to write it. And that's why he had so many kids, to help him get the parts done in time.

You know, Mozart had to write for the court. He didn't have a choice in the matter, he did it so he could live. So how is that different from what a composer today does, when he has to write music for a film that's on a deadline? He doesn't wait for the muse to visit. He has to go write and go work for somebody else. That's what those guys did, and that's what we do. When you say "new classical," it's the classical music of our day, I think that's true in multiple levels.

MM: It sounds like a fun job.

PA: At times it's a great job. Other times it's just a job. But more often than not it's a great job.

> **WHOLE NOTE**
>
> This is an excerpt from a longer interview I conducted with Pete Anthony. You can read the entire interview online at www.idiotsguides.com/conducting.

The Least You Need to Know

- The goal of a studio conductor is to accurately reproduce the music the composer wrote, not to interpret that music.
- Studio conducting is a high-pressure job, in terms of schedule and in managing all the individuals involved—including the score's composer and the movie's director.
- A soundtrack conductor typically gets the score the night before the session—if then.
- Many studio conductors also serve as orchestrators of the music.
- The latest form of studio conducting involves conducting video game soundtracks—which are often longer and more involved than movie soundtracks.

Glossary

Appendix A

a cappella   Vocal music, without instrumental accompaniment.

a tempo   Return to the previous tempo.

accelerando   Gradually speed up. (Abbreviated as *accel.*)

accent   A note played louder or with more emphasis than a regular note.

accidental   A marking used to raise and lower the indicated pitch. Sharps raise the note a half-step, flats lower the note a half-step, and naturals return the note to the original pitch.

adagietto   Moderately slow tempo, slightly faster than *adagio*.

adagio   Moderately slow; stately.

adante   Moderate, walking tempo.

adantino   Moderate tempo, slightly faster than *adante*.

allegretto   Moderately fast, but not quite as fast as *allegro*.

allegro   Fast, cheerful.

artistic director   The lead executive of a musical organization, responsible for all music-related tasks.

baton   A short wooden or composite stick used by conductors to direct a musical performance.

beat pattern   A pattern a conductor draws in the air, via hand movements, to indicate the time signature of a musical piece.

beats per minute (bpm)   An expression of tempo in terms of how many beats are played per 60-second period. (In some older pieces you may see the notation M.M. instead, for "metronome marking.")

bulb   The large, rounded end of the baton held in the conductor's right hand.

cadenza   An improvised passage by a solo performer, typically in a free rhythmic style.

canon   An informal list of respected and influential works.

cantor   In Christian and Jewish religious services, a solo singer to whom the choir or congregation responds. (In some Jewish traditions, this is an ordained position.)

chant   *See* plainsong.

chironomy   The use of hand gestures to show the rhythmic elements of a musical work, as practiced in the singing of Gregorian chant in the Middle Ages.

choir   An ensemble consisting of vocal musicians; the voicing may vary but is normally one of the following: men, women, or men and women (known as a mixed choir).

clef   A graphic symbol placed at the beginning of the staff to indicate the pitch of the notes on the staff.

click track   A sound that plays on each beat of a measure, defining the tempo of a piece, much like an electronic metronome.

coda   A short section at the end of a composition.

common time   The 4/4 time signature.

complex meter   A time signature that does not divide into two or three equal parts.

composition   The art of creating music.

compound meter   A time signature in which the prevailing beat may be divided into three equal parts, as with 3/8, 6/8, and so forth.

concert band   A large instrumental ensemble with brass, woodwind, and percussion instruments, but no strings. Also called a symphonic band, wind ensemble, wind symphony, or symphonic winds.

concertmaster/concertmistress   The leader of an orchestra's first violin section.

conducting   The art of directing a musical performance via a large vocabulary of standard hand gestures.

conductor   The person who leads a musical ensemble.

crescendo   Gradually louder.

cue   An indication that a performer should begin playing or singing at a certain spot in the score.

cut time   The 2/2 time signature.

D.C. al Coda   Navigation marking meaning to go back to the beginning and play to the Coda sign; then skip to the Coda section.

D.C. al Fine   Navigation marking meaning to go back to the beginning and play through to the end.

D.S. al Coda   Navigation marking meaning to go back to the Segno sign and play to the Coda sign; then skip to the Coda section.

D.S. al Fine   Navigation marking meaning to go back to the Segno sign and play through to the end.

decrescendo   Gradually softer.

diminuendo   Same as *decrescendo*; gradually softer.

doppio movimento   Play twice as fast.

downbeat   In the conducting world, the first beat of a measure.

drum corps   A marching band that consists primarily of percussion and brass instruments, with a focus on competition.

drum major   The leader and field conductor of a marching band or drum corps. If a band has more than one drum major, the senior drum major is sometimes designated the *field major*.

dynamics   The relative volume level of a musical work or passage.

falsetto   A voice that sounds a register above a singer's normal range, typically with different vocal characteristics than the singer's normal range.

fermata   Symbol used to indicate that a note should be held indefinitely; sometimes called a "bird's eye."

flat   The lowering of any pitch by a half-step; signified by the ♭ sign.

forte   Loud. (Abbreviated as *f*.)

fortissimo   Very loud. (Abbreviated as *ff*.)

fortississimo   Very, very loud. (Abbreviated as *fff*.)

French six pattern   A beat pattern, typically used in 6/8 or 6/4 time, that mixes a standard triple pattern (for the first three beats) with an ascending center-based pattern for the final beats; this ascending pattern looks something like the top of a Christmas tree.

front line   The nonmarching section of a marching band, lined up at the front of the field. Also called the *pit*.

glissando   A mechanism for getting from one pitch to another, playing every single pitch between the two notes as smoothly as possible.

grace note   One or more notes, played lightly and quickly, that precede a main note.

grave   Slow and solemn.

Harmon mute   A type of trumpet mute designed to elicit a particular sound from the instrument.

ictus   Any beat in a conducting pattern.

key one   In musical theater, the first keyboard chair.

key signature   The sharps or flats that are placed at the beginning of a staff to indicate the key of the music.

larghetto   Slow, slightly faster than *largo*.

larghissimo Very, very slow.

largo Slow and dignified; broadly.

legato A marking that indicates consecutive notes are to be played smoothly together.

lento Slow.

mace A large staff used by some drum majors that functions as a type of oversized baton.

measure A group of beats, indicated by the placement of bar lines on the staff.

mezzo forte Medium loud. (Abbreviated as *mf*.)

mezzo piano Medium soft. (Abbreviated as *mp*.)

moderato Moderate tempo.

modulate To change the key.

molto Modifier for tempo markings; means "very."

motif A brief melodic or rhythmic idea.

movement Self-contained part within a larger musical work.

music director A person who performs multiple creative and managerial tasks for a musical organization, including conducting, auditioning, and managing musicians.

music theory The study of how music works.

orchestra An instrumental ensemble consisting of strings, winds, and percussion, typically with 80 to 100 musicians in total.

orchestration The art of assigning parts within a composition to individual instruments and/or voices.

perfect pitch The innate ability to recognize the exact pitch of any note played.

phrase A connected group of notes, played one after another without a breath or break.

pianissimo Very soft. (Abbreviated as *pp*.)

pianississimo Very, very soft. (Abbreviated as *ppp*.)

piano Soft. (Abbreviated as *p*.)

pit *See* front line.

pizzicato The technique of plucking the strings on a bowed instrument.

plainsong A musical passage in which biblical text is sung with its natural, unmetered speech rhythms. Also known as *chant* (as in Anglican chant and Gregorian chant).

podium A small platform, situated in front of an ensemble, on which a conductor stands.

preparatory beat The silent beat conducted before the first downbeat of a piece.

prestissimo Extremely fast.

*** presto*** Very fast.

programmer The person who chooses the music for a given musical program.

programming The act of choosing music to play on a given program.

rallentando Gradually slow down. (Abbreviated as *rall.*)

rebound The small bounce after every downward stroke, or ictus, in a conducting pattern.

recitative A musical passage by a solo singer that utilizes the rhythms of ordinary speech in an unmetered style. Typically found in operas, oratorios, and cantatas.

rest A symbol used to denote silence or not playing a particular note.

ritardando Gradually slow down. (Abbreviated as *rit.* or *ritard.*)

ritenuto Hold back the tempo. (Abbreviated as *riten.*)

SATB Shorthand for soprano, alto, tenor, and bass. (Choral scores are sometimes called SATB scores.)

score The written representation of a musical composition; the conductor's score typically contains all the parts of the ensemble, arranged one below another, grouped by section.

score order The accepted order of instruments, top to bottom, in a written score.

sight reading The ability to sing or play a piece of music at first sight, without prior preparation.

sitzprobe A seated rehearsal in a musical production where the singers first sing with the orchestra.

soli In big band music, an entire section playing in harmony.

*** staccato*** A marking that indicates a note is to played with a shortened duration.

staff An assemblage of horizontal lines and spaces that represent different pitches.

syncopation A rhythm that places notes on unexpected or normally unaccented beats or parts of beats.

tactus The prevailing beat of a given meter.

tempo The speed of the beat in a musical work or passage.

tempo primo Return to the tempo designated at the beginning of a piece.

tenuto A marking to hold a note its full duration.

tie   A curved line over or under two or more notes that "ties" the two notes together into one.

time signature   A symbol with two numbers, one on top of the other (like a fraction), that indicates the basic meter of a song. The upper number indicates how many beats are in a measure; the bottom number indicates the type of note that receives one beat.

tremolo   In bowed string instruments, the technique of moving the bow rapidly back and forth on the string while playing a single pitch.

trill   The technique of rapidly alternating between higher and lower tones.

triplet   A group of three notes performed in the space of two.

unmeasured prelude   A free-form introductory passage in some 17th century music, typically played on the harpsichord.

unmetered music   A musical passage without a steady, pulsed meter, where the duration of each note is essentially left to the performer(s).

vivace   Lively tempo.

Online Videos

Appendix B

The following videos illustrate conducting concepts discussed in this book, and can be viewed online at www.idiotsguides.com/conducting.

1. **The Basics of Conducting.** Demonstrates proper stance and how to hold the baton.

2. **Conducting the Downbeat.** Demonstrates how to conduct a clear downbeat and rebound.

3. **Conducting in Two.** Demonstrates beat patterns for 2/8, 2/4, and 2/2 time signatures.

4. **Conducting in Three.** Demonstrates beat patterns for 3/8, 3/4, and 3/2 time signatures.

5. **Conducting in Four.** Demonstrates beat patterns for 4/8, 4/4, and 4/2 time signatures.

6. **Conducting in Five.** Demonstrates beat patterns for 5/8 and 5/4 time signatures.

7. **Conducting in Six.** Demonstrates beat patterns for 6/8 and 6/4 time signatures.

8. **Conducting in Seven.** Demonstrates beat patterns for 7/8 and 7/4 time signatures.

9. **Conducting in Nine.** Demonstrates beat patterns for 9/8 and 9/4 time signatures.

10. **Conducting Subdivisions.** Demonstrates how to conduct subdivisions of the beat.

11. **Conducting Tempo Changes.** Demonstrates how to indicate tempo while conducting, including how to speed up and slow down the tempo.

12. **Conducting Dynamics.** Demonstrates how to indicate dynamics while conducting, including how to conduct *crescendos* and *decrescendos*.

13. **Conducting Phrasing.** Demonstrates how to indicate musical phrases while conducting, as well as how to indicate other articulations, such as *legato* and *staccato* passages.

14. **Conducting Cues and Entrances.** Demonstrates how to signal entrances during a performance.

15. **Conducting Accents and Syncopation.** Demonstrates how to conduct accents, hits, and syncopated rhythmic patterns.

Index

A

accelerando tempo change marking, 103
accented notes, cueing, 116
adagietto tempo, 99
adagio tempo, 99
Aho, Kalevi, 137
allegretto tempo, 98-99
allegro tempo, 98-99
Amazing Grace, 87
American in Paris, An, 98
andante tempo, 98-99
ansantino tempo, 99
Anthony, Pete, 204-208
artistic directors, 20
audience acceptance, programs, 17
Autumn in Paris, 87

B

Bach, Johann Sebastian, 174, 177, 208
Baker, David, 161
Baroque music, pitch level, 38
Bartok, Bela, 136
"Basics of Conducting, The," 50
Basie, Count, 155, 160-163
batons, 45
    beat patterns, 60
    benefits, 46-47
    choosing, 47-48
    detriments, 47
    holding, 49-50
    indicating dynamics, 109-110
    left hand, 56
    Mollard P-series, 48
    origins, 46
    tapping, 45
beat patterns, 52
    choosing, 80
    compound triple meters, 69
        fast, 73
        nine-beat, 71-72
        six-beat, 69-71
        twelve-beat, 72-73
    five-beats-per-measure, 76-77
    four-beats-per-measure, 63-65
    general principles, 59-60
    one-beat-per-measure, 60-61
    seven-beats-per-measure, 77-78
    simplicity, 57
    three-beats-per-measure, 67-69
    two-beats-per-measure, 61-62
beats, 57
    bpm (beats per minute), 89, 98
    changing number, 81-82
    click tracks, 98
    downbeats, 52-54, 59
    final upbeat, 55
    ictus, 52
    preparatory, 53-54
    rebounds, 54-57
    repeats, 55-56
    setting, 100-101
    subdividing, 79-80
    versus rhythms, 57
beats per minute (bpm), 89, 98
Beck, Christophe, 197-198, 204
Beethoven, Ludwig Van, 87, 100, 137, 177
Bernstein, Leonard, 47

best practices, 57-58
big band scores, 25
both hands, utilizing, 95-96
Boulez, Pierre, 47
bpm (beats per minute), 89, 98
breathing exercises, 38
"Broadway Sings the Music of Jules Styne," 188
Buselli, Mark, 157-163
Buselli-Wallarab Jazz Orchestra, 161

C

cadenzas, 120-123
cantors, 121
changing
    dynamics, 109
    tempos, 102-104
chants, 120-122
chironomy, 46
choirs, conducting, 165, 171-177
    chorales, 166-167
    church, 169-170
    community, 168-169
    professional, 170
    youth, 167-168
chorales, conducting, 166-167
chords, 38
church choirs, conducting, 169-170
click tracks, 98
colored pencils, 30
communication skills, 10
community choirs, conducting, 168-169
Complete Idiot's Guide to Arranging and Orchestration, The, 6
Complete Idiot's Guide to Music Composition, The, 6
Complete Idiot's Guide to Music History, The, 9
Complete Idiot's Guide to Music Theory, The, 6
Complete Idiot's Guide to Singing, The, 171
Complete Idiot's Guide to Solos and Improvisation, The, 158
complex meters, 75
    five-beats-per-measure, 76-77
    seven-beats-per-measure, 77-78

compositions, 6
    interpreting, 87-88
        dynamics, 90
        energy, 90-91
        mood, 90-91
        phrasing, 89
        tempo, 89-90
        timbre, 88-89
compound triple meters, 69
    fast, 73
    nine-beat, 71-72
    six-beat, 69-70
        French, 70-71
    twelve-beat, 72-73
concert band scores, order, 26
concert bands, conducting, 130-139
concertmasters, 8
    befriending, 128
Concerto for Orchestra, 136
conducting, 3-5
    best practices, 57-58
    choirs, 165, 171-177
        chorales, 166-167
        church, 169-170
        community, 168-169
        professional, 170
        youth, 167-168
    concert bands, 130-139
    drum majoring
        military technique, 146-147
        standard technique, 144-145
    jazz bands, 155-163
    live shows, 181-194
    marching bands, 144-153
    musical theater, 179-194
    opera, 181-194
    orchestras, 133-139
        instruments, 127-128
        sound, 129-130
        youth, 131-132
    preparation, 32-33
    rehearsals, 35-40
    soundtracks, 197-208

conductors, 3-4
  great, 12-13
  programming, 15-18
  skill requirements, 5
    communication, 10
    conducting, 11-12
    instrumental, 7-8
    language, 9
    leadership, 10
    listening, 7
    music history, 9
    music theory, 5-6
    performance, 8-9
    rehearsal, 11
    self-confidence, 10
    sight reading, 6-7
    teaching, 11
    vocal knowledge, 7-8
Connick, Jr., Harry, 185-187
controlling performances, 91
crescendos, 109-110
cues
  accented notes, 116
  entrances, 113-114
  making contact, 115-116
  syncopation, 116-117
cultural appropriateness, programs, 17
cutoffs, 56

D

Davies, Tim, 197-203
Deck the Halls, 91
decrescendos, 109-110
different tempos, conducting, 102
diminuendo, 109
discipline, rehearsals, 40-41
doppio movimento tempo change marking, 103
double meter beat pattern, 61-62
downbeats, 52-54, 59
drum corps, 142-143
  conducting, 144-153
    military technique, 146-147
    standard technique, 144-145

drum majors, 143
    military technique, 146-147
    modern, 144
    standard technique, 144-145
Dvorak, Antonin, 129
dynamics
  changing, 109
  indicating with baton, 109-110
  indicating with left hand, 110-111
  influencing, 90
  markings, 107-108
  scores, 29

E

electronic components, tempo, 98
elementary school choirs, conducting, 167
Elfman, Danny, 204
Elijah, 173
Ellington, Duke, 155, 161-163
energy, influencing, 90-91
entrances, cueing, 113-114
Evans, Gil, 161

F

Ferguson, Maynard, 155, 162
fermati, conducting, 104-105
final upbeat, 55
five-beats-per-measure patterns, 76-77
Follies, 186
form analysis, scores, 28
fortissimo, 108
four-beats-per-measure beat pattern, 63-65
French six pattern, 70-71
front lines, marching bands, 142
Fulford, Phyllis, 171
full vocal scores, 28
fundraising, 20

G

Gershwin, George, 98, 174
Goodman, Benny, 155
Goodwin, Gordon, 155
gradual tempo changes, conducting, 103-104
grave tempo, 99

H

Hahn, Dave, 182-185
Harmon mute, 160
harmonic structure, scores, 28
Herman, Woody, 160-162
high school choirs, conducting, 168
holding batons, 49-50
Howard, James Newton, 204

I

ictus, 52
Indianapolis Symphonic Choir, 175
Indy Sings blog, 171
instrumentation, scores, 29
instruments, orchestras, 127-128
interpreting musical works, 87-88
    dynamics, 90
    energy, 90-91
    mood, 90-91
    phrasing, 89
    tempo, 89-90
    timbre, 88-89

J-K

Jablonsky, Steve, 197
jazz bands, conducting, 155-163
jazz ensemble scores, order, 27
JazzMN Orchestra, 162
Joy of Music, The, 47

Kenton, Stan, 162
key one, 184

L

Lane, Nathan, 185-187
language skills, 9
larghetto tempo, 99
larghissimo tempo, 99
largo tempo, 99
Laureano, Manny, 133-139
leadership skills, 10
leading rehearsals, 18
left hand, 93
    indicating dynamics, 110-111
    mirroring, 94-95
    things to avoid, 93
    utilizing, 94-95
left hand conduction, 56
lento tempo, 99
liaison role, 206
listening skills, 7
live shows, conducting, 181-194
Lurie, Deborah, 197

M

MacDonald, Audra, 188
maces, 144
marching bands, 141-143
    conducting, 144-153
        military technique, 146-147
        standard technique, 144-145
    drum corps, 142
    drum majors, 143-144
    front lines, 142
    modern, 141-142
markings
    dynamics, 107-108
    measures, 201
    scores, 30-31
    tempo, 99-100
Masur, Kurt, 47
measures, marking, 201
melodic lines, scores, 29
Mendelssohn, Felix, 46, 173

meter
    complex, 75-76
        five-beats-per-measure, 76-77
        seven-beats-per-measure, 77-78
    compound, 69
        fast, 73
        French, 70-71
        nine-beat, 71-72
        six-beat, 69-70
        twelve-beat, 72-73
    conducting through changes, 80-83
    four-beats-per-measure, 63-65
    one-beat-per-measure, 60-61
    three-beats-per-measure, 67-69
    two-beats-per-measure, 61-62
middle school choirs, conducting, 168
military technique, drum majoring, 146-147
Miller, Glenn, 155
Minnesota Youth Symphonies (MYS), 133
mirroring
    marching bands, 145
    right hand, 94-95
moderato tempo, 99
Mollard P-series batons, 48
molto vivace tempo, 100
mood, influencing, 90-91
movie soundtracks, conducting, 195-208
Mozart, Wolfgang Amadeus, 173, 208
Muppets, The, 198
music directors, 19
music history, 9
music stands, positioning, 50
music theory, 5-6
musical difficulty, programs, 17
musical instruments, orchestral, 127-128
musical theater, conducting, 179-194
musical work, interpreting, 87-88
    dynamics, 90
    energy, 90-91
    mood, 90-91
    phrasing, 89
    tempo, 89-90
    timbre, 88-89
Musicians Wages website, 182-183
MYS (Minnesota Youth Symphonies), 133

N-O

New World Symphony, 129
nine-beat patterns, 71-72
nonbaton hand, utilizing, 93-95
Northern, Glenn, 147-153
number of beats, changing, 82

On a Clear Day You Can See Forever, 182, 185
On Conducting, 97
one-beat-per-measure beat pattern, 60-61
opera, conducting, 181-194
operatic recitatives, 120-121
orchestral scores, 22
orchestras, 127
orchestras, conducting, 127-139
    instruments, 127-128
    sound, 129-130
    youth, 131-132
orchestration, 6
order, scores
    concert band, 26
    jazz ensemble, 27
    symphonic orchestra, 25
over conducting, avoiding, 57

P

Patinkin, Mandy, 188
pencils, 40
performance skills, 8-9
performances
    controlling, 91
    studying, 31
phrasal analysis, scores, 29
phrasing
    indicating, 111
    influencing, 89
piano, learning benefits, 9
pitch level, Baroque music, 38
pits, marching bands, 142
plainsongs, 120-122
planning rehearsals, 36-37

podiums, 4
    positioning, 50
Porgy and Bess, 161
positioning, 50-52
Powell, John, 204
"practice perfect," 36
preludes, unmeasured, 120-123
preparatory beat, 53-54
preparing scores, 21, 28-30
    comprehension, 22-29
    dynamics, 29
    form analysis, 28
    harmonic structure, 28
    instrumentation, 29
    marking up, 30-31
    melodic line, 29
    outside source material, 31-32
    phrasal analysis, 29
    rhythm, 29
    special effects, 29
    study, 21-22
    tempo, 29
    transpositions, 29
prerecorded material, tempo, 98
prestissimo tempo, 99
presto tempo, 99
Priscilla, Queen of the Desert, 182-184
professional choirs, conducting, 170
programming, 15-18
programs
    audience acceptance, 17
    constructing, 16-17
    cultural appropriateness, 17
    musical difficulty, 17
    unity, 17
    variety, 16

Q-R

quadruple meter patterns, 63-65

Rachmaninoff, Sergei, 174
rallentando tempo change marking, 103
rebounds, 54-57
recitatives, 120-121, 181
recordings, studying, 31
rehearsal skills, 11
rehearsals
    conducting, 35-40
    importance, 35-36
    leading, 18
    maintaining discipline, 40-41
    planning, 36-37
    "practice perfect," 36
    tuning, 37-38
    warmups, 38-39
    wrapping, 41
rhythmic values, changing, 82
rhythms versus beats, 57
Rich, Buddy, 155, 162
right hand, mirroring, 94-95
ritarando tempo change marking, 103
ritenuto tempo change marking, 103

S

SAB (soprano, alto, baritone) pieces, 169
scales, 38
Schneider, Maria, 155, 158, 161
scores, 6
    big band, 25
    concert band, order, 26
    dynamics, 29
    form analysis, 28
    full vocal, 28
    harmonic structure, 28
    instrumentation, 29
    jazz ensemble, order, 27
    melodic line, 29
    orchestral, 22
    order, 25
    phrasal analysis, 29
    preparing, 21, 28-30
        comprehension, 22-29
        marking up, 30-31
        outside source material, 31-32
        study, 21-22
    rhythm, 29

special effects, 29
symphonic orchestra, 25
tempo, 29
transpositions, 29
two-staff vocal, 27
self-confidence, 10
setting
    beat, 100-101
    tempo, 97, 101
seven-beats-per-measure patterns, 77-78
Shalman, Marc, 204
Shaw, Robert, 33
sight reading music, 6-7
sitzprobes, 185-186
six-beat patterns, 69-70
    French, 70-71
skill requirements, 5
    communication, 10
    conducting, 11-12
    instrumental, 7-8
    language, 9
    leadership, 10
    listening, 7
    music history, 9
    music theory, 5-6
    performance, 8-9
    rehearsal, 11
    self-confidence, 10
    sight reading, 6-7
    teaching, 11
    vocal knowledge, 7-8
slower tempos, 79-80
soli, 159
soloists, 8
soundtracks, conducting, 195-208
special effects, scores, 29
splaying fingers, 145
stance, 50-52
standard technique, drum majoring, 144-145
Stark, Eric, 171-177
steady tempo, setting, 101
Stern, Eric, 188-194
Stokowski, Leopold, 47
string instruments, orchestras, 127

subdividing beats, 79-80
sudden tempos changes, conducting, 102-103
symphonic orchestra scores, order, 25
symphonic orchestras, conducting, 127-139
    instruments, 127-128
    sound, 129-130
    youth, 131-132
syncopation, 116-117

T

Take Five, 76
tapping batons, 45
Tchaikovsky, Pyotr Ilyich, 136
teaching skills, 11, 18-19
television soundtracks, conducting, 197-208
tempo, 97
    bpm (beats per minute), 89, 98
    changing, 102-104
    choosing, 98
    conducting different, 102
    electronic components, 98
    influencing, 89-90
    markings, 99-100
    prerecorded material, 98
    scores, 29
    setting steady, 97, 100-101
    slower, 79-80
tempo change marking, 103
tempo primo change marking, 103
Tennstedt, Klaus, 135
three-beats-per-measure beat patterns, 67-69
timbre, influencing, 88-89
time changes, practicing, 82-83
time signatures, conducting through changes, 80-83
tone, concert bands, 131
transpositions, scores, 29
Trask, Stephen, 197
triple meter patterns, 67-69
    compound
        fast, 73
            nine-beat, 71-72
            six-beat, 69-71
            twelve-beat, 72-73

tuning, rehearsals, 37-38
twelve-beat patterns, 72-73
two-beats-per-measure beat pattern, 61-62
two-staff vocal scores, 27

U

underlying pulse, changing, 81-82
unison notes, 38
unity, programs, 17
unmeasured preludes, 120-123
unmetered music, 119-123
upbeats, final, 55
Upshaw, Dawn, 188

V

variety, programs, 16
Vänskä, Osmo, 134
video game soundtracks, conducting, 197-208
vivace tempo, 99

W-X

Wagner, Richard, 97
Walden, Snuffy, 206
Wallarab, Brent, 157, 160-161
warmups, rehearsals, 38-39
Watson, Bobby, 161
West Wing, The, 206
Wonderful Town, 182
wrapping rehearsals, 41

Y-Z

Young, Christopher, 204
youth, conducting, 131-132, 167-168
Yurman, Larry, 185-188